REMOTE
LAN
CONNECTIONS

WILLIAM WONG

M&T BOOKS

M&T Books

A Division of MIS:Press, Inc.
A Subsidiary of Henry Holt and Company, Inc.
115 West 18th Street
New York, New York 10011

Library of Congress Cataloging-in-Publication Data

```
Wong, William
     Remote LAN connections / Bill Wong.
         p.      cm.
     ISBN 1-55851-438-4
     1. Local area networks (Computer networks)   I. Title.
  TK5105.7.W64   1995
004.6'8--dc20                                        95-22152
                                                         CIP
```

10 9 8 7 6 5 4 3 2 1

Associate Publisher & Vice-President: Paul Farrell

Managing Editor: Cary Sullivan **Development Editor:** Jono Hardjowirogo

Copy Edit Manager: Shari Chappell **Production Editor:** Maya Riddick

Copy Editor: Bud Paulding **Technical Editor:** Greg Nunemacher

DEDICATION

This book is dedicated to my wife Ann
and my children Jenny, Bobby and Laura.

ACKNOWLEDGEMENTS

I would like to thank my wife who supported me in this venture and who listened to my late night altercations with modems and other stubborn hardware and software.

I would like to thank Jono Hardjowirogo. Without his persistence this book would not have been completed.

I would like to thank the people at Nu-Moga technologics for their understanding when I had to meet my book editorial deadlines.

While I cannot list all the people who assisted my research I would like to thank all the companies and their respective public relations departments or companies that supplied technical support, evaluation products and documentation for this book.

WHO SHOULD READ THIS BOOK

This book is designed for LAN managers supporting telecommuters, a mobile workforce, and even remote access by customers and clients. It covers different methods to link people with your LAN and addresses the advantages and trade-offs for putting these methods into place. The book covers methods suitable for single users as well as hundreds of users.

The book is also for users who want to use a LAN remotely. It addresses their point of view and explains how the various methods work. Numerous examples from real products are shown to give you an idea of what you will see and what you can do.

Only a very basic knowledge of LANs is required to read this book, so even casual LAN users will feel comfortable with it. While some of the remote access methods may be already familiar to you there are probably some new ones you have not even thought of.

Contents

CHAPTER 1

REMOTE LAN ACCESS

Local area networks (LANs) are usually found in a company that has more than a dozen PCs. Companies with fewer PCs, on the other hand, have found peer-to-peer networks running a network operating system (NOS) like LANtastic, Personal NetWare, POWERLAN, and Windows for Workgroups to be more appropriate. During the last several years, improved software quality and lower hardware costs have also made LANs more desirable in all parts of a company. LANs are becoming a standard feature in the home office and even in the home itself. A home PC is very common, and we are seeing a tremendous increase in the number of homes with two or more PCs. In homes with multiple PCs, connecting them to each other is routinely done.

WHAT IS REMOTE LAN ACCESS?

In this age of electronic interconnection, LANs clearly play more than just a file-serving role. Access to a LAN is becoming extremely important, as a big part of our business existence is tied to it–LANs provide electronic mail, scheduling, and shared resources.

    With the use of a modem and a telephone line, you can now access your office PC that is wired to a LAN from almost anywhere: from a branch office, while on the road, even from home. A variety of remote LAN access methods can help you do this. Each has advantages and disadvantages, depending on what kind of information you need to access. Knowing several different methods of access is a good idea since there may arise a situation in which your favorite method of access is not suitable. While access to your mail and files should be fairly straight-forward, getting access to shared and other corporate resources may lead to complications, such as security and inefficiency, and may actually require a dedicated method of access. In a business where LAN access may be made available to a number of different types of users, including customers, clients, and employees, the need for multiple methods of access is clear.

Most chapters in this book are dedicated to individual remote LAN access methods. Each of these chapters describes how a particular method accomplishes remote LAN access and addresses issues such as security, efficiency, and performance. Each chapter also includes a section on actual products that provide support for that particular remote LAN access method, so you have a starting point if you want to implement that method on your LAN. The product presentations are not intended as endorsements or detailed reviews but rather as a way to show actual products that implement the method presented in the chapter. The product lists are not exhaustive; remote LAN access products are available from a very large number of vendors, and new versions and products are continually being released.

Each chapter addresses the product from both a user's and the LAN manager's points of view. The LAN manager is usually charged with installation and maintenance of the LAN-resident portion of the system. Users need to be concerned with hardware and software requirements, so we will take a look at these issues as well.

The other chapters in this book cover the following methods of remote LAN access:

✧   Chapter 2 "Mail Gateways"

✧   Chapter 3 "Remote Workstation"

✧   Chapter 4 "Remote Control Programs"

✧   Chapter 5 "Network Bulletin Board System"

✧   Chapter 6 "Remote Faxing"

✧   Chapter 7 "Wireless Connections"

✧   Chapter 8 "Specialized Tools"

✧   Chapter 9 "Accessing the Internet"

Let's look at an overview of each chapter.

Mail Gateways

Chapter 2 covers mail exchange between LAN users and remote users. A mail gateway allows free exchange of messages, which can usually include attached files, but does not provide complete access to the rest of the LAN. It normally requires custom remote client software (see Figure 1.1).

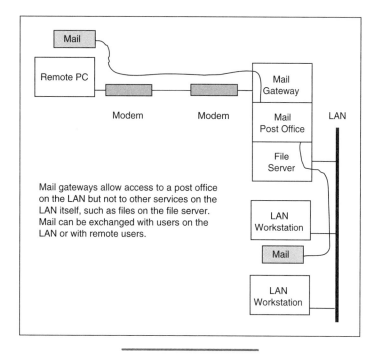

FIGURE 1.1 MAIL GATEWAYS.

Mail gateways work well when the interaction is between users and the response does not have to be immediate. For example, suppose you are on the road and you need a file later that day; you write a mail message to a coworker and send it through the mail gateway. Your coworker receives the message and responds with a message, with the file attached. You pick up the response and the file. Mail systems with work-flow support can often handle routing and requests automatically. In this case, a work-flow program takes the place of the coworker. For example, a customer could send a message containing an order. The mail gateway would forward the message to the work-flow program, which recognizes the order and starts processing it. This processing may include a response message confirming the order and a message to Accounts Receivable to send out a bill.

If you currently use mail on your LAN and you need remote LAN access, a mail gateway is an ideal choice. Most mail gateways are provided by the vendor of the LAN mail package, but in some cases third-party mail gateways are available.

Remote Workstations

Chapter 3 deals with a method at the other extreme from that covered in Chapter 2: remote workstations. With this method, the remote PC is part of the LAN during the call, and typically the only difference between the remote PC and a local PC is the speed of moving data across the LAN. The local PC has faster access to servers (10 megabits per second (Mbps) for Ethernet and 4 or 16 Mbps for Token Ring). A remote PC uses a modem that operates at speeds like 9600 to 28,800 baud, faster if data compression can be used (see Figure 1.2).

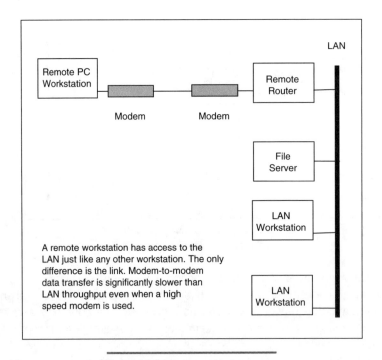

FIGURE 1.2 REMOTE WORKSTATIONS.

Remote workstations should be examined with care. They are versatile and provide a way to do remote network management, but they can also provide the remote user with access to the entire LAN. This security risk can be minimized by using passwords to restrict users and to control the time they can use a remote workstation link. Additional security can be implemented using callback modems, so that the caller can only initiate a connection from a particular location, such as from home or a branch office.

Remote workstation products are usually available from your NOS vendor. Third-party support is available for popular NOSes like Novell NetWare 3.x and 4.x. Remote workstation products also often provide LAN-to-LAN support and they can often use a single modem for both types of connection, but only one at a time.

Remote Control Programs

Remote control programs are covered in Chapter 4. This type of program requires a matching local host PC that is attached to the LAN. What is typed on the remote PC is sent to the remote control host PC, which thinks its own local keyboard is being used. The remote control program also sends a copy of the screen to the remote PC so the remote user can see what the host is doing (see Figure 1.3). Remote control programs can be used with PCs that are not on a LAN, but there are many advantages to using remote control programs with LAN-based PCs.

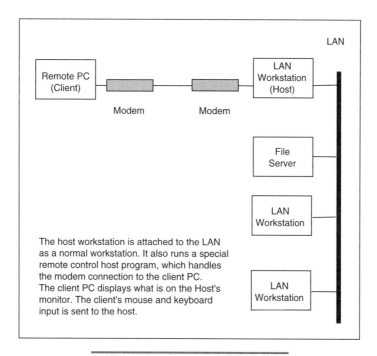

FIGURE 1.3 REMOTE CONTROL PROGRAMS.

Remote control programs usually have their own security system, which can be used in place of, or in addition to, the LAN security system. Remote control programs usually reside on either the LAN or the local workstation, so callers do not have to have or maintain these programs. The same is true for data, which is the usual reason for calling into a LAN. Access through a remote control program is more efficient than access via a remote workstation if there is a lot of LAN-based data to be processed by the local application and only a little data to be exchanged with the remote PC. Remote control programs are also ideal for LAN management, since the management programs are already on the LAN and the local workstation has direct access to the LAN.

Network Bulletin Board Systems

Network bulletin board systems (BBSes) are the subject of Chapter 5. Network BBSes provide an interesting remote LAN access method because the remote PC can use just about any terminal emulation program to access the BBS. The BBS has its own security system, so it can be managed independent of the LAN security. LANs are often installed without any security controls enabled, and users are often adverse to imposing restrictions. A network BBS can let you have external security while maintaining the status quo on the LAN (see Figure 1.4).

A BBS lets callers leave mail and upload and download files, and it often provides other services such as databases that can be searched. Order-entry and other custom programs can often be implemented with today's BBS products. A network BBS can give controlled access to files and services without providing direct access to the LAN. Files can be kept on a LAN file server so that LAN users can access and update them. Some BBS products even have network access programs, so you can use the BBS from a LAN workstation as if you had called in using a modem.

A network BBS is ideal when the callers have a variety of backgrounds and needs. Clients and customers with a PC and a terminal emulation program can access your BBS and, indirectly, your LAN. BBS add-ons, some of which are available from third parties, can provide mail gateway services between the native BBS mail and your LAN mail.

The BBS approach has another advantage over a basic mail gateway because of the way users are added and maintained. Mail gateways usually require a LAN manager to add new users. With a BBS, you can have a LAN manager do this, or you can set up the BBS to automatically add new users, with new users choosing their own passwords and entering their own background information.

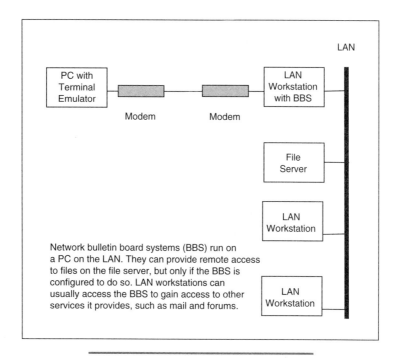

FIGURE 1.4 NETWORK BULLETIN BOARD SYSTEMS.

Remote Faxing

Chapter 6 covers remote faxing, a special case wherein information is exchanged using a fax machine instead of a PC, although a PC with a fax modem is a suitable alternative to a fax machine. A variety of products exist for sending faxes to a LAN, picking up faxes sent to a LAN fax server, and receiving faxes you request using a computer or Touch-Tone phone (see Figure 1.5). The fax method can often be used in combination with other means, such as a remote BBS or a mail gateway.

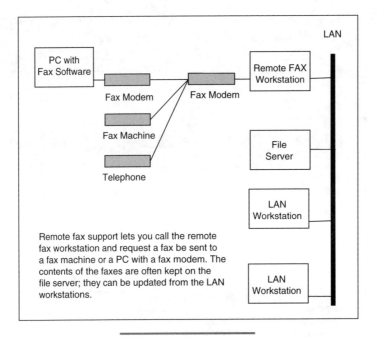

FIGURE 1.5 REMOTE FAXING.

Wireless Connections

Chapter 7 covers wireless connections, which are the alternatives to telephone-based modems. For the local solutions there are wireless LAN adapters (see Figure 1.6). For the road, we have radio modems and modems that attach to cellular telephones.

A wireless LAN adapter is a network interface card (NIC) that uses radio waves to communicate with other wireless NICS. A conventional Ethernet NIC is connected to other Ethernet NIC using coax cable or twisted pair wire. Wireless LAN adapters let you use standard NOS drivers. They provide the same support as a remote workstation except that a wireless LAN adapter is used instead of a modem. Wireless LAN adapters cost more than wired Ethernet or Token Ring adapters, but the main disadvantages of the wireless products are that they are slow and can only work over limited distances: they tend to be five to ten times slower than their wired counterparts, and you must be within 100 to 1000 feet of a receiver, depending on the product and the objects between the PC and the receiver.

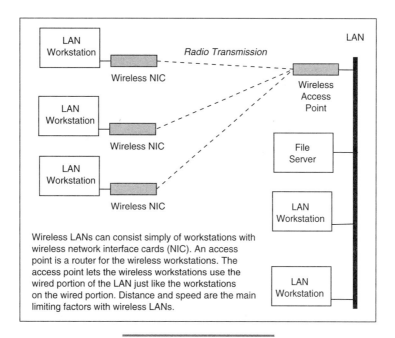

FIGURE 1.6 WIRELESS NETWORK.

There are two types of radio modems: normal modems with radio links and specialized modems with custom software. The former let you use any of the modem-based remote LAN access methods already discussed, while the latter normally interact with a specialized mail gateway. This type of system is useful if users need access to your LAN when they are traveling without a telephone and are farther away than the limited distance allowed by a wireless LAN adapter.

Specialized Tools

Chapter 8 takes a look at some of the hardware you might want to check out when implementing remote LAN access methods. For example, a remote power control box can turn on the local modem and PC when a call comes in, so that you don't have to keep the local PC turned on all the time. The chapter also covers specialized modems and software, such as white board software. Whiteboard software lets multiple users view and edit a common window. The contents of the window are replicated on each users screen. A user's annotations are immediately displayed on all screens.

Accessing the Internet

Chapter 9 is included as an initial introduction to Internet-related systems. These actually warrant their own book, and there are many books and products that address this method of remotely accessing LANs.

There are many advantages to Internet access to and from a LAN. You can share data with millions of users and provide services directly to both the Internet and your LAN users. You need to be careful of security, however; you probably don't want to open up all your LAN's resources to users of the Internet. Firewalls and dedicated gateways can often minimize the security risk (see Figure 1.7).

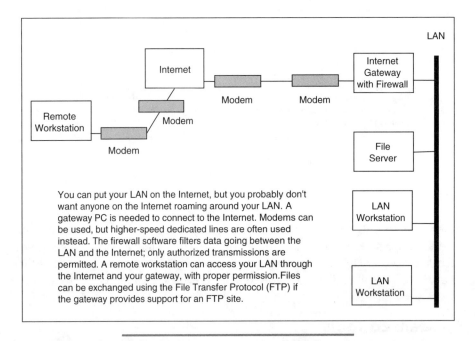

FIGURE 1.7 INTERNET, FIREWALLS, AND GATEWAYS.

This type of access should not be chosen casually. While other remote LAN access methods can be implemented for less than $1000 for hardware and software, Internet access can run this much, with additional monthly charges. A dedicated gateway PC must be powerful and should include a hefty bit of disk storage, which adds to the cost. The person who installs and maintains the system will also need to be familiar with TCP/IP and Internet tools. At this time, Internet access is typically done only by large or technically adept companies.

On the other hand, you may be accessing someone else's LAN through the Internet. While this often entails a cost for the Internet connection and the supporting software, the cost and required technical expertise are significantly lower than on the LAN side.

Are these access methods specific to a particular NOS? No, the methods are not. Often the products that implement the methods are, however, so you may have to do some shopping around to find one that fits your requirements. Novell NetWare 3.x and 4.x tend to have the widest support due to the popularity of these NOSes, but products are typically available for any major NOS, including IBM's LAN Server, Banyan's VINES, and Microsoft's Windows NT Advanced Server, as well as for peer-to-peer NOSes like Artisoft's LANtastic, Performance Technology's POWERLAN, Novell's Personal NetWare, and Microsoft's Windows for Workgroups.

If you are already convinced of the necessity and desirability of remote LAN access, then you can plunge right into the chapters that interest you. However, if you need a few ideas or reasons for implementing remote LAN access methods, check out the rest of this chapter. It will take a look at who needs remote LAN access, why it is needed, and what is needed to implement a remote LAN access method.

WHO NEEDS REMOTE LAN ACCESS?

If you are looking into remote LAN access, you probably need it. There are a number of different types of people who can make good use of remote LAN access, including:

❖ telecommuters

❖ traveling workers

❖ branch office workers calling into the main office

❖ LAN managers doing remote network management and diagnostics

❖ tech support

❖ clients and customers

Telecommuters work at home and call into the office (see Figure 1.8). Having access to their company's LAN is as important—if not more important—for telecommuters as for workers in the office. Electronic mail is an extremely useful tool for telecommuters, since their hours are often more flexible; being able to exchange messages with coworkers is a good way to augment voice telephone calls.

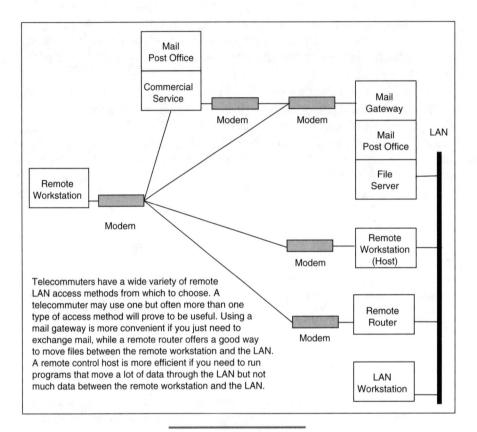

The figure contains the following text:

Mail Post Office

Commercial Service

Modem

Modem

Mail Gateway

LAN

Mail Post Office

File Server

Remote Workstation

Modem

Remote Workstation (Host)

Modem

Telecommuters have a wide variety of remote LAN access methods from which to choose. A telecommuter may use one but often more than one type of access method will prove to be useful. Using a mail gateway is more convenient if you just need to exchange mail, while a remote router offers a good way to move files between the remote workstation and the LAN. A remote control host is more efficient if you need to run programs that move a lot of data through the LAN but not much data between the remote workstation and the LAN.

Remote Router

Modem

LAN Workstation

FIGURE 1.8 TELECOMMUTING.

Traveling workers can keep in touch via their office LAN if they have remote access to it. Sending and receiving mail while on the road can be very important, and having the ability to access files on the LAN—or even on their own office PCs—can be very handy if they forget to bring an important file with them (see Figure 1.9).

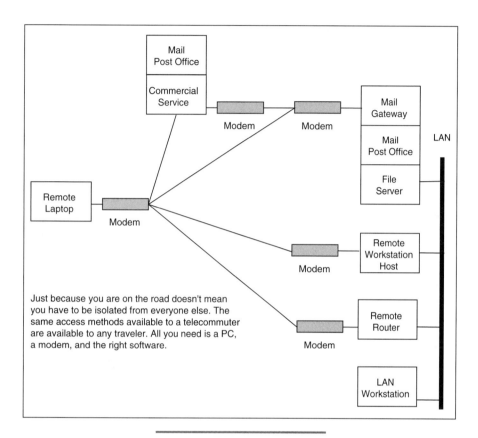

FIGURE 1.9 LAPTOPS ON THE ROAD.

Branch offices often have their own LANs, and more sophisticated companies often have wide area network (WAN, i.e., remote LAN-to-LAN) connections (see Figure 1.10). In this case, the WAN appears as a single LAN to users. The difference is local LAN access is faster than accessing something across a WAN link. A typical local LAN uses Ethernet which operates at 10 mbits/sec. A typical WAN connection using a V.34 modem runs at 28.8 kbits/sec. WANs are great if you have a need for regular or dedicated LAN-to-LAN connections, but remote LAN access is often a more suitable and less expensive alternative. Calling into the LAN can occur between the main office and the branch office in either direction depending on what needs to be done.

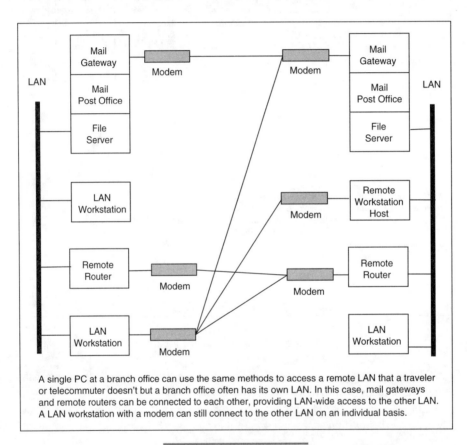

A single PC at a branch office can use the same methods to access a remote LAN that a traveler or telecommuter doesn't but a branch office often has its own LAN. In this case, mail gateways and remote routers can be connected to each other, providing LAN-wide access to the other LAN. A LAN workstation with a modem can still connect to the other LAN on an individual basis.

FIGURE 1.10 BRANCH OFFICES.

One person who might need to call a branch office is the LAN manager. Branch offices are often too small to warrant a dedicated LAN manager, but a company may be large enough to have a full-time LAN manager at one site. Remote LAN access allows a LAN manager to perform normal LAN management and remote LAN diagnostics (see Figure 1.11). This same technique can even be used on the main LAN if the LAN manager is on the road or is a telecommuter.

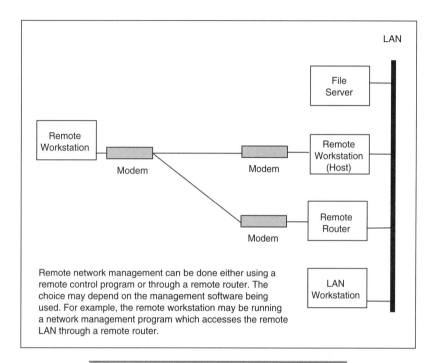

FIGURE 1.11 REMOTE MANAGEMENT AND DIAGNOSTICS.

LAN managers are not the only people who might use remote LAN access to do their jobs. Technical support can often be done remotely, perhaps even by a third party that you hire. Tech support can include answering questions via electronic mail or updating files on the LAN. The ultimate remote tech support uses remote control programs to interact directly with the users and their PCs. Having remote LAN access set up ahead of time can make remote tech support practical and easy to use.

Finally, there are users who would not normally have access to your LAN, such as clients and customers. The best interchange may be between mail gateways, one on your LAN and one on their LAN. This configuration can require a sophisticated LAN manager for installation and maintenance, but it is very transparent to users; they can send mail to people on another LAN the same way they communicate with their own local users. Direct access to your own mail gateway or network BBS are other alternatives. The advantage of this less-sophisticated approach is that a number of different clients and customers can use the same access method. Remote LAN access is one way to provide tech support and services to clients and customers.

Once you have remote LAN access for one type of user you will probably want to expand support to others. Multiple remote access methods on a single LAN are not uncommon, and it often pays to use an access method suitable to the type of user. Remote LAN users may also use more than one type of access method, depending on their needs and resources.

WHY YOU NEED REMOTE LAN ACCESS

Why do *you* need remote LAN access? Are you a telecommuter? Do you travel with a laptop? Are you a LAN manager who needs to provide support to a number of different LANs? Do you need to provide tech support to a large number of clients or customers? Remote LAN access methods may be appropriate if the answer to any of these questions is *yes*.

Remote LAN access keeps people in touch with each other. It can be used to provide services remotely such as tech support and LAN management, diagnostics, and maintenance. In many cases, it is impossible, impractical, or undesirable to have the necessary people in the office using the LAN locally.

Remote LAN access lets you exchange data, access services, and control PCs on the LAN. The kind of data and services and the type of control vary and can dictate what access methods are required and desirable.

Many types of data exchange or services can be provided using different remote LAN access methods. For example, electronic mail can be used via mail gateways, remote workstations, remote control programs, and a network BBS.

WHAT YOU NEED FOR REMOTE LAN ACCESS

Remote LAN access hardware consists typically of a high-speed modem (see Figure 1.12). The remote user needs one and there needs to be at least one on the LAN. The actual number of modems on the LAN may be dictated by the number of simultaneous connections required and the number of methods used. LAN modem pools are often available for dial-out use by local LAN users, but coordinating these pools with remote LAN access modems is often difficult—if not impossible. The problem occurs when a modem setup to answer a call is needed for an outgoing call when one comes in. Typically both operations fail.

FIGURE 1.12 HIGH-SPEED MODEM.

Some remote LAN access methods can be accomplished with 2400-baud modems, but most require higher-speed modems. V.32 modems running at 9600 baud should be your minimum choice. The current crop of modems is actually faster; V.32bis modems run at 14,400 baud and cost less than $150. The price difference between these modems and their slower brethren is negligible. The fastest modems you can get these days are V.34 modems, which operate at 28,800 baud. They currently command a premium price, but prices tend to drop as demand and availability rise.

Early modems simply sent data as it was received from the computer. Today's modems include built-in data compression, so the actual throughput can exceed the stated transfer rate. Hardware handshaking takes care of controlling data flow from the PC to the modem, so the PC transfer rate is usually set higher than the modem transfer rate. Hardware handshaking uses dedicated wires to let the modem and PC know when data can be exchanged without data being ignored. Handshaking allows the modem to tell the PC its buffer is full and that the PC should wait before sending data to the modem.

Hardware is not much good without software. Each access method requires software running on the LAN and on the remote PC. Where the LAN-based software runs depends on the access method and the actual product. It may run on a file server, on a user's PC, or on a dedicated PC acting as a specialized server. It can also run on a specialized server box connected to the LAN. For example, remote workstations connect to the LAN through a device called a *remote router*. The router can be software running in the file server with a modem attached to it, or a specialized device called a dedicated remote router. This little box contains a simplified version of a PC, a network interface card (NIC), a modem (or serial interface to attach an external modem), and the software to perform the routing function.

Most access methods require custom software at both ends. The software product you use typically comes with both parts, but some, such as remote control software, is often sold as individual parts. Licensing and related costs may be a consideration when you are choosing a remote LAN access method.

Of course, you will need a telephone line and a PC running an operating system that supports the software you choose. Nothing else is needed; this makes remote LAN access practical almost anywhere.

Alternatives to Remote LAN Access

Two alternatives to direct LAN access are to use the Internet or a commercial computer communication service provider such as CompuServe, America OnLine, Delphi or MCI Mail (see Figure 1.13). The latter typically provide electronic mail exchange only, while the others can provide electronic mail and other services.

What is the Internet? It is actually a worldwide network that has been popularized as the Information Superhighway. Hook up a server on your LAN to the Internet, and now your LAN is part of it. Access the Internet from any one of millions of access points and you can access your LAN. Sound great? Sound easy? We should be so lucky. Hooking your network into the Internet has many advantages and some disadvantages. Security and cost are major issues when considering the Internet as a remote LAN access method.

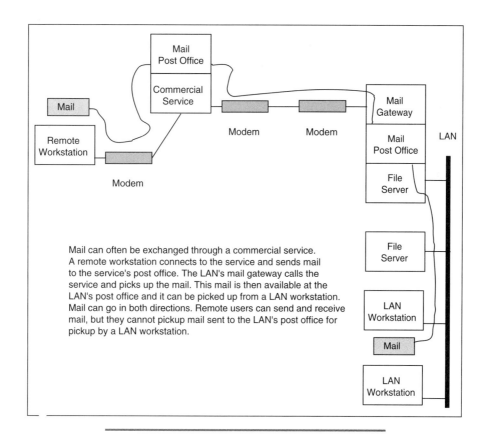

FIGURE 1.13 COMMERCIAL SERVICE AND ACCESS TO A LAN.

Using the Internet to access your LAN is overkill if you have only a few remote users. Internet links also require significant technological support compared to the other remote LAN access methods. In addition, for small to medium-size companies, Internet access must be through an Internet service provider. For more details, check out Chapter 9, "Accessing the Internet."

Commercial service providers such as Compuserve can act as extensions to mail gateways, which are covered in Chapter 2. The mail gateway on your LAN calls the commercial service provider's mail gateway and exchanges mail. This type of connection requires compatible mail gateways on both sides and is appropriate only for a limited collection of LAN-based mail packages. Technical support requirements are less demanding than those required for Internet access but greater than for other remote LAN access methods covered in this book.

Like Internet access, use of commercial service mail gateways is usually impractical for small companies with limited telecommunication requirements. Security is less of an issue—mail exchange does not allow direct access to your LAN—but cost is an issue. Commercial service mail gateway costs are much higher than a single user on the same service. Connection fees, minimum monthly fees and connection time costs can add up to a significant expense. These costs are significantly higher than a single user's costs.

There are two major reasons for using the Internet or a commercial service to provide access to a LAN. The first is a large number of access points around the country and, for the Internet, around the world. This can lower the cost of accessing your LAN and may be an issue when you are providing remote LAN access to a large number of users. The second reason is the number of potential users. Commercial service providers have millions of users and the Internet has even more. Even a small percentage of these users would be a large number of potential users. If you are providing or selling a service or data through your LAN, these alternatives may be economically and technically practical.

Regardless of which remote LAN access methods you choose to implement, you will find the added flexibility very useful. LAN-based mail and common file and service access provide local users with a powerful way to interact with each other. Remote LAN access brings this power to users outside the building that contains the LAN.

Chapter 2

Mail Gateways

Electronic mail (E-mail) was not invented for local area networks (LANs), but it has been popularized and has grown significantly with the growth of LANs. E-mail can also be used to remotely exchange information on a LAN.

Mail, LANs, and Mail Gateways

E-mail use is analogous to real (physical) mail, only the components are electronic. E-mail itself is simply computer documents that you create and send to someone else. E-mail, like real mail, goes through a post office. An E-mail post office can be a shared database or an active program on a server, often a network file server (see Figure 2.1).

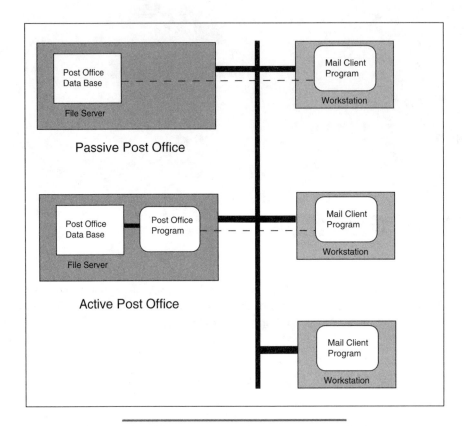

FIGURE 2.1 BASIC POST OFFICE CONFIGURATION.

A separate program is normally needed to create, send, retrieve, and view E-mail. Graphical environments like MacOS, Windows, and OS/2 and their applications are incorporating mail support to a greater degree, so that many applications such as word processors and spreadsheets provide the front-end program.

E-mail systems, however, do not totally duplicate real mail. Where mail is kept, for example, is one difference between them. Whereas an E-mail system's post office can act as both a delivery system and a repository, the post office in a real mail system simply delivers the mail and you take possession of it. You might read your E-mail at your PC, but it remains in the post office until you delete it. There are advantages to both approaches. Keeping the mail in the post office allows you to read and reread your mail from any access point on the same LAN. You can, of course, move the mail to your own PC for greater security, but by doing so you limit your access point. The analogy between real and electronic mail goes even further. A single post office does not serve the entire country; instead, there are local post offices that act as local delivery mechanisms for local mail and provide exchange of nonlocal mail with other post offices.

The interface between two electronic mail post offices is called a *mail gateway*. Actually you need a pair of mail gateways for two post offices to exchange mail and they must be compatible with each other. Just as there is a standard letter address format and ZIP code system, so there is a standard electronic exchange standard between a pair of compatible mail gateways. Mail gateways act as a buffer between the post office and a remote source. The remote source does not have to be another post office. It can often be a single PC, such as a remote E-mail user's laptop. The connection between the post office's mail gateway and the remote source is usually accomplished with a telephone line and a pair of modems. There are other ways to make the connection, including going through the Internet or using other connection methods like ISDN, but more on that later.

A modem-based mail gateway can often handle multiple simultaneous remote users, as well as multiple remote post offices. Put the post office onto a LAN with local mail users and add a mail gateway for remote users, and you have a form of remote LAN access.

Electronic mail gateway products, normally available from an E-mail vendor, connect a pair of the vendor's post offices together. These often use proprietary *protocols*, which prevent one vendor's post office from being connected to another vendor's post office. A protocol defines how two post offices will communicate with each other including data format and the order of data exchange. Connecting different vendor post offices together often means finding mail gateways that work with different post offices and communicate with a common gateway format. Another alternative is to add a third post office, as shown in Figure 2.2, which is common to both post offices. In this case, the mail gateways exchange mail with the common post office. Mail can move from one vendor's post office to the other, with an extra hop through the common post office.

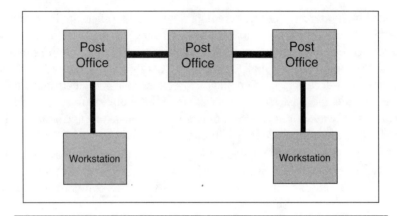

Fɪɢᴜʀᴇ 2.2 Tʜʀᴇᴇ ᴘᴏꜱᴛ ᴏꜰꜰɪᴄᴇꜱ ᴡɪᴛʜ ᴛʜᴇ ᴍɪᴅᴅʟᴇ ᴏɴᴇ ᴀᴄᴛɪɴɢ ᴀꜱ ᴀɴ ɪɴᴛᴇʀꜰᴀᴄᴇ
ʙᴇᴛᴡᴇᴇɴ ᴛʜᴇ ᴏᴛʜᴇʀ ᴛᴡᴏ.

Mail can even move through multiple post offices to get from a remote E-mail sender
to a remote E-mail recipient. Likewise, a pair of remote E-mail users can exchange mail
on the same post office. Figure 2.3 shows some of the combinations that can occur.

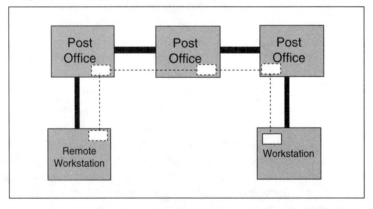

Fɪɢᴜʀᴇ 2.3 Rᴇᴍᴏᴛᴇ ᴍᴀɪʟ ᴇxᴄʜᴀɴɢᴇ ʙᴇᴛᴡᴇᴇɴ ʀᴇᴍᴏᴛᴇ ᴜꜱᴇʀꜱ, ᴛʜʀᴏᴜɢʜ ᴍᴜʟᴛɪᴘʟᴇ
ᴘᴏꜱᴛ ᴏꜰꜰɪᴄᴇꜱ.

Basic electronic mail exchange is between mail users, either remote or local. In
this case, a person must be at both ends of the exchange to make it work. If attach-

ments are sent, then the sender selects the files to attach to the mail message. A response will be sent when the receiver reads the message.

Work-flow software can remove the need for active user intervention at either end of the exchange. Work-flow support can be implemented in a number of ways, but the end result is that messages can be sent under program control and processed in the same fashion. The work-flow processing can be specified using rules, menu selections, or a programming language, depending on the work-flow product. The user is allowed to setup the rules or write the program. Work-flow software is often used to process messages such as expense reports, orders, and technical support calls. Sending a message to someone may cause the message to be filed and forwarded. It may also cause other messages to be generated. Work-flow support can also be set up to process messages as requests for data to be sent back to the original sender; this automatic data exchange is possible, and the main enabling technology is the mail system. For example, a manager could setup a rule to forward incoming expense reports to accounts payable and to send a confirmation to the sender. Bringing such functions to remote users requires the addition of a mail gateway.

If you think that mail messages are just for text, you are in for a pleasant surprise. Many mail systems are limited to text messages or messages that can be either text or binary data, but newer mail programs and post offices support a variety of data types. The next step up from a message with a single text or binary block of data is a message with attachments. The message is typically text, and the attachments are files of any type. The file name is normally included with the message. More sophisticated mail systems support documents with embedded data. Three document standards are emerging: *Mail Interchange Multimedia Extensions* (MIME), *Common Object Model/Object Linking and Embedding* (COM/OLE), and *OpenDoc*. All three have a base document format, with the ability to include data or references to data in the document. The document viewers can display this embedded data at the appropriate position within the document; this differs from a message with attachments, where the files are not part of the message itself. Document viewers can be the application that created a document or a special program that can display a particular document format. These document standards also include formatting information, so your mail message may contain mixed fonts, drawings, pictures, and even sounds and multimedia presentations. The document standards are designed for general data exchange, not just mail messages, but the two fit together very well.

The bottom line is that mail provides an excellent way for remote users to access a LAN, its data, and its users. The way that a remote user accesses the LAN is through a mail gateway.

MAIL GATEWAYS: A USER'S VIEW

Using a mail gateway is relatively easy once the software is installed on the LAN and the remote PC. The installation procedure is specific to the product you use, and the gateway normally matches the remote PC mail gateway access software. The gateway and remote gateway access software normally come from the same vendor. Mail gateways usually support a variety of remote PC operating systems and PC types, but for the purposes of discussion we will be looking at Microsoft Windows–based software with mail gateways that operates on Novell NetWare or Microsoft Windows NT Advanced Server servers or on DOS-based LAN workstations. Microsoft Windows–based mail client software will be on the remote PC.

Using a basic electronic mail system requires user input at both ends. Figure 2.4 shows how the process operates. Mail is created at the remote PC or at a workstation on the LAN using a built in text editor (see Figure 2.5). The messages are kept at the creation point until they are ready to be sent. Sending a message from the LAN-based PC moves the message immediately to the server-based post office, where it can be picked up; sending a message from the remote PC places the message in an output queue or out-box for subsequent delivery. Immediate delivery could be done, but then your PC winds up making a telephone call for each message you write. This approach lets you write multiple messages and send them all at once. You can also delay the pickup time to a more convenient time, such as the evening, when telephone toll charges are lower or when you have access to a telephone.

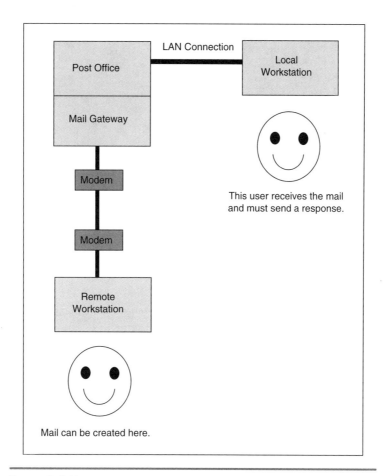

FIGURE 2.4 MAIL CREATION AND EXCHANGE PROCESS CHART (FOR BOTH ENDS).

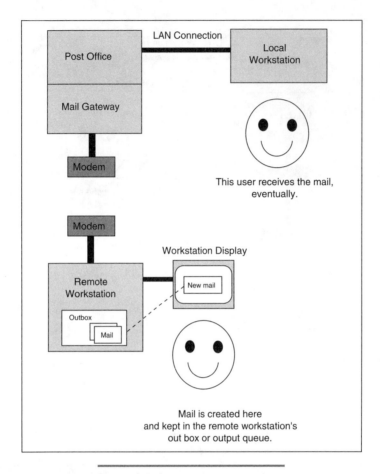

FIGURE 2.5 CREATING A MAIL MESSAGE.

The next step for the remote PC user is to send the messages in the output queue to the LAN-based post office (see Figure 2.6). This is where the mail gateway comes into play. Most post office products are designed to interact directly with LAN-based workstations and gateways. The remote mail gateway is just one possible gateway; other gateways include fax gateways and gateways to other post offices. Post office gateways can be used to connect post offices from the same vendor or different vendors' post offices. In the latter case, a common mail exchange protocol may be used, so a LAN manager or post office manager needs to buy the matching gateway packages.

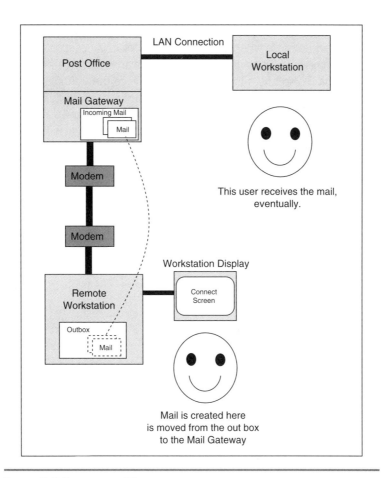

FIGURE 2.6 THE REMOTE PC USER SENDS THE MESSAGE IN THE OUTPUT QUEUE TO THE LAN-BASED POST OFFICE.

Some remote mail packages let you work with a single post office. Others are capable of working with more than one, although you must initiate a call between all post offices to deliver or pick up mail with the respective post office. Products with this type of support typically integrate the post office address within the address book entries used to address a message. Products that access a single post office can be used to access multiple post offices by manually changing the post office name and phone number before calling the post office. The mail software can then determine which messages need to be sent to a particular post office when a connection is made.

Mail exchange can be initiated manually or automatically; the latter is often done at scheduled times or when a sufficient number of messages are in the output queue. The mail program on the remote PC uses an attached modem to call the mail gateway, which also has a modem attached. Once the connection is made, a status window like the one shown in Figure 2.7 will be displayed. The number of messages, and possibly the estimated transfer time, is displayed while the messages are exchanged. The connection is broken after all the mail is transferred.

FIGURE 2.7 ONCE THE CONNECTION BETWEEN THE REMOTE PC AND THE POST OFFICE IS MADE, A STATUS WINDOW LIKE THIS ONE WILL APPEAR.

The remote mail program communicates with the mail gateway program to exchange messages. The mail gateway, in turn, works with the post office on the LAN. Normally the gateway does not maintain messages, it just passes them between the post office and the remote PC.

Some mail programs will let you maintain the connection so you can read mail and send a response immediately. This type of connection is helpful for users, but it can incur additional telephone toll charges and it ties up the mail gateway's modem. The latter may not be desirable if there are few modems on the mail gateway and a potentially large number of remote users. A quick-connect/disconnect procedure makes efficient use of the mail gateway's phone line. The automatic nature of the connection makes it relatively easy for a remote user to respond to a message after leisurely examining the message (see Figure 2.8), while not racking up long distance telephone charges.

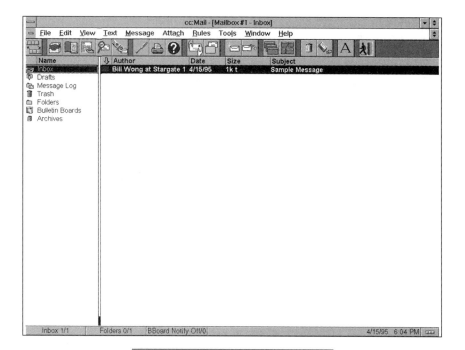

FIGURE 2.8 READING AN EMAIL MESSAGES.

From a user's standpoint, there is not much to it, other than to send and read messages. The mail program installation procedure must be done once, and often the program can be installed for you. There are four pieces of information that are used to customize your installation:

✧ the post office name
✧ the post office phone number
✧ your mail name
✧ your post office password.

The post office name is only needed if you work with more than one mail gateway. The phone number is needed to initiate a call using the modem, but the number may have to be changed depending on where you are calling from. A PC at home will use the same phone number all the time, but a mobile user may need to modify the phone number to accommodate changes in area code, dialing prefixes, or even different phone numbers, depending on the priority of a message. Your mail name will probably differ from your full name, but it is how other mail users will send you mail. It must be entered in your PC's mail software so it knows whose mail to pick up. If you are also a LAN-based mail user, your post office mail name may be the same or different for LAN and remote use. Different names may be required by the post office software or gateway software, or it may be required for security reasons. Many LAN-based post offices can use the LAN's user name and password for managing mail; this means that a LAN user need only remember one name and password to both use the LAN and to send and receive mail. The LAN user also needs to remember just one name to give others for sending mail. The problem with this approach, in that a single name and password provides mail and LAN access, is that a LAN manager may have remote users who will never be official LAN users but may have occasional access to LAN-based PCs. In this case, the LAN manager would like to be able to give the remote user a name and password that does not give them access to the LAN.

One advantage to giving remote users two mail names, and hence two associated passwords, is to allow users to selectively send messages to remote users; what may be a small file attachment for a LAN-based user could take an hour to transfer for a remote user. The throughput differences between LAN access and modem access are very large. For example, Ethernet runs at 10 megabits/second. A one-megabyte file can be sent in a few seconds, depending on the efficiency of the file server, the network interface card (NIC), and the load on the network due to other network traffic. A modem connection is significantly slower. Slow 2400-baud modems used to be common, but today 14,400-baud modems with data compression are standard. The new V.34 modems operate at twice that speed, 28,800 baud, and you can often double that with built-in compression. Still, 57,600 bits/second is much slower than Ethernet's 10,000,000 bits/second. A one-megabyte file takes more than four minutes to send if it cannot be compressed, and about half that if the file can be compressed by the modem during transmission. A remote user can request that LAN users send small files and messages to one mail name and larger files sent to the LAN-based user name. The remote user can call in and pick up the small messages to minimize connection time.

Two mail program features found in some products give users the ability to control what mail is exchanged. One feature is selective pickup. In this case, the user is presented with a list of messages, and all or some messages can be designated for pickup. Messages are normally listed with size or transfer time estimates, so a remote user can determine how long a connection will be. The second control feature is thresholds on message size, possibly combined with priority settings if the mail programs allow them. In this case, you might accept large files with high-priority messages but limit the size of messages or attachments for normal or low-priority messages. Although I have not seen a product with the following feature, it would be possible to have the settings based on transfer time instead of message size. This actually makes more sense, since the modem settings may differ for a variety of reasons; for example, some modems can adjust their transfer rate based on the quality of the telephone line, which can vary from call to call. A connection may thus have to be made at 2400 baud even though both modems are capable of connecting at 14,400 baud.

The use of work-flow mail support does not change the basic operation of remote mail LAN access, but it does provide some benefits. In particular, it allows a remote user to interact with the LAN in a controlled fashion without requiring the active intervention of another user. Figure 2.9 shows how a remote user's mail message might invoke a response, which the remote user can then pick up at a later time.

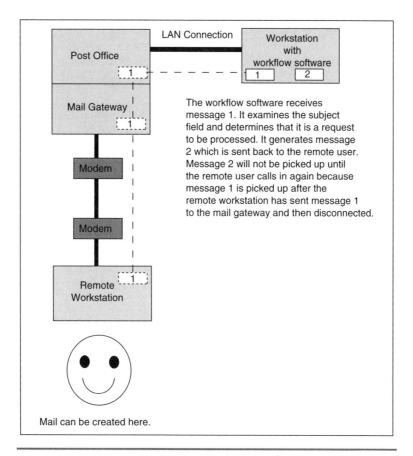

FIGURE 2.9 WORK-FLOW METHOD CHART. A REMOTE USER'S MAIL MESSAGE MIGHT INVOKE A RESPONSE, WHICH THE REMOTE USER CAN PICK UP LATER.

Essentially, a work-flow product uses the mail transport system to exchange data. It may have access to its own set of mail names or messages to actual users. The messages are scanned for various criteria, which are programmed into the work-flow system. The work-flow system can forward messages or generate new messages in response to a received message. A work-flow system is usually put in place for LAN-based users, but it works equally well with remote users. It can often be customized for remote users to provide remote data access; for example, a message sent to a special work-flow user name could include a list of files to be sent back as attachments in a response message.

Remote LAN access using a mail gateway is a useful way to let a variety of users gain access to a LAN and its users. It requires only a remote mail access program on the remote PC. It does not require knowledge, understanding, or access to the LAN, so access security can be maintained if necessary. Most mail programs use the same interface for both remote and LAN-based access, so mobile or remote users who also use a workstation on the LAN do not have to use two different interfaces.

MAIL GATEWAYS: A LAN MANAGER'S VIEW

Planning, installing, and maintaining a mail gateway is not a piece of cake, but neither is installing and maintaining a LAN-based post office. Luckily, most product manufacturers try to make the job as easy as possible. In general, you will need to set up a LAN-based post office before installing a mail gateway. Some products include and integrate mail gateway support into their post offices, but most are separate programs that add onto the main post office product. Post offices and mail gateways can be installed in a number of different ways, as shown in Figure 2.10, although most products use only one architecture.

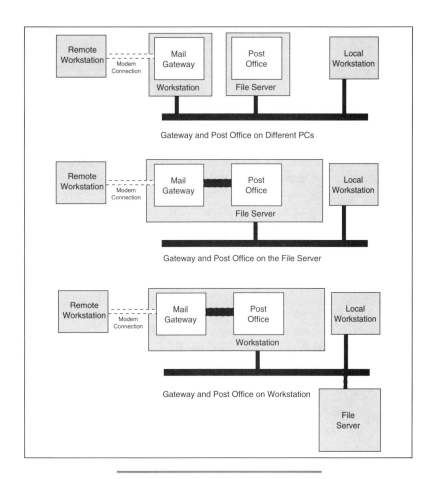

FIGURE 2.10 MAIL GATEWAY ARCHITECTURE.

Post offices can be divided into two categories: *passive* and *active*. A passive post office uses a database on a file server; mail client programs on workstations access the post office database. Active post offices have a server-based program that is accessed by mail client programs. The post office server program maintains its own database that the mail client programs cannot access directly. The mail client programs work directly with the post office program. Some active post offices can run on a server along with other programs such as file and print services, while other active post offices must run on their own dedicated PCs. A single active post office may maintain a single post office or multiple post offices, depending on the product and the needs of the users. A post office that can be placed on either a server or a dedicated PC has the advantage of being able to minimize the amount of hardware on the LAN by sharing the server's hardware or distribute the load imposed by the mail system. Some post office products can only be used on a server or a dedicated PC.

Mail client programs on a LAN workstation access the post office directly, while those on a remote workstation must access the post office through a mail gateway. In many respects, the mail gateway operates like a LAN-based mail client program, but typically a mail gateway has more flexible access to the post office because it needs to be able to access mail for multiple users.

A mail gateway, like a post office, may be placed on a file server or a dedicated PC. The mail gateway may be on the same PC as the post office or on a different PC, depending on the product and its options. One product may require the post office database to be placed on a file server with a PC needed for an active post office and a second PC to run the mail gateway. A more consolidated approach has all three parts on a single file server. From a user's point of view, there is little, if any, difference; from a LAN manager's point of view, the difference is in performance, availability, and cost of hardware, support, reliability, and security.

A mail gateway is installed after the post office is installed. Some mail gateways require a gateway product in addition to the mail gateway. The gateway product provides the interface for specific types of gateways such as fax gateways or remote mail gateways. A remote mail gateway uses at least one modem; most products support at least two, and many provide support for a whole bank of modems. In the latter case, special multiple-port serial adapters are used. The adapters are the same ones used with multiterminal UNIX systems and BBSes.

Mail gateways require maintenance and support in addition to the post office itself. The amount of support depends on how the gateway is configured and what jobs it performs. Mail gateways can provide remote mail access by individual users. Mail gateways can also provide remote post office–to–post office connections. The latter is more complicated and requires coordinated support at both ends of the connection. It does provide remote LAN access to a whole group of users instead of individual users.

Mail gateways often let you specify which users can send and receive messages through the gateway, when calls can be accepted, and which modems are used for various functions. For example, it may be desirable to dedicate one modem for connecting to other mail gateways. The modems attached to the mail gateway may have different capabilities, and as a LAN manager, you may want to restrict who can use the faster modems. The mail gateway manager is not involved when the gateway makes a connection with remote users, and most connections to other mail gateways are done on a timed basis.

MAIL GATEWAYS: WHAT ARE THEY AND HOW DO THEY WORK?

A *mail gateway* is a special communications program that communicates with a remote PC and a post office via a modem. It works with a post office to allow messages to be exchanged between the post office and something on the other side of the gateway. The two things that are typically on the other side of a mail gateway are a remote user's PC or another mail gateway. Although what happens over a connection between a mail gateway and a PC and between two mail gateways is different, they are conceptually the same: an exchange of messages. For the purposes of discussion we will look at the mail-gateway-to-PC connection only. In particular, we will be looking at a modem-based mail-gateway-to-PC connection.

The mail gateway can access the modem and the post office using different techniques, depending on the product. Typically the serial port for the modem is on the same PC as the mail gateway. The alternative has the mail gateway using a network-based modem. In this case, the LAN is used to communicate between the mail gateway and the network-based modem. Network-based modems are typically part of a *modem pool*, which is a collection of modems that can be accessed by programs on the LAN. Modem pools are typically used for outgoing calls, but they can also be used for incoming calls. Mail gateways normally handle incoming calls from remote PC users and initiate outgoing calls to connect with other mail gateways.

A mail gateway initializes its modem or modems to accept incoming calls when the mail gateway starts up. It then monitors the modems for a call. After a call is detected, the mail gateway goes through a *handshaking* protocol with the calling program (in this case, the calling program is the mail client software on the remote PC). The handshake procedure identifies the two programs to each other.

The remote PC then lets the mail gateway know the name and password of the user on the remote PC. This information is forwarded by the mail gateway to the post office. The post office software then checks the name and password, just like it does when a mail client program on the LAN tries to access the post office. Assuming all goes well at the post office, the mail gateway can then accept messages from the remote PC and forward them to the post office, and then pick up any messages for the user that are at the post office and send them to the mail client program on the remote PC.

Although the kind connection between the post office and the mail gateway is really irrelevant to operation, it is important in terms of performance and hardware requirements. Where the mail gateway is placed is usually a function of a particular product. For example, a cc:mail remote gateway runs on a workstation. A mail gateway can be on the same PC as the post office or on another PC. The only functional difference between the two is how the post office and gateway communicate. Fast, *interprocess communication* (communication between two programs) is used when the two are on the same PC; the LAN is used when they are on different PCs. Putting the mail gateway on its own PC does add traffic to the LAN. It is also slower than when both are on one PC, but remember that the slowest link is actually the modem used to connect the mail gateway to the remote PC. Mail exchange is also a procedure that requires little turn-around time. Messages are actually *buffered* at the mail gateway, so there is no perceived transmission time over the LAN. A message is received in its entirety by the mail gateway before it is sent to the post office. Likewise, the recipient of a message will probably not notice the fraction of a second it takes to move a message across the LAN if the post office is on one PC and the gateway on another.

Although we have been talking about a mail gateway and a single remote PC, mail gateways typically handle multiple modems simultaneously. The mail gateways that run on a single-tasking operating system like DOS implement their own multitasking system within the mail gateway program. Mail gateways that run on multitasking operating systems like OS/2 or Windows NT typically take advantage of the underlying multitasking support.

One special type of mail gateway is implemented as part of a bulletin board system (BBS). Network BBS support is covered in Chapter 5. BBS-based mail gateways differ from the mail gateways already discussed. A BBS typically has its own mail support; it essentially acts as its own post office. In this case, the BBS mail gateway acts more like the mail gateways between post offices. The main difference between using a remote mail client with a mail gateway and using the BBS mail gateway is the user interface. The BBS is normally accessed using a terminal-emulation program and the mail is created while you are connected to the BBS. A mail client does not include the terminal emulation support but it will be similar in operation to the interface presented by the BBS in the terminal emulation window.

The advantage of a BBS mail gateway is the ability to use a simple terminal-emulation program to access the post office. Terminal-emulation programs are easy to obtain, and almost any one will work with most BBS programs. The disadvantages, compared to the remote mail client software, are the comparatively primitive interface and the more complex connection procedure to access the BBS. Remote mail client operation is relatively simple and automatic.

MAIL GATEWAYS: WHY USE THEM FOR REMOTE LAN ACCESS

Mail gateways have a number of advantages and disadvantages when they are used to remotely access a LAN. The following table summarizes these.

Advantages

Simple user interface
Access to LAN mail system
Telephone time minimized
Automatic connect/disconnect
Mail users do not have to be LAN users
Security is independent of LAN security
No direct access to other LAN services

Disadvantages

No direct access to other LAN services
Requires user interaction
Delayed response to requests

On the positive side, the mail client interface is relatively simple. We are not talking about how many menu options there are or if the program has a toolbar, but rather about the logical operation that all products in this category share. In its most basic form, the mail client has an in-box, an out-box, and possibly a folder filing system. This interface is easy to describe and use. You create messages and put them in the out-box. Messages in the out-box get sent to a post office.

Messages are picked up from the post office and placed in the in-box, where the user can read them at his or her leisure. Messages can also be placed into the filing system so that the in-box does not get cluttered and so you can keep copies of messages sent via the out-box.

Access to the LAN mail system is the primary goal of the techniques presented in this chapter, but it is possible to set up a mail gateway solely to service remote users; having further access to LAN mail is an added benefit when a LAN-based mail system is already in place and in use. Direct access to the office's mail system while on the road or at home means you can get your mail without having to be in the office.

Telephone time is minimized if the mail client and post office operate in a connect/exchange/disconnect mode. The connection between the remote PC and the mail gateway remains in effect only long enough to determine what messages need to be exchanged and to perform the exchange. The connection is not maintained while a user reads his or her mail. A subsequent call may be required if a response is created and must be sent immediately, but this is relatively easy and automatic. This automatic connect/exchange/disconnect is probably the hallmark of the mail gateway approach. Other remote LAN access methods can take significantly longer to perform the same task.

Although remote mail users can also be LAN users they do not have to be. This can be a definite plus for companies that want to provide non-employees access to the LAN and its users. Remote mail access is well-defined in scope, operation, and security.

A mail gateway's security is normally independent of LAN security. Small companies may omit security measures on their LAN because of the physical security of the LAN (it is inside a secure building), but they probably do not want unsecured modem access. A mail gateway's use of individual names and passwords for remote mail users can provide this security.

Finally, remote mail users do not have direct access to other LAN services such as file and print services. This is an advantage from a security viewpoint. These services do not have to be secured from remote users because the mail system does not provide direct access to these services. Of course, a LAN user can send a file located on a LAN to a remote user, but that is a desirable option.

On the negative side, the mail gateway does not provide direct access to other LAN functions such as file and print services. This is a disadvantage from a user's point of view. Users that require access to file services or other LAN-based services must use another remote LAN access method to gain access to them.

The use of work-flow products aside, remote mail access requires user interaction to get any work done. Remote users can send all the mail they want, but unless someone checks the mail or sends mail to the remote user, little gets done. Other remote access methods such as remote workstation software or remote control programs let a remote user access files on the network without other users, LAN or remote, being involved.

Delayed response to remote user requests goes along with the need for remote users to interact with other mail users. Messages are not typically examined immediately, or at least not during a mail exchange between the remote mail client software and the mail gateway. A remote user creates a message and it is sent to the post office; after the connection is broken, the recipient can read the message and respond to it. The response message will be picked up by the remote user the next time they call in. This delay can be minutes, hours, or days.

Remote LAN access using a mail gateway is a suitable approach if the remote users can live within the limitations. Using a mail gateway is not a suitable way to access a database located on a LAN-based server. It *is* an ideal way to exchange mail. Mail gateways are suitable for use by users who may not be employees.

MAIL GATEWAYS: CONSIDERATIONS ON USING THEM FOR REMOTE LAN ACCESS

There are a number of basic considerations that need to be examined before a mail gateway should be implemented. These considerations can help determine if mail gateways are suitable, practical, and desirable. The following is a list of considerations we will examine in more detail:

- ✦ Access to LAN users (yes)
- ✦ Access to LAN services (no)
- ✦ Ease of use by remote users (good)
- ✦ Telephone time (minimal)
- ✦ Number of simultaneous active lines (high)
- ✦ Performance (good)
- ✦ Scalability (good)
- ✦ Hardware requirements (variable)

- ✧ Client licensing (required)
- ✧ Cost (high)
- ✧ Adding users (manual)
- ✧ General maintenance (minimal)
- ✧ Security (good)
- ✧ Auditing (minimal)
- ✧ Automation (good with work-flow support)

Mail gateways provide outside users access to LAN users via mail exchange, but they do not provide direct access to LAN operations such as file or print services. Remote users that need to communicate with LAN users or other remote users can make good use of a mail gateway. If other LAN services must be accessed, it is time to look elsewhere.

The remote mail client software is typically easy to use for both message creation and viewing, as well as message exchange with the remote post office through the mail gateway. Installation is usually straightforward, even for novices. Proper configuration of the modem is the most difficult task. Using a mail gateway is a good choice if the remote users are not well versed in computers and telecommunications. The automatic nature of the mail client and mail gateway connection is also a benefit to the user. Although the remote PC must be running, the user can often be doing other things or the connection can be handled without user intervention. Other remote LAN access mechanisms require the active participation of the user during the connection. The remote user can initiate a connection and have the mail client program complete it automatically or even schedule an automatic connection for a later time.

Telephone connect time can be of concern for a number of reasons, and keeping connect time low is usually important. Long distance connections cost money. Mail gateways can support more than one modem, but even a bank of modems can be kept busy with enough users calling in. Keeping the connect time to a minimum allows other callers to connect using the mail gateway. Typically, connection times can be kept to minutes unless large files are being sent. This means a single mail gateway can handle a relatively large number of remote users.

Performance for a single user is good because there is little unused connection bandwidth; most of the connection time is spent exchanging messages. Other remote LAN access methods may have nothing being transferred while a user is reading messages or examining files. Likewise, a mail gateway and post office update the post office's database for a remote mail user. Using another remote LAN access method such as a remote workstation, covered in Chapter 3, requires additional manipulation using the remote connection. Here a connection is first made as a remote workstation. The next step is to login and then run the mail client. Finally mail can be exchanged.

A single mail gateway can handle more than one modem. Mail gateways provide both a growth path and the ability to support multiple telephone lines from a single PC. Other remote LAN access methods need a matching PC and modem, which can get expensive quickly.

The ability to add more than one modem to a mail gateway makes scalability good. A telephone line, a modem, possibly another serial port, and the appropriate license, if necessary, are all that is needed to provide each additional user access to the mail gateway. A rotary telephone line lets a single telephone number be used to access all the modems for a single gateway. This approach lets a mail gateway be scaled up transparently to the remote users.

The actual cost for hardware varies depending on how the mail gateway is implemented and installed. A mail gateway that can be placed on the same PC as the post office saves the cost of a PC. Small gateways, with one or two modems, can be installed on standard PCs using COM1 and COM2 (PC serial ports). Gateways that have more modems normally require multiple-port serial adapters. Some adapters have up to sixteen serial lines; often these adapters have their own microprocessor to assist in communications tasks. The adapters are expensive compared to single- or dual-port serial adapters, but they are significantly less expensive than a PC.

One way mail gateways can add to the overall cost is in licensing fees. A mail gateway may require a single license for any number of supported modems, or the fee may be based on the number of modems or users supported. Regardless of the cost of the mail gateway, the cost for mail client software may easily overshadow it. It is also possible that the mail client software can be freely distributed for use with a post office, but then the post office is licensed based on the number of users. In this case, the number of users is typically not divided into local and remote users. In fact, a user that accesses the post office both remotely and locally will normally be licensed as a single user.

Total cost estimates based on licensing fees and support hardware should be made before looking at a mail gateway as a remote LAN access method. Although the cost is typically high for a large number of users, the incremental cost for adding additional remote mail users is usually not high, especially if the remote users are also local users.

One area where a mail gateway can be more difficult to manage than other remote LAN access methods is in maintaining the user population. Mail gateway users are normally managed through the post office. Most post office products maintain their own user list or synchronize with the network operating system's user list. In either case, adding a new user (local or remote) to the post office is a manual process for the LAN manager. The mail gateway or mail post office administration program must be run to add a new user. This is good from a security point of view, but it does not allow a user to add him- or herself to the post office address list. Mail gateways are good if the user population is relatively static or where growth is controlled; they do not work well if arbitrary users need to be added to the post office access list. An added problem in providing a user access to a post office through a mail gateway is the availability of mail client software. This software is not something that is generally available, and most software licenses will not provide for free distribution.

General maintenance of a mail gateway and a post office is usually minimal. Adding or deleting users from the post office's list of valid users is the usual kind of maintenance a LAN manager can expect. Occasionally clearing a modem line or changing access schedules are typical chores.

LAN security with a mail gateway is relatively good. Remote users can only send and receive mail; they do not have direct access to other LAN services, regardless of the security settings for local LAN users. Using a gateway typically requires a valid user name and password, so even mail exchange is validated.

Auditing is one way to verify and maintain security. It is also useful in determining the load on the mail gateway. A heavy load may indicate the need to increase the number of modems or mail gateways. Unfortunately, most mail gateway software does not include auditing support. Occasionally post offices do, but they often do not differentiate between remote and local access. You are fortunate if auditing support is available for either the post office or mail gateway you choose or are required to use.

Remote mail clients connect to a post office through a mail gateway automatically, but this is not what one would consider automation. The addition of work-flow software can bring automation to a mail environment. Work-flow software can be a very powerful tool, although it does involve some programming to make it work. Work-flow automation is an excellent solution to a number of problems, but it is not suitable where interaction between the remote PC and the LAN occurs quickly and repeatedly. For example, querying a database is best done using other remote LAN access methods.

Mail gateways make an excellent solution for remote LAN access if the users can live within the limitations.

MAIL GATEWAYS: SOME EXAMPLES

Mail gateways come in all flavors. We can't take examine all of them, but we will take a look at some representative products: cc:Mail from Lotus; Microsoft Mail; and Novell's Message Handling System (MHS). The last is not a full mail product, but rather it is a mail backbone. We will also take a look at LANShark's SharkMail! for Banyan VINES. cc:Mail is a conventional mail product with a remote gateway architecture as we have presented earlier in the chapter. It uses a passive post office and a gateway on a dedicated PC. The products are available in an incremental fashion and the remote mail client is built-in. Microsoft Mail does not currently have a remote mail gateway; instead, you must make the PC a remote workstation. Although this remote LAN access method is covered in Chapter 3, we will take a look at Microsoft Mail to contrast the use of a mail gateway with accessing a mail system from a remote workstation. Novell's MHS is a server-based passive-post office architecture. It is also commonly used by third-party mail products, and many mail products, like Lotus cc:Mail, have a gateway product that moves messages between an MHS post office and the product's own post office. Banyan VINES comes with a *mail backbone* called the Intelligent Messaging System (IMS). A mail backbone is a way to connect together multiple post offices on one network which are often found on very large networks. It is the same as using post office-to-post office gateways where all gateways have access to a common interchange system. IMS is an active post office and it runs on a VINES server. LANShark's SharkMail! is mail client software for IMS; a remote version is available. A matching mail gateway runs on the LAN and accepts connections using the same serial interface card used for remote workstation access, although a single serial interface can be used only for one service at a time.

Lotus cc:Mail

Remote LAN access using Lotus cc:Mail requires three Lotus products: cc:Mail for a LAN, cc:Mail Router, and cc:Mail Mobile. The LAN product comes in a number of different forms, depending on the operating system involved. Licensing is by the number of post office users. LAN-based mail client software is included. DOS, Windows, and Mac clients are supported. The Router product includes both a DOS and OS/2 version in the same box. cc:Mail Mobile is a special version of the mail client software that works with the cc:Mail Router. The normal LAN-based mail client does not work with the cc:mail Router.

Figure 2.11 shows the cc:Mail post office and Router architecture. The post office is passive and resides on a file server. The passive nature allows cc:Mail to work with most network operating systems. The Router can run on the same file server if it is capable of running DOS applications or if the base operating system is OS/2. Otherwise, the Router runs on another PC on the LAN. It is even possible to use the OS/2 version of both the post office and the router on a single PC to provide a remote-access-only post office. No LAN is needed. OS/2 is a multitasking operating system, so it is even possible to use the post office PC as a workstation that can send and receive mail to and from the post office. A multitasking operating system lets you run more than one program at a time.

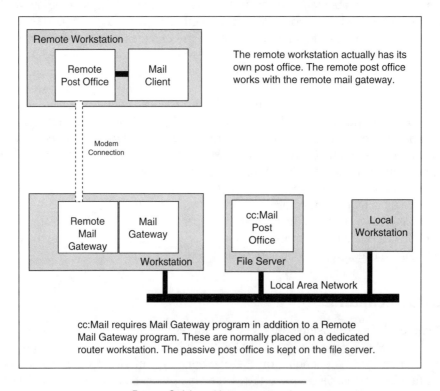

FIGURE 2.11 CC:MAIL ARCHITECTURE.

The post office supports the Vendor Independent Messaging (VIM) interface. This is a client-level interface that is also used by the cc:Mail client. VIM is transparent to mail client users, but it may be of interest to programmers or sophisticated developers.

Figure 2.12 shows the cc:Mail Windows Client Message Creation screen. Attachments can be included with messages. cc:Mail can view some files directly, such as text files and AmiPro documents. You can also configure your own viewer programs to view files not directly supported by cc:Mail.

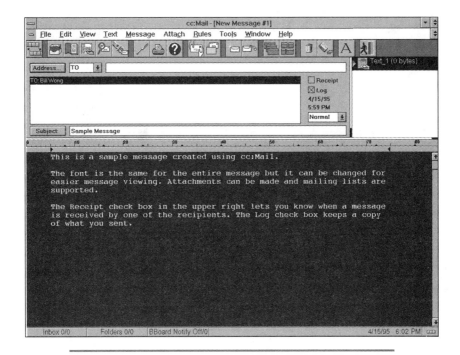

FIGURE 2.12 CC:MAIL WINDOWS CLIENT MESSAGE CREATION SCREEN.

Addressing a message is done using an address book entry. Figure 2.13 shows an address book dialog box. There is no indication of an address being local or remote to the post office. This allows cc:Mail to transparently deliver messages.

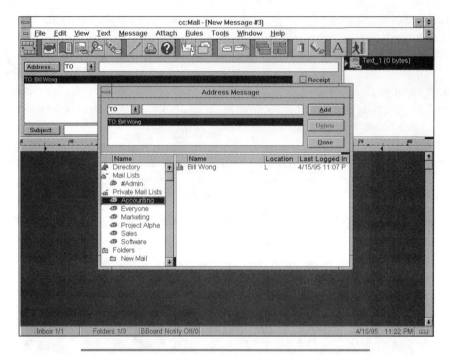

FIGURE 2.13 CC:MAIL WINDOWS CLIENT ADDRESSING SCREEN.

The cc:Mail client goes farther than a basic mail client program. It also provides basic work-flow support. cc:Mail lets you optionally apply rules to process mail exchanges. The rule system is implemented with a simple dialog box interface, shown in Figure 2.14. The rule system is far short of a full-blown work-flow programming environment, but it does perform the functions most often requested by the average mail user; for example, it can move messages to folders based on the sender or the message topic. cc:Mail Mobile extends the rule system, with rules for controlling which messages will be picked up from a post office.

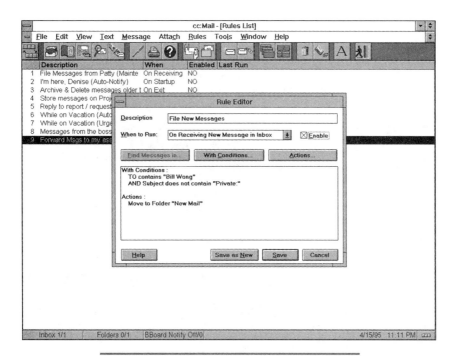

FIGURE 2.14 cc:Mail Windows Client Rules screen.

The mail client package supports private in- and out-boxes, as well as folders created by users. Mail can be moved between the boxes and folders as necessary. The folders provide a way to organize messages. The post office also supports public bulletin boards, where files and messages can be placed for access by more than one user. Bulletin board messages can include a text description with file attachments. Mail users can examine the contents of bulletin boards just as if they are viewing a private folder. Searches can be performed on both bulletin boards and folders.

The cc:Mail Post Office Management screen, shown in Figure 2.15, is an application used to add or delete users and to perform other maintenance operations on the post office, including backup. cc:Mail does not require extensive maintenance and even supports *directory synchronization*, which uses a cc:Mail program to read and convert the network user list to a cc:Mail address list.

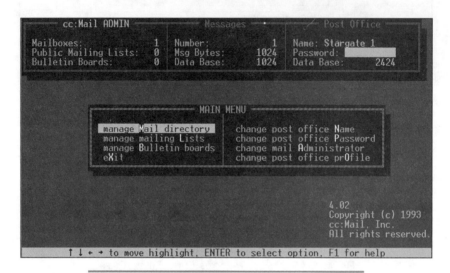

FIGURE 2.15 CC:MAIL POST OFFICE MANAGEMENT SCREEN.

The cc:Mail Router program is required for any type of external cc:Mail post office access. This does not include remote access using the LAN-based mail client software, which can be done using either remote workstation software (described in Chapter 3) or by using a remote control program (as described in Chapter 4).

The cc:Mail Router comes with two kinds of external router support: remote access and an MHS gateway. The remote access support works with cc:Mail Mobile. The MHS gateway works with an MHS post office. MHS is Novell's passive post office system. An MHS and cc:Mail post office can exist on the same file server. The cc:Mail Router also supports gateways to fax servers, like the cc:Mail FAX gateway, as well as to other mail systems.

The cc:Mail Router supports *Automatic Directory Exchange* (ADE) through gateways. This allows the Router to send its post office's public address list to remote users and other post offices, so people can have the latest address list. Otherwise, users must obtain the address of a new user through other means.

The single-session DOS version of the cc:mail Router supports a single modem. The multiple-session OS/2 version supports a single or more modems attached to the same PC. A standard PC will support two modems, while a PS/2 MicroChannel will support three. Multiple-port serial adapters, including Stargate Technologies' ACL II or II+, Digiboard's DigiChannel, and IBM's ARTIC, support up to eight serial ports.

One of the cc:Mail Router Management screens is shown in Figure 2.16. Other screens provide access to modem configuration and report generation. The Router can be remotely managed from a LAN-based workstation, but not via cc:Mail Mobile.

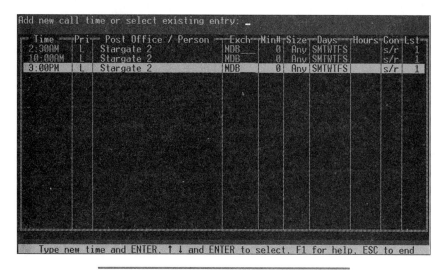

FIGURE 2.16 cc:MAIL ROUTER MANAGEMENT SCREEN.

The router also supports a task manager, which can perform scheduled operations for post office or non–post office support. You can program a Router to call other Routers on a timed basis or to run other applications at a prescribed time. You can even send mail when a procedure is complete or if an error is detected.

Lotus created a special version of the mail client software for mobile users called cc:Mail Mobile. It starts with the basic Windows cc:Mail client package and adds special features. In fact, if you look at the Message Creation screen in Figure 2.17, you will see little difference between it and Figure 2.12, which is the LAN-based cc:Mail Windows Client Message Creation screen.

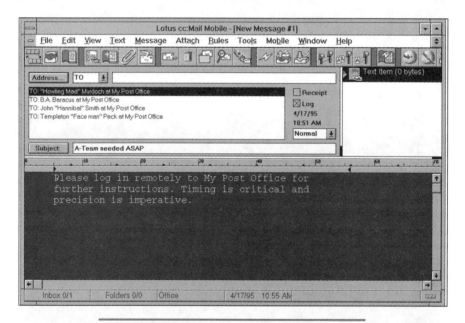

FIGURE 2.17 CC:MAIL MOBILE CREATE MESSAGE SCREEN.

One of the special features cc:Mail Mobile adds is location profiles (Figure 2.18). Many mobile users will call in from many different locations: home, a hotel, a branch office. The phone numbers, dialing characteristics, and other parameters may be different at these locations and changing them can be a nuisance. Location profiles let you set up the parameters for each location or type of location and then to simply select the appropriate one by name. You don't have to remember what the settings are once a profile is created, just remember its name.

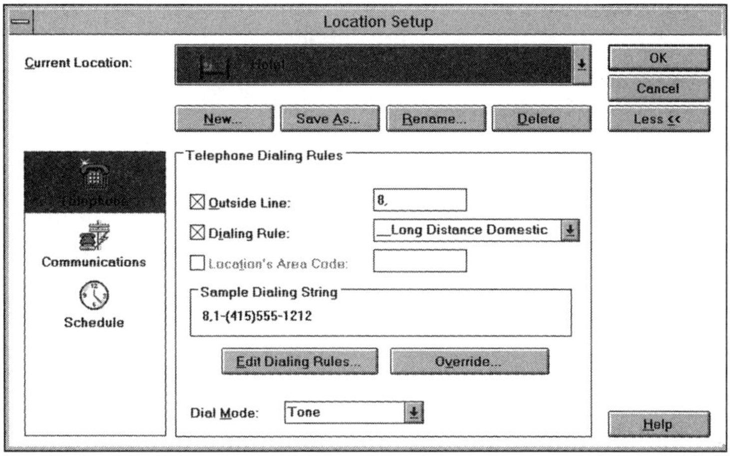

FIGURE 2.18 CC:MAIL MOBILE LOCATION PROFILES SCREEN.

Another special feature of cc:Mail Mobile is the Client Rule System (see Figure 2.19), which is enhanced for mail pickup. Incoming messages can automatically be screened by a number of criteria. The most useful is message size. This prevents the post office from sending files that are too large or that would take too long to transfer. cc:Mail Mobile can let you select messages to download, but the rule system normally precludes the need to do so.

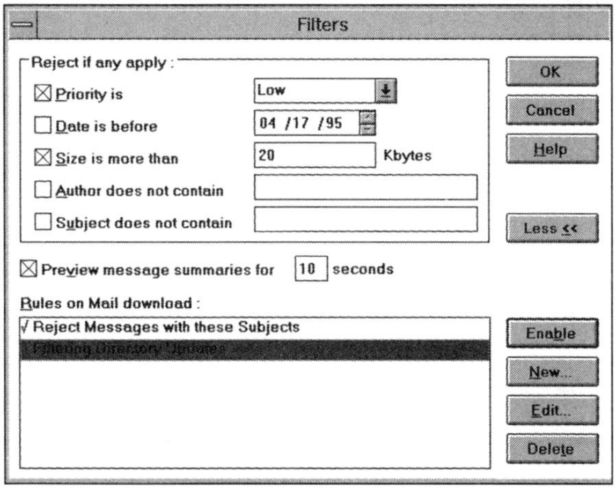

FIGURE 2.19 CC:MAIL MOBILE RULES SCREEN.

The Login screen (Figure 2.20) is presented when calling into a post office. It lets you use a password so someone cannot simply make use of your PC or laptop to gain access to your mail. An activity log (Figure 2.21) is made while there is a connection. It lets you track what messages are transferred, and it can be handy in debugging a bad connection.

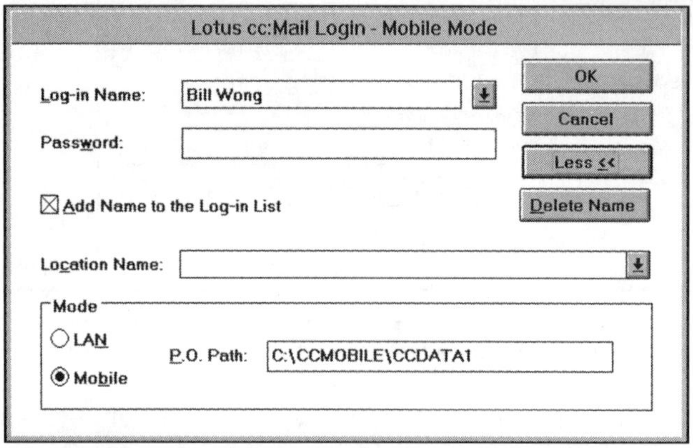

FIGURE 2.20 CC:MAIL MOBILE LOGIN DIALOG BOX.

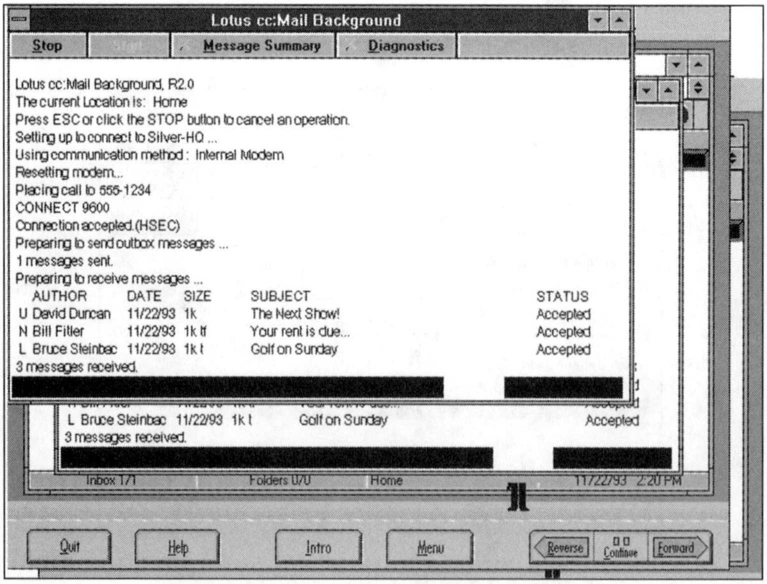

FIGURE 2.21 CC:MAIL MOBILE ACTIVITY LOG SCREEN.

Scheduled pickup and delivery lets you leave your PC running and lets cc:Mail Mobile call a post office for you (see Figure 2.22). You can create messages and leave them in the out-box to be sent later. The rule system lets cc:Mail Mobile screen messages for you.

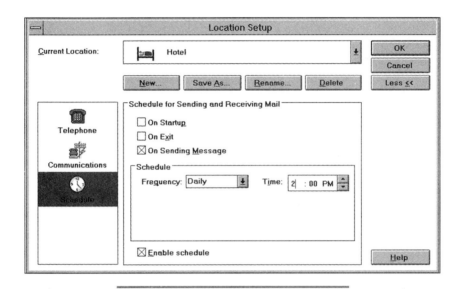

FIGURE 2.22 CC:MAIL MOBILE SCHEDULE SCREEN.

The cc:Mail product line and cc:Mail Mobile contain many features not presented here, which may make it more useful to you, so you will want to check out the latest version to see if it suits your needs. For example, cc:Mail Mobile has a feature that lets a laptop synchronize its folders and boxes when connected to the LAN, which is often the case for users who visit the office and have a PCMCIA network interface card for direct access to the network. PCMCIA cards are a little larger than a credit card and plug into a laptop PC. Overall, the cc:Mail products make a flexible remote LAN access method. The cc:Mail Mobile product lets remote users access the LAN without even knowing what kind of LAN it is. In fact, the post office may be on a standalone PC. This package also has a user interface that is consistent with the LAN version, so users can switch between the two without additional training.

Microsoft Mail

Microsoft Mail is available as a standalone product that runs under DOS and Windows. There are also versions that run under Microsoft Windows NT and

Windows 95. Microsoft Mail uses the Messaging Application Program Interface (MAPI), which incorporates just 12 functions. MAPI is an interface available to third-party companies, and it is also used by Microsoft applications like Excel and Word so mail can be sent directly from them. The Microsoft Mail client program also uses MAPI.

Microsoft Schedule+ is a MAPI-based scheduling program that uses the Microsoft Mail post office. Messages are sent from one user to another to handle scheduling chores. It is just another example of how an application can use mail to get a job done.

Microsoft Mail does not include a remote mail gateway, but it is possible to access a Microsoft Mail post office from a remote PC. In fact, this technique can be used with any post office on a LAN with remote workstation access. Remote workstation support is actually covered in Chapter 3. We will look at how Microsoft Mail works with remote workstation support to contrast it with a mail gateway. Figure 2.23 shows the Microsoft Mail architecture as used with a remote workstation. The main difference between this architecture and a mail gateway is the replacement of the mail gateway with a remote router. There is little difference in operation, but there can be a major difference in performance. Mail gateways transfer mainly messages and update post office files for the remote client. The client does not access the post office directly nor is he or she involved in the movement of data necessary to perform the update. A remote workstation is involved with the post office files and must move data across a connection, even though the data is not directly related to the messages being exchanged. Figure 2.24 shows the Microsoft Mail directory structure. This may give you an idea of how complex an update could be.

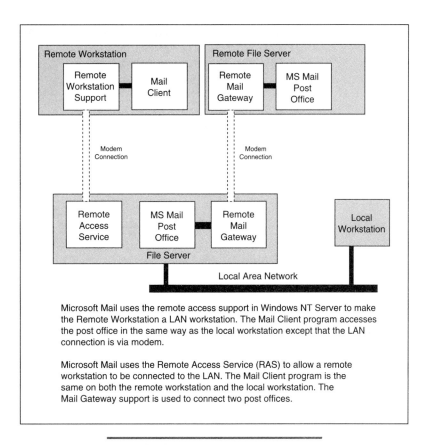

Microsoft Mail uses the remote access support in Windows NT Server to make the Remote Workstation a LAN workstation. The Mail Client program accesses the post office in the same way as the local workstation except that the LAN connection is via modem.

Microsoft Mail uses the Remote Access Service (RAS) to allow a remote workstation to be connected to the LAN. The Mail Client program is the same on both the remote workstation and the local workstation. The Mail Gateway support is used to connect two post offices.

FIGURE 2.23 MICROSOFT MAIL ARCHITECTURE.

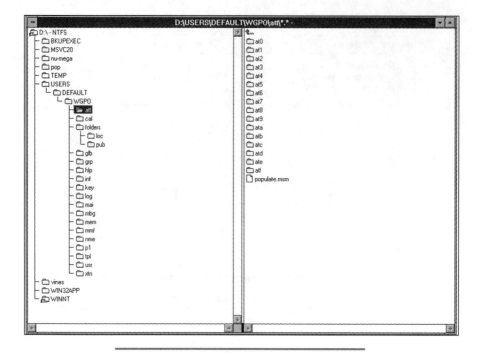

Figure 2.24 Microsoft Mail directory structure.

The major disadvantage and/or advantage of a remote workstation connection is its direct access to LAN resources in addition to the post office. This includes files and printers plus any other services that may be provided through the LAN. Security is provided by the network operating system, so it is possible to restrict access to services, but the user must have a network name and password. Protection must be explicit, not implicit, as with a mail gateway.

The Microsoft Mail client program (see Figure 2.25) is similar to other mail client interfaces. It supports file attachments, mailing lists, and most features found in other mail products.

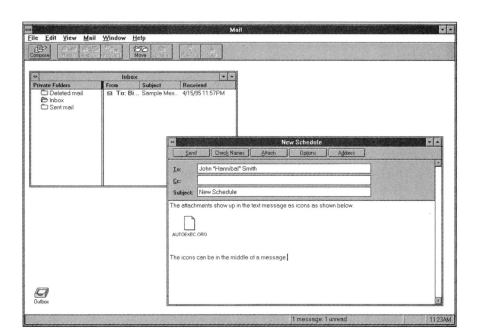

FIGURE 2.25 MICROSOFT MAIL CLIENT.

Microsoft provides RAS support with Windows for Workgroups (WFW) and Windows NT Server (NTS). The WFW support is available from Microsoft's technical support areas, such as the one found on Compuserve, while NTS ships with RAS support. All you need to add to the network server is a modem. Alternatively, and for almost any LAN, you can use a remote router, which is typically a small box with a modem or with a connector for a modem. Chapter 3 covers these alternatives and general uses for remote workstations.

Novell MHS

We will take a look at Novell's Message Handling Service (MHS) because of NetWare's popularity and because MHS has become one of the *de facto* standards for mail exchange. Most post office products have a LAN-based MHS mail gateway option, or they may use MHS as their post office.

MHS is a passive post office. It is actually a standard, covering message file contents, directory structure, and message exchange protocol. Figure 2.26 shows how MHS-related products, including those available from Novell, interact. Mail users have directories created for them by the post office software. Messages are files placed in these directories.

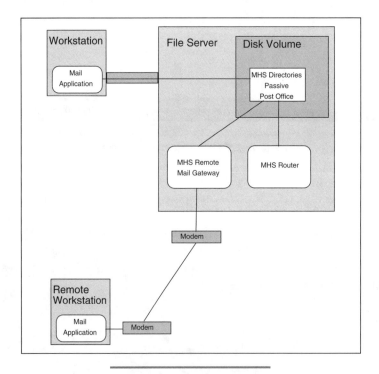

Figure 2.26 MHS architecture.

MHS-based mail products do not have to operate on a Novell NetWare LAN, although most are installed on NetWare LANs. Most remote mail gateways that operate with an MHS-based post office will work with any other product that also operates on the same post office. The software on the remote PC must match the mail gateway product.

Most MHS-based mail gateways run on a LAN workstation, but it is possible to find some NetWare 3.x and 4.x NLM-based gateways. The MHS post office resides on a NetWare file server. An NLM (NetWare Loadable Module) is a program written to run on a NetWare file server. An NLM mail gateway lets you use the file server as the gateway as well. A file server is typically I/O-*bound*, moving data between its hard disk and the LAN. An I/O bound server is limited by how fast data is transferred between peripherals. The other extreme is a computer bound server that spends most of its time running programs that rarely access the peripherals. It normally has plenty of extra processing power that is unused. This power can often be efficiently used by an NLM mail gateway.

LANShark's SharkMail!

LANShark's SharkMail! is designed to run with Banyan VINES Intelligent Messaging System (IMS). Banyan VINES is a network operating system like Novell's NetWare. VINES is typically found in very large enterprise-wide networks with thousands of workstations and hundreds of servers connected into one very large network. Banyan's Enterprise Network System (ENS) is a network support system that runs on top of other network operating systems such as Novell's NetWare. ENS also runs IMS. Both VINES and ENS are based on Banyan's global naming system, StreetTalk. Every item is given a StreetTalk name, which is made up of three parts: Item@Group@Organization. The at sign, @, is a separator. Mail users have a StreetTalk name. The name is not based on the user's post office. IMS spans VINES and ENS systems, and a network can encompass a wide variety of servers running different network operating systems.

IMS is an active post office architecture. Figure 2.27 shows the basic IMS architecture. IMS is designed as a back end program (the part a user does not see); mail clients provide the front end (the part of the program a user sees). IMS provides a programming interface, which is made available to the vendors of mail front-end applications. The interface is similar to Microsoft's MAPI in operation. The difference is that IMS accepts messages and manages the post office database internally. Microsoft's Mail MAPI implementation has the mail application modifying the post office directly, although the support is provided through program modules supplied with Microsoft Mail.

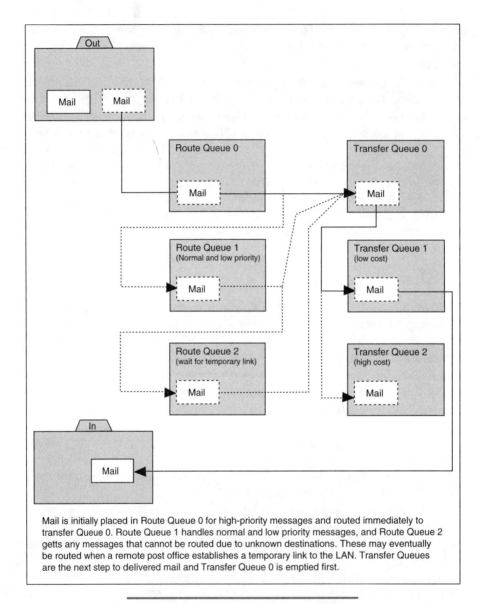

Mail is initially placed in Route Queue 0 for high-priority messages and routed immediately to transfer Queue 0. Route Queue 1 handles normal and low priority messages, and Route Queue 2 getts any messages that cannot be routed due to unknown destinations. These may eventually be routed when a remote post office establishes a temporary link to the LAN. Transfer Queues are the next step to delivered mail and Transfer Queue 0 is emptied first.

FIGURE 2.27 BANYAN VINES IMS ARCHITECTURE.

IMS also has a mail gateway programming interface. LANShark uses this interface for its remote access support. The LANShark mail gateway program runs on a VINES file server and uses a Banyan Integrated Communications Adapter (ICA) for serial support for a modem. An ICA supports multiple serial ports, and these can be used for the mail gateway or for other VINES-related communication services.

SharkMail! is the mail client. It runs on a LAN workstation or a remote PC. The remote version communicates with the LANShark mail gateway through the ICA and an attached modem. The mail client screen (Figure 2.28) is the same for the LAN and remote versions.

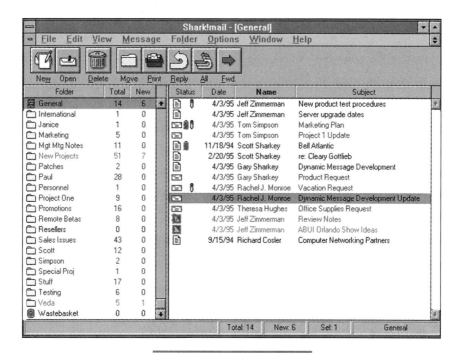

FIGURE 2.28 SharkMail! client.

SharkMail! supports basic rules just like cc:Mail Mobile. Figure 2.29 shows SharkMail!'s Rule dialog box. LANShark also sells a work-flow package that runs on the file server, just like the mail gateway. The advantage of an active post office and a work-flow program that run on the same PC is that mail does not normally have to be moved across the LAN. The work-flow program simply updates the post office database.

FIGURE 2.29 SHARKMAIL! RULES DIALOG BOX.

Functionally, SharkMail! and cc:Mail Mobile are very similar. The main differences include the active nature of the IMS post office and the fact that a third party, LANShark, supplies the client software. Banyan has its own client software, but it is possible to mix client software on the same network. A user can send a message using Banyan's mail client software to a user who reads it using SharkMail!

From a user's standpoint, there is little difference between using cc:Mail Mobile from Lotus and LANShark's SharkMail! You write a message and leave it in the out-box. It gets delivered when you call the mail gateway, and the process requires minimal user intervention. The difference concerns how the mail gets to the post office PC and what can be done with it once it is there using server based workflow support. Banyan's IMS is extremely sophisticated, and LANShark's work-flow software can make it more so.

MAIL GATEWAYS: SPECIALIZED PRODUCTS

Mail gateways provide access to users with PCs and the appropriate software. Laptops and desktop PCs are equally applicable. Unlike many other remote LAN access methods, mail gateways also let users with specialized computers exchange mail. Palmtop computers like Hewlett Packard's HP-200 fit into this category. These small computers have limited processing power, memory, and disk storage, if they have any at all, but this is often more than sufficient for accessing a mail gateway. All that is needed is the proper software and a modem. PCMCIA modems fit nicely into these palmtop computers.

Personal digital assistants (PDAs) fall into the same category as palmtop computers. Palmtop computers are just small laptops, but PDAs are usually a different breed. Many are pen-based, such as Apple's Newton. PCMCIA slots are standard fare so a PCMCIA modem is a relatively simple addition. A PDA works well for viewing mail. The PDA is also well equipped in terms of processing power to exchange mail. Creating mail is the more difficult task, if text is the desired message medium. Most PDAs support handwriting recognition, but at this point accuracy is not great. Luckily many PC-based mail clients are quite capable of displaying graphic files sent as messages. PDAs are also capable of capturing pen input as graphic files, which can be sent using mail software.

Although palmtop computers and PDAs make interesting and useful remote mail clients, the choice of using these tools is not always open to every user because the selection of the post office and mail gateway software may already have been made. Palmtop computers can often be loaded with PC-compatible software, which often allows them to be used with a variety of mail gateways. Unfortunately, the limitations of a palmtop's processor, memory, and screen may prevent some PC-compatible software from operating on the palmtop. Some, like the HP-200, have the mail software already built in.

PDAs tend to be unable to run PC-compatible software unaltered for a variety of reasons. As such, custom mail client software must be available for the PDA to operate with a particular mail gateway. Unfortunately, there is no universal mail gateway interface, so it is unlikely that a particular PDA will work with an arbitrary mail gateway.

CHAPTER 3

REMOTE WORKSTATIONS

Remote workstations are PCs that have the same access capabilities to LAN services as a PC that is *locally* (directly) attached. The only difference between the two types is the *throughput* (speed); local PCs operate at the speed of the network interface used. Ethernet and Token Ring, two popular network interfaces, run at 10 Mbps (megabits/second) and 4 or 16 Mbps, respectively. On the other hand, remote PCs are normally connected using modems, and the fastest high-speed modem standard is V.34, which operates at 28,800 bits/second, which is significantly slower. Integrated Services Digital Network (ISDN) is a higher-speed alternative to modems, but ISDN is not available in all areas of the country.

REMOTE WORKSTATIONS

Users of remote workstations have all the network's services available to them, but there are trade-offs compared to other remote LAN access methods. A LAN's security with a remote workstation is based on the same LAN security as local workstations. Most network operating systems support user names and passwords, but not all network managers avail themselves of these features. It is not uncommon to find a LAN that does not require password access. Add in remote workstation access, and anyone with a PC and the right software will have free reign in your LAN.

The slow transfer rate of the remote connection can be a major factor in the performance of applications that access the LAN. A program that operates nicely on a local PC may slow to a crawl or be completely unusable from a remote workstation. On the other hand, some operations work reasonably well even with the slower connection, and having direct access to the LAN, their resources and network protocols can be beneficial. Many network management tools work just fine from a remote workstation.

A remote workstation requires a *remote router* connected to the LAN. A remote router passes or routes LAN data from the remote workstation to the LAN or vice versa. A remote router is often called a *communications server*. The remote router is also connected to a modem. The modem attached to the remote workstation calls the remote router's modem to make a connection between the remote workstation and the LAN. A remote router can be located in a number of places on a LAN, as shown in Figure 3.1. A remote router can be a software package on a network file server; it can also be a dedicated workstation with a similar software package. A third type of remote router is a box that attaches to the LAN and one or more modems. This device operates just like a dedicated PC running the router software; the main difference is that the remote router device does not require a keyboard or monitor and often has no floppy disk or hard disk drive.

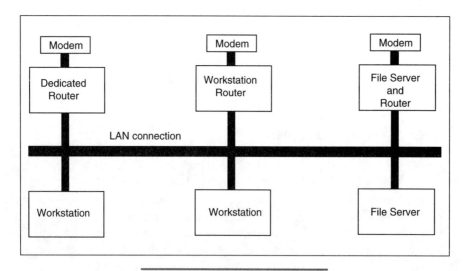

FIGURE 3.1 REMOTE ROUTER LOCATIONS.

In basic terms, the remote workstation runs the same type of network software that a local workstation does; the difference is in the network interface support. A local workstation has a device driver that works with the *network interface card* (NIC) that plugs into the workstation, such as an Ethernet or Token Ring NIC. The remote workstation has a modem device driver that works like a communications program. Data sent from an application on a *local* workstation to the LAN is sent through the device driver and NIC, as shown in Figure 3.2; data sent from an application on a *remote* workstation to the LAN is sent through the modem device driver to the *remote* router, as shown in Figure 3.3. The router then sends the data through its local device driver and NIC to the LAN. Incoming data follows the reverse routes.

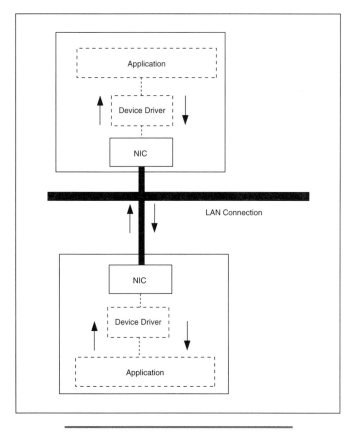

FIGURE 3.2 LOCAL WORKSTATION DATA ROUTING.

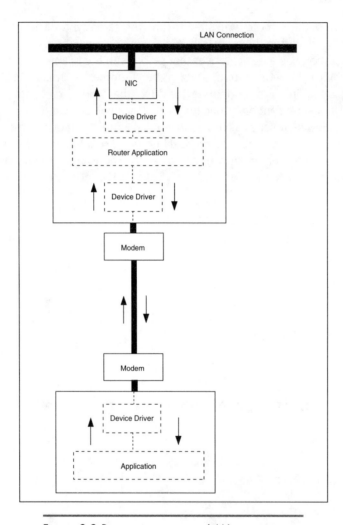

FIGURE 3.3 REMOTE WORKSTATION LAN DATA ROUTING.

A utility program on the remote workstation initiates a connection with a remote router. The connection program is often supplied in two forms: one with a menu-driven interface and the other with a command-line interface. The menu-driven interface lets users select the router's phone number and displays the initial connection process in an easy-to-view display; the command-line interface lets other programs initiate a connection. For example, a batch file can use the command-line interface to make a connection to the LAN and then move data to or from the LAN. The same command-line interface can normally be used to terminate the connection.

Remote workstations have the advantage of using the same programs and presenting the same interface as a local workstation. Mail programs, word processors, and even graphical user interfaces (GUIs) like Windows work just fine on a remote workstation. The remote workstation runs all the programs the user works with. Files there are available to these programs as are the files on the LAN. The only difference is that LAN access is much slower.

Remote workstations provide an excellent way to remotely access LAN services. Security issues and throughput to the LAN are important considerations when choosing remote workstation access to a LAN.

A USER'S VIEW

A remote workstation user's view of the world is similar to a local LAN workstation user's view. Both have network device drivers loaded when they start up the workstation. Both eventually have to log onto the LAN, which normally requires a user name and a matching password for security. In between, the remote workstation user must also initiate a remote connection. Figure 3.4 shows a sample remote connection screen.

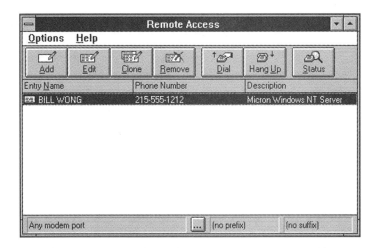

FIGURE 3.4 REMOTE ROUTER CONNECTION INITIATION SCREEN.

Once connected and logged in, a user can run applications that access files on the remote workstation or on the LAN. A user can log out and log in again as long as the connection is maintained. Figure 3.5 shows a sample remote disconnect screen. Typically, the network software will automatically log out a user when a disconnect occurs without first logging out.

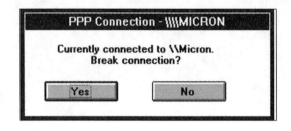

FIGURE 3.5 REMOTE ROUTER CONNECTION TERMINATION SCREEN.

Once connected, a remote workstation user has access to all the LAN services they would normally have, either all services or a subset of them, depending on the network operating system (NOS) in use. Most NOSes can selectively provide services to users. Simpler NOSes provide all users access to all services; more sophisticated NOSes can restrict service based on the time of day and the type of connection, so remote users may have access to fewer or different services than when they log on from a local LAN workstation.

File and print operations are services most users think of when dealing with a LAN, but there are many others. Database servers and application servers are just two starting to crop up in this age of *client/server* computing. Client/Server computing places a server program on one or more client programs on other workstations. The client programs communicate with the server by making requests. The server processes the requests. A client/server database system has the server performing a search. A client only database system has the client reading the database to do a search. These services are also accessible to a remote workstation user.

A remote workstation user using a GUI like Windows will see network drives when using a file-manager program, just like a local workstation user will. What the remote workstation user does not see is the difference in speed when LAN files are accessed using the comparatively low-speed modem connection and local files.

Unfortunately, there are a couple problems that arise when a user has access to the LAN using a remote workstation, and they are all related to the speed of the connection. The higher the connection speed, the lower the chance a problem might arise.

The first problem is simply slow response time when copying small files. This is to be expected, and it simply results in a user waiting from a few more seconds to a few more minutes for an operation to complete, depending on the size of the file and the speed of the connection. Good remote workstation software will provide users with a visual feedback cue while remote transfers are taking place, so they do not assume that a nonresponse from their application is due to a failure. Visual displays in DOS often include a flashing character in the upper-right corner. GUIs like Windows are a bit more amenable to this type of indicator, which is normally a small status window a user can place anywhere on the screen.

The second problem is similar but on a much larger scale. LANs move megabytes of data quickly, but modems do not. Unfortunately, moving megabytes of data on a LAN can occur much more often than you might think. For example, many Windows applications (not to mention supporting dynamic link libraries or DLLs) are often around one megabyte in size. Start the application from the LAN, and your workstation moves all this data from the LAN, over the modem connection, to your workstation while you wait, and wait, and wait. The status indicators may tell you that data is being transferred but it normally does not tell you how long you will have to wait. One solution is to keep a copy of the program files on the remote workstation, but this does not solve the problem if the data files are also large. Large data files can be kept on the remote workstation, but accessing the data files on the LAN is the primary reason for remote LAN access. For example, I use a personal information manager (PIM) application. The database has grown from a few thousand bytes to two megabytes. Accessing this database, even with the PIM program, on the remote workstation is impractical because the first thing the program does when it starts is to scan the entire database.

I know the size of the database and I have used modem connections before, so it did not come as a surprise to me that this type of application would not work as well from a remote workstation. Unfortunately, many users would not know this or be able to guess what the problem is with their remote workstation when they tried to use the same application that works quickly from a local LAN workstation. Figuring out the problem is only half the battle. Breaking the connection is another. Often the only recourse is to disconnect the modem or telephone line or to reset or turn off the remote workstation. Unfortunately, these actions can produce undesired results, such as corrupted files or directory entries. Luckily, most initial operations, such as loading a program or scanning a database, involve reading files and directories, which will not result in corrupted information if the connection is prematurely terminated.

The moral is to estimate network traffic for a particular application before using it remotely. This normally needs to be done just once for each application, but it may change if the program, its use, or the data it uses is changed.

One useful tool often supplied with remote workstation software is a special file manager. Data transfer status, as well as duration, is normally displayed, so you know how long a transfer will take. Transfers can be easily and safely canceled, and some file managers allow transfers to occur in the background. Remote workstation users should not assume that all applications will work well or the same over a modem connection. Even mail programs may scan a significant portion of the post office database, causing problems like those already discussed.

Remote workstations can be used effectively with client/server applications. Mail applications with active post offices work as well as mail gateways presented in Chapter 2, since the post office handles database updates. Many remote control programs, covered in Chapter 4, can also be used via a remote workstation. In this case, the LAN protocol is used instead of a custom modem connection. This approach has the benefits of remote control programs, and they also provide the benefits of remote workstation access.

A LAN Manager's View

WARNING

Stop! Read This: If you do not want to provide unrestricted remote LAN access to all network services, then read this section carefully and read the documentation to any product that you consider for providing remote workstation support. A remote workstation can provide the same access as a local workstation. Although most network operating systems provide security measures that can restrict general access, they often allow some access without using the security measures. The bottom line: Beware, be careful, be smart.

Considering and implementing remote workstation support is a relatively straight-forward process. A remote workstation operates and is managed in the same fashion as a normal LAN workstation. A remote router or server-based support is required in addition to a modem. These require additional management support, such as resetting a modem, but most of the work occurs during the initial setup, with regular maintenance being minimal.

One aspect of remote workstation *support* that is not always apparent is that most products are also integrated with network modem support. This typically includes *dial-out support*. Dial-out support lets a user on a LAN workstation access a modem on the communications server; the workstation software uses the modem as if it were located on the workstation. The workstation software is typically a terminal-emulation program or a front-end program for a communication service such as Compuserve or the Internet.

A communication server is like a network file server except that it provides access to communication devices like modems instead of files. Communications servers usually support multiple modems. Modems can often be grouped into *modem pools*. Modems are allocated from the pool on a first-come, first-served basis. Unfortunately, modem pools are suitable for dialing out, but not for calling in. Incoming lines must be dedicated to remote workstation support; they can also be used for fax servers, network BBS support, and other communication services. This large number of possibilities makes planning important.

Communications servers can be divided into two types: those integrated into a file server, and standalone communications servers. Figure 3.6 shows the different server architectures. Integrated communications servers can be further divided into servers that provide access to the file server and those that provide access to the rest of the network. Standalone communications servers provide access to the entire network.

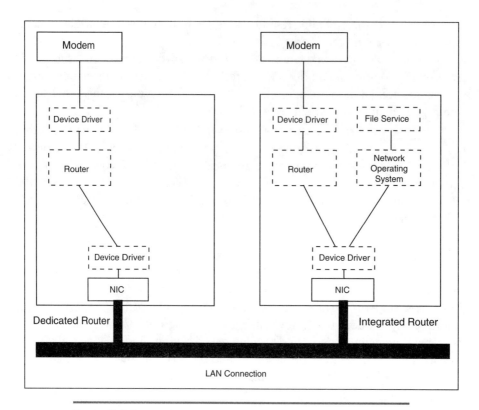

FIGURE 3.6 INTEGRATED VERSUS STANDALONE COMMUNICATIONS SERVERS.

Integrated servers that do not provide access to the rest of the network do not have to be concerned with *network protocol*, because remote workstations only interact with the file server. A network protocol defines how data is formatted and exchanged on a network. Other communications servers must be concerned with the network protocol. Three popular network protocols are Novell's IPX, NETBIOS, and TCP/IP. Some network operating systems support a choice of protocols, and some even support multiple protocols, often on the same cable. The protocol supported at the remote workstation is important not only for connecting with a file server, but also for accessing other services on the LAN. Network management often operates directly between a workstation and managed devices using the network protocol instead of going through a file server.

As if these choices were not enough, there is also a lower-level protocol specific to the network. For example, Ethernet supports four different *frame types*. A frame type is the lowest protocol level. Ethernet frame types include 802.2, 802.3, Ethernet_II, and Ethernet_SNMP. As with higher-level protocols, the lower levels can be mixed on the same network. Integrated communications servers are appropriate if a remote workstation only accesses the integrated file server. Standalone communications servers are a better choice if multiple servers are to be accessed from the remote workstation, or if the remote workstation needs to support multiple network protocols.

Modem speed will be important to LAN managers because they are usually charged with justification of telephone costs associated with remote LAN access. Modem speed is critical for more large amounts of data, but it is also important for a responsive remote workstation. Applications actually run on the remote workstation, which makes them inherently responsive, but a program's user interface can slow to a crawl when LAN data is being accessed. Slow response can even occur with small amounts of data, if the modem is slow. The prices for high-speed V.34 modems are so low that it is important for LAN managers to consider these, and even ISDN lines, when they consider remote workstation support. One approach is to put the highest-speed modems on the remote router, even if all remote workstation users do not have matching modems. V.34 modems work with slower modems such as V.32 and V.32bis; high-speed modems can be issued on a per-need basis.

Modem performance is important to LAN managers, but security is usually more important. Remote workstations are a major security risk because they usually have the same access to the LAN as a local workstation. Most network operating systems provide various levels of security, and user names and passwords can be required by the LAN manager. Unfortunately, this level of security, although useful, is not always airtight. Figure 3.7 shows how many protocols allow a workstation to access another workstation or server without having the user log in with his or her name and password.

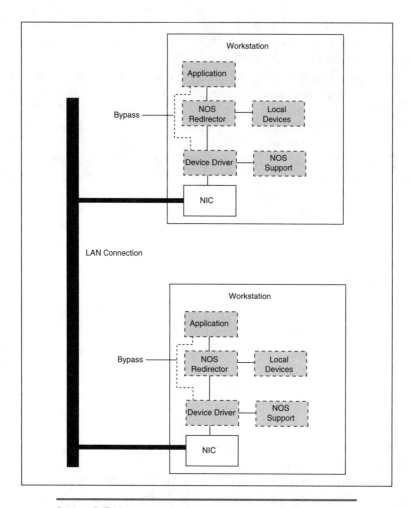

Figure 3.7 Network protocols bypassing network security.

The possibility of breaching conventional network security is one reason that additional security features are found on remote routers; some include: modem callback support; access names and passwords independent of the user's network operating system name and password; required network login; protocol restrictions; and restricted access times. Modem callback is often implemented by remote routers; this feature is also often found in more expensive modems. The *callback* feature, shown in Figure 3.8, lets a user call in from a remote workstation. The router's modem answers and goes through a handshake protocol to identify the remote router. The handshake may include the phone number of the caller or the number may be preprogrammed in the router or its modem. The router's modem then hangs up and places a second call back to the original caller. The remote workstation's modem answers and the resulting connection lets the remote workstation communicate with the LAN.

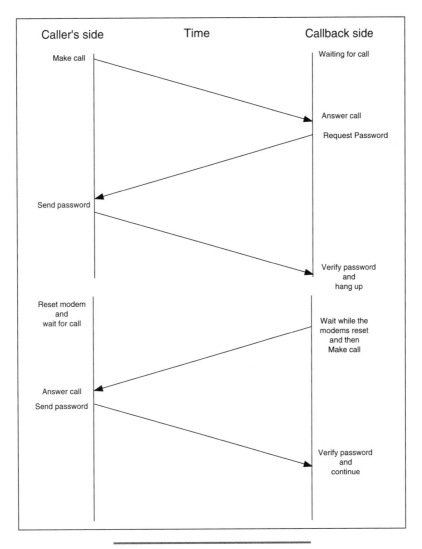

FIGURE 3.8 MODEM CALLBACK PROTOCOL.

Callback support requires at least an identification name; passwords are often an additional requirement. Even if callback support is not used, a router can require a user name and password before the remote workstation can access the LAN. An even better alternative is to have the remote router use the same user name and password as the network operating system. In this case, the remote router can perform the login for the user when the connection is made and prevent access to the network if the login is unsuccessful. Unfortunately, this type of interaction means the router must support the network operating system. The configuration is rarely available if multiple network operating systems and protocols are to be used from the same remote workstation. Luckily, most users only deal with a single network operating system.

Restricting protocols and access times can also cut down on the ability of people to access the LAN without proper permission. Restricting remote access during office hours may allow a LAN manager to more easily monitor who is using the LAN remotely. Likewise, some users may be given different access rights depending on their clearance and needs. The actual security procedures you implement may be a combination of these and others provided by a particular product. The end result is to provide LAN access only to certain people, and that access should be to only those services the LAN manager allows.

Network operating systems often support user-auditing features of varying degrees. Some let you track user logins and logouts, while others let you track what services are accessed. Remote routers often provide some of this support, and it usually pays for a LAN manager to use it. A good remote router will let you track unsuccessful and successful connection attempts and will notify the LAN manager, using electronic mail or other messaging techniques, when too many unsuccessful attempts are made within a specific time period.

Overall, the level of security and auditing used by a LAN manager will depend on the data available on the network, company policy, the capabilities of the remote router and the network operating system, and the ability of the LAN manager to implement and manage these features. It is important to consider these factors before implementing remote workstation support, because not all products provide every security and auditing feature.

Technical support of remote users and for the remote router tends to be minimal once a reliable system is installed. Getting to that point may require significant configuration work and trial and error. Router operation is relatively automatic, and the remote workstation interaction is normally apparent only during the initial connection and when the connection is broken. Much of the router maintenance will include programatically resetting modems to break a connection or resetting a modem that did not make or break a connection properly. Most other tech support calls will involve users who encounter problems with transferring large amounts of data. A training program for remote workstation users can help eliminate the need for much of this type of support.

Remote workstations provide power and familiarity to network users, but remote workstation support is not a solution to all remote LAN access situations; while it provides the greatest access to the LAN of all methods, this may not be desirable. There are many remote users to whom you may not wish to grant network access, even if the network operating system does provide good security measures, for example, customers or even strangers.

How do Remote Workstations Work?

The basic concept of remote LAN access using a remote workstation has been presented earlier in the chapter; in this section we look in detail at the various ways remote workstation support is actually implemented. Figures 3.9 and 3.10 show the two methods we will consider. Figure 3.9 shows server-based access, while Figure 3.10 shows a dedicated communications server.

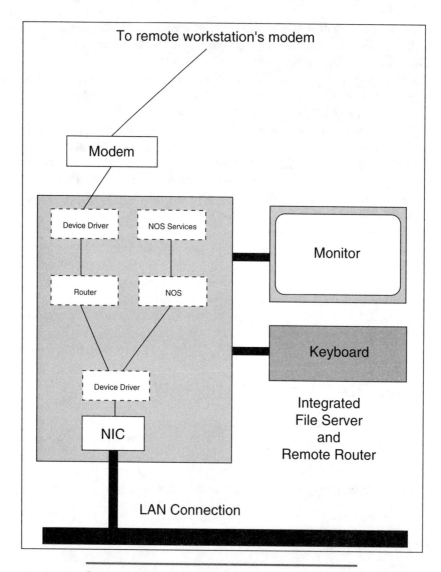

FIGURE 3.9 SERVER-BASED REMOTE WORKSTATION SUPPORT.

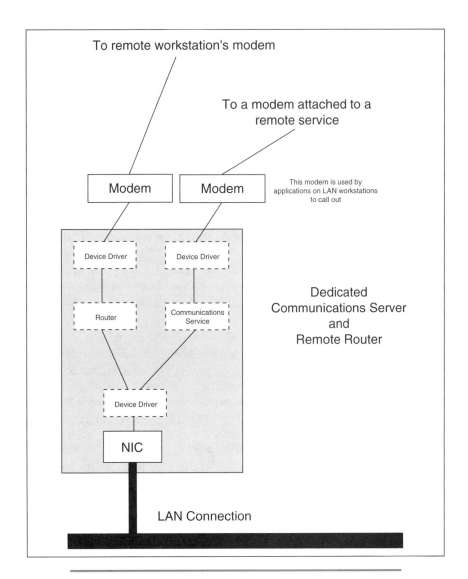

FIGURE 3.10 COMMUNICATIONS SERVER REMOTE WORKSTATION SUPPORT.

In the simplest case, the server-based architecture provides remote workstation access to the server itself; a more complex case allows the server to act as a bridge to other servers. Generally the remote workstation support software is designed to work with the network operating system on the server it is connected to; the bridging support may provide access to servers running different network operating systems.

Matching the remote workstation support to the network operating system on the server has advantages. It can be designed more efficiently because the type of operations is known and it can be optimized accordingly. Security is integrated with the network operating system security since the remote user must login to the server when a connection is initiated.

Server-based remote workstation access to a LAN starts with a modem-handling layer with a network operating system redirector built on top. A redirector is a piece of software that intercepts operating system calls. It forwards calls to local devices to the operating system. It forwards calls to remote devices to the remote workstations network access software that uses the modem to communicate with the server. A connection-initiation program is normally used to make a call to the server. This program may be integrated with the login program.

On the server side, there is also a modem-handling layer with a remote workstation server application above it. The server application acts as a proxy for the remote workstation. A proxy does the same operations for the remote workstation. Requests from the remote workstation are sent over the modem connection to the remote workstation server application, which then sends the requests to the network operating system. Bridging support requires an additional proxy. The remote workstation bridge works with the remote workstation server support; requests from the remote workstation for servers other than the main one will be forwarded to the bridging proxy support, which is connected to local network interface drivers. The proxy sends the request, appropriately formatted, to the appropriate server. Responses or interactions between servers and the remote workstation operate in the reverse fashion.

The main difference between server-based remote workstation support and dedicated communications server support is that the remote workstation software operates at the network operating systems level for the server-based support, instead of the LAN protocol used with a dedicated communications server.

A dedicated communications server normally operates in a different fashion from its server-based counterpart. The remote workstation and communications server both have a modem-support layer like the server-based approach, but the next layer is at the LAN network interface level instead of the network operating system functional level; the network interface is built on top of this LAN interface level. A remote workstation application sends its network request to the network interface support level on the remote workstation. The request is then formatted and packetized (additional protocol information is added), just like on a local workstation. The packets are then passed to the network interface support level and sent across the modem connection. The packets received at the communications server are then sent to the LAN. The packets are sent across the LAN to the respective server, which analyzes the packets and processes the request accordingly. The LAN-based server does not necessarily "know" that the request is coming from a local workstation or a remote workstation. Responses and server-to-workstation requests are sent back in the opposite fashion.

A call-initiation program is also used with a dedicated communications server, but the security it may implement is based on the server and not on the network operating system. In some cases, remote workstation support and the server are not matched to a particular network operating system; this is possible because the remote workstation software looks like a standard network interface card driver to the workstation network support. No special support is required at the file server or other server, since the communications server appears as a workstation to the file or other servers.

The advantage of this approach is the ability to access different types of network operating systems from one remote workstation, if the appropriate software is on the remote workstation. Also, LAN-based management tools like SNMP (Simple Network Management Protocol) work with a remote workstation and a dedicated communications server, because the low-level interface needed to access SNMP is available to the software on the remote workstation, and the messages are passed through to the LAN transparently through the connection and the dedicated communications server.

WHY USE A REMOTE WORKSTATION FOR REMOTE LAN ACCESS?

Remote workstations have a number of advantages and disadvantages when used to access a LAN remotely. The following list summarizes these.

Advantages
══

Simple user interface

Access to LAN resources

Requires no user interaction to access resources

Access to LAN protocols

Disadvantages
══

Security is dependent on LAN security

Delayed response to requests

Telephone time not minimized

Manual connect/disconnect

Significantly slower than LAN transfer rates

Network broadcast messages can overload remote connections

On the plus side, the remote workstation represents a simple and familiar user interface for network users. LAN servers provide the same disk and printer services that local network users see. Login and logout procedures are changed only by the additional requirement of making and breaking a modem connection. These may be integrated with the login and logout procedures, or they may be provided through separate programs.

Remote workstations have access to LAN resources other than disk and print services, such as SQL database servers. Client applications running on the remote workstation can access the database server more efficiently than directly accessing database files. The modem connection is used to send requests and receive results while the database server processes its own local database.

Accessing LAN resources normally requires no additional user interaction other than the initial login. This is typically the same for local and remote users because remote workstations operate just like local workstations. Of course, if a local user must perform a special process to use a LAN function, then the same will be true for a remote workstation user.

Access to LAN protocols lets a remote workstation access some network services, such as SNMP devices, which are accessed directly from applications that run on the remote workstation. Direct access often means the remote workstation may not have to be logged into a network server. Some network management chores can be performed in this fashion, so remote workstation access allows these management chores to be performed remotely. In fact, a network manager may want to keep the network management programs on his or her remote workstation so other users do not have access to them.

On the minus side, remote workstations are dependent on the security provided by the network operating system and on the accessibility through direct access using LAN protocols. Most remote workstation support programs use their own user name and password system for making a connection, or they are integrated with a required network login, using the network operating system's name and password system. This approach works fine for verifying the remote user, but it provides full network access once a connection is made. Most network operating systems can restrict access to services based on the user, but direct access often bypasses conventional security measures. Access at this level may be fine for users that work for the company running the LAN, but this level of access may be undesirable for users that do not work for the company. Other remote LAN access methods may be preferable due to security issues.

There are other negative issues related to remote workstation use, assuming the security issues are addressed. Chief among these is the delayed response (the time it takes for the screen to update after you press a key) for remote workstation requests to servers on the LAN, because of the slow remote-workstation-to-LAN connection. All network transfers are slower because the connection throughput is slower compared to a local workstation, but the effect varies depending on the amount of data being transferred. Operations that work acceptably on a local workstation can be divided into three categories for remote workstations. The best category is small transfers, which simply decrease application response time within a noticeable but acceptable range. What may be instantaneous on a local workstation may have a one-second delay on a remote workstation. The next category occurs with larger transfers that may take seconds on a local workstation but tens of seconds on a remote workstation. This delay can range from acceptable to unacceptable. The third category occurs when the transfer to the remote workstation will take so long that it is impractical; transfers that take hours or even days fit into this category. Unfortunately, remote users cannot always recognize which category an operation fits into; delays caused by the second and third categories may be wrongly attributed to connection failures.

Remote workstation connections by themselves do not necessarily minimize telephone connect time. Batch files or work-flow programs can help by placing all or most of the control of the connection under program control. The remote user can initiate the connection process, with the batch file or program completing the desired operation and automatically breaking the connection. If the user were to type the commands instead of using the batch file the connection would not be used while user is typing or viewing the contents of the screen. For example, a remote user may wish to drop off and pick up mail. This process is similar to using a mail gateway, discussed in Chapter 2. The alternative has the remote user running the mail program to check his or her mail, possibly reading and writing messages before finally terminating the mail client application running on the remote workstation, and then breaking the connection. In this case, the majority of the connect time has the user reading or typing. The connection is not used, or is used very little, during this time, which prevents the connection from being used by others. Of course, the connection cost may be a minor concern, such as with local telephone calls, or it may simply be necessary, such as a remote network monitoring application.

Manual connect and disconnect procedures may be required by the support software, or automatic connections may simply be difficult to implement with remote workstations. Some remote workstation software requires users to enter their access name and password from the keyboard. This prevents someone from taking the remote workstation and having access to the name and password, but it means an automatic login procedure is not possible. Why would you want an automatic login procedure? Let's say you wanted to automatically drop off and pick up mail in the evening when telephone rates or remote network use is low. You can automatically start up a procedure at a given time, which could perform this operation for you, but it will not work if you're not there to enter the name and password.

Obviously, most remote workstation connection rates are significantly slower than LAN transfer rates. V.34 modems, the fastest standard modem for conventional telephone lines, run at 28,800 bits per second, but this pales in comparison to Ethernet, which runs at 10,000,000 bits per second. ISDN connections, which are becoming more common, are significantly faster than V.34 modems but still slower than a LAN connection. Of course, faster remote connections must also be compared to emerging LAN connections, such as 100-MHz Ethernet. The problem here is that application development takes advantage of the faster LAN connections, keeping remote workstations, even with fast connections, in the slow lane. For example, many newer programs employ multimedia presentations in their help support. A multimedia presentation can easily be a megabyte or more in size. The presentation will run smoothly on the LAN but the added delay over a modem connection will cause pauses or lost frames in the presentation.

Optimally, a remote workstation sends data to a server on the LAN and gets back only the data it requests; the problem is that networks use broadcast messages to perform some operations. Broadcasts are typically used by the network operating system (a message sent to all workstations instead of a specific one) on workstations and servers to notify programs of new services, search for services, or indicate a change in status. Remote workstations often need these broadcasts but broadcasts can be used for other purposes as well. Network games are one example of applications that may use message broadcasts. It is a simple and efficient way to keep multiple workstations in sync, but it can overburden the connection to a given remote workstation, which may or may not be involved in the game. The problem occurs because most local LAN connections have bandwidth (transmission speed) to burn, but a remote workstation's connection does not. A game that uses 10% of a local LAN's bandwidth with broadcast messages can amount to more than the total bandwidth of the remote workstation connection; what may be unnoticed by local LAN users will cause a remote workstation's access to come to a complete halt. This is even true when the remote workstation is not involved with the application doing the broadcasts, because message broadcasts are usually indiscriminate.

One solution to the message broadcast problem is to put the remote workstations on a different segment where network broadcasts are minimized. A segment is a collection of workstations that access the file server using the same NIC on the file server. A file server can have multiple NICS. Partitioning of this sort can often be done in a logical fashion. The same local LAN connection can be used by servers, workstations, and communications servers, but messages from one partition are not seen by network nodes in another partition. It is possible for one server to be in both partitions using a single NIC.

Remote LAN access using remote workstations is great if you need direct LAN access, if you want to run applications locally, or if you want to run the same applications as a LAN user. Remote LAN access may not be suitable if security is an issue.

SHOULD YOU USE REMOTE WORKSTATIONS FOR REMOTE LAN ACCESS?

There are a number of basic considerations that need to be examined before a remote workstation should be implemented. These considerations can help determine if remote workstations are suitable, practical, and desirable. The following is a list of considerations we will examine in more detail.

- ✧ Access to LAN users (yes)
- ✧ Access to LAN services (yes)
- ✧ Ease of use by remote users (good)
- ✧ Network operating system (important)

- ✧ Network protocol (important)
- ✧ Telephone time (high)
- ✧ Number of simultaneous active lines (high)
- ✧ Performance (good)
- ✧ Scalability (good)
- ✧ Hardware requirements (variable)
- ✧ Client licensing (variable)
- ✧ Cost (variable)
- ✧ Adding users (manual)
- ✧ General maintenance (minimal)
- ✧ Security (LAN security)
- ✧ Auditing (varies)
- ✧ Automation (possible)

Remote workstations allow access to LAN services. Access to remote users is possible through a variety of means that are available to local LAN users as well. These means typically include electronic mail, chat programs, possible remote control programs, and white board programs.

Remote workstations are easy to use if users are already familiar with LAN workstations. There is added overhead if remote users only want to send mail, because they must first make a remote workstation connection, log onto the network, and finally run the mail program. Logging out and terminating the connection are also necessary tasks. The extra procedures are simple, repetitive, and short so they become less significant as more operations are done during a connection.

The network operating system is important for remote workstations because they interact directly with each other. Most network operating systems support remote workstations, but the way this support is implemented may vary. For example, some network operating systems, such as Microsoft's Windows NT Server, have built-in support for remote workstations. Communications servers can also be used with a Windows NT Server and a remote workstation. The remote workstation software is different in both cases.

The network communication protocol is important if the remote workstation goes through a communications server, or if the file server that provides remote workstation support also provides access to the rest of the network. For example, many Simple Network Management Protocol (SNMP) devices attached to the network communicate using TCP/IP. A remote workstation can run an SNMP front-end application that communicates with these devices if the remote workstation is also using TCP/IP. The front-end application displays information obtained from the SNMP devices. In many cases, the network protocol is not important because this type of operation cannot be done by most users. Many applications, such as mail and word processors, operate independently of the underlying network communication protocol.

Telephone time is typically high compared to using other remote LAN access methods such as a mail gateway. It is possible to automate the connect and disconnect procedure, but normally the user is interacting directly with the remote workstation during the connection. Time spent viewing an application's screen uses connection time, regardless of how long you view the screen; if the connection is a long distance telephone call, this time costs money.

The number of simultaneous active lines can be high, but the actual number and the cost are based on the implementation chosen. Some network operating systems provide built-in remote workstation support, but only with a PC's standard serial ports. This limits the number of active lines to two for a typical IBM PC-compatible. More sophisticated implementations support multiple-port serial boards, which usually raise the limit to 8 or more. Communications servers are normally the answer if you need a large number of active lines; large enterprise-wide networks often have multiple communications servers and thousands of users.

Remote workstations offer good performance when moving data between the workstation and the LAN but you need to be careful not to overload the communication link with too much data. The network operating system's overhead tends to be low, so most of the connection's throughput can be used by an application. More importantly, any application can be run on the remote workstation.

Remote workstation support scales well if support for more lines are needed. Communications servers can often handle multiple lines. The only items that must be added to support a new telephone line are a modem and a cable. Some communication servers support only one or two lines. You need multiple servers to support more lines. It is possible to have an installation with only one line.

Hardware requirements vary depending on the implementation. A modem is required for each telephone line, but the cost of modems is relatively low these days. Network operating systems that provide remote workstation support in the file server often use the two standard serial communications ports. Multiport serial adapters are needed for more lines. Communications servers come in a variety of forms. Some are expandable, while others provide a fixed number of lines, some as few as one or two. Exceeding this number of lines requires an additional server. Modems cost less than $150 while a two line communication server is about $1000.

Licensing of the remote workstation software varies depending on how the network operating system vendors sell their products, but typically the cost is on a per-workstation basis. The remote workstation typically requires two licenses: one for the network operating system and the other for the remote workstation support. Both are normally inexpensive, but it is a consideration nonetheless. Communications servers are typically sold with the workstation software included at no additional cost. The software can be distributed to any number of remote workstation users because the costs are based on the number of lines supported by the communications server. The network operating system client license is still required, but you may want to determine whether the number is based on the number of active lines or the number of remote workstations.

The cost of using remote workstations can vary quite a bit depending on the necessary support hardware and software, remote workstation software, modems, and, of course, telephone charges. A single line into a file server with a network operating system that includes built-in support for remote workstations can be quite inexpensive, with the only additional cost being the cost of the modems. At the other end of the spectrum are sophisticated communications servers with many active lines supported.

Adding new remote workstation users is normally a manual operation that entails adding them as new network users. Additional work may be required if the remote workstation support at the LAN requires a separate user name and password. Local LAN users can often be remote LAN users with no additional administrative work. Automatic addition of users is typically not supported for security reasons; otherwise, anyone could have complete remote access to your LAN.

General maintenance is low for remote workstation support. Communications servers operate automatically. The two typical maintenance operations are to check the access log and to clear connections that have failed without breaking the connection. A LAN manager may also be notified of illegal entry attempts.

Security is a major consideration when using remote workstations because, in theory, a remote workstation can have access to all services on a LAN. Poor security procedures can let remote users have access to services you may not want them to access such as network printers or particular network disks. Unlike other remote LAN access methods, it is difficult to restrict remote workstation users to particular LAN services, other than to use the network operating system's security measures. Other remote LAN access methods often provide or even force additional security measures to ensure that remote users can only access authorized services. Of course, if you are confident that the network operating system and communications server you are using provides the necessary security, then remote workstation access may be a suitable remote LAN access method Some remote workstation communication servers can restrict protocol level access by the remote workstation.

Tracking remote access is important for security and administrative purposes. Auditing support varies greatly for remote workstation products. Some provide no auditing features, placing the audit burden on the network operating system—which also may not provide this support.

Remote workstations have the potential for providing very flexible automation support, the most flexible of any remote LAN access method. Batch files provide an easy way for almost any user to perform basic operations. Custom programs can provide more sophisticated support. Client/server applications are at the extreme end of the spectrum. The remote workstation would have the client program on its disk and the program would run on the remote workstation. The client application communicates with a server application that is running on a PC on the LAN. The communication data is usually much smaller than the LAN data the server processes.

Remote workstation support is a very powerful remote LAN access method, but it is not for everyone. Security issues are very important, especially if the LAN is currently being used with no security—often the case for small LANs.

SOME EXAMPLES OF REMOTE WORKSTATION PRODUCTS

Remote workstation support offers a variety of choices. We now take a look at a number of different examples, which represent some of the various approaches taken to implement remote workstation support. The end result should be a remote workstation that has the same capabilities as a local workstation. Most products are designed to work with modems; high-speed modems, such as V.34 modems, are preferred but most products will operate just as well, although less quickly, with slower modems.

The products we examine include:

✧ Xylogic's ANNEX

✧ Microsoft's Remote Access Service

✧ Novell's Net Connect

✧ Artisoft's LANtastic Z and Central Station II

✧ LAN Distance

Xylogic's MICRO ANNEX is actually the low cost, low end of an entire family of ANNEX remote access products based on the standard communications-server approach. We will concentrate on these low-end products because they are more suitable for small to medium networks, while the higher-end products are more applicable to the enterprise-wide network.

Microsoft's Remote Access Service (RAS) is available for Windows for Workgroups (WFW) and Windows NT Server. The WFW version is available free from Microsoft but is not included in the 3.11 product. Windows NT Server ships with a more flexible and powerful version of RAS.

Novell's Net Connect is a NetWare Loadable Module (NLM) designed to run on a NetWare file server. It provides modem-pooling support for calling out from local workstations as well as for remote workstations calling in.

Artisoft's LANtastic Z is specific to Artisoft's popular LANtastic peer-to-peer network. The simplest case has a remote workstation calling into a single PC. The two PCs represent a simple two-workstation/server network. LANtastic Z can also be used to access a server on a larger LANtastic network. Artisoft's Central Station II is an alternative if more than one remote workstation is needed; Central Station II is a combination communications and print server that supports two dial-in lines. Multiple Central Stations can be used on one network.

LAN Distance is designed to work with a variety of network operating systems. It represents a software-based communications server; you supply the hardware for the server and IBM supplies the software.

Whichever approach you choose, you can usually find more than one product that will work with your network. Novell NetWare networks have the widest variety of choices because of their popularity.

Xylogic's LANModem

Xylogic sells a line of communications servers, from the simple two-port LANModem (see Figure 3.11) to an expandable multiport communications server (see Figure 3.12.) Figure 3.13 shows the architecture used by Xylogic's communications servers. The server attaches to the network and passes remote workstation messages to the network through this connection.

The LANModem is a complete diskless networkable PC with a built-in modem and serial port. In addition to RAM and a processor, the LANModem contains an EEPROM, which allows software upgrades to be performed from a LAN workstation. The built-in Ethernet LAN adapter is used for upgrades and to provide access for the management program and the connection to the LAN for the remote workstations that call in.

FIGURE 3.11 LANMODEM BY XYLOGIC.

FIGURE 3.12 XYLOGIC'S MULTIPLE-PORT COMMUNICATIONS SERVER.

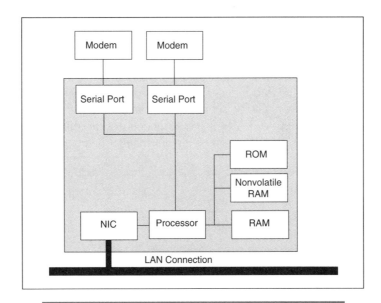

FIGURE 3.13 XYLOGIC'S COMMUNICATIONS SERVER ARCHITECTURE.

Many vendors provide products that are similar in function, price, and performance. Most of the features covered here are equally applicable to these other products. Remote workstations are very popular, and the variety of available options reflects this popularity.

Communications servers typically provide both dial-in and dial-out support for local workstations. The modems and telephone lines used by the communications server can often be used for both purposes, although some products restrict themselves to one or the other. Dial-out support typically collects multiple modems into a *modem pool*, which lets users access the modems on a first-come, first-served basis. Modem pools are useful for LAN users and they can even be accessed from a remote workstation. We will not dwell on this because it is not a required item to support remote workstations; although some communications server products do not provide dial-out support, most will.

Xylogic's LANModem represents the low end of the communications server spectrum; it is typical of them. It is a self-contained communications server and modem. All you need to do to use the LANModem is plug it into an AC outlet, plug the modem connection into a telephone jack, and connect the built-in network adapter to the LAN. LANModem management software is used to configure the LANModem. The management software runs on a LAN workstation, including a remote workstation. Figure 3.16 shows the initial dial-in screen on the remote workstation. The remote workstation's requests are passed through the LANModem to the network, which is typical for remote workstation support found in communications servers.

The LANModem's additional serial port can be connected to an external modem. There is no perceptible functional difference between the internal and external modem support. The LANModem can support two remote workstations simultaneously. The modems can also be set up for dial-out support. The LANModem can also be set up to support LAN-to-LAN connections. In this case, a pair of LANModems, one attached to each network, exchange data from one LAN to the other. Broadcast messages are exchanged, but most data is sent specifically between workstations or servers on either LAN. LAN-to-LAN connections are practical as long as the modem throughput can handle this message exchange.

Multiple LANModems can be placed on the same LAN to provide support for more telephones, but this approach is economical for only a few telephone lines. Larger expandable communications servers make more sense if you have more than ten telephone lines. In fact, many communications servers are nothing more than PCs with custom software. Additional lines are supported by plugging multiple-line serial boards into the communications server. Larger servers can support hundreds of remote workstations.

Microsoft's Remote Access Service

The Windows Remote Access Service (RAS) is Microsoft's answer to remote workstation support. RAS is available for Windows for Workgroups (WFW) and is bundled with Windows NT Server. It is also promised for Windows 95, which was not shipping when this was written but should be functionally the same as the Windows NT Server version. The Windows NT Server version is more sophisticated than the WFW version, so we will concentrate on it.

RAS is a software program that runs on a file server, as shown in Figure 3.14. It can provide access to just the server or to the rest of the network using TCP/IP or NETBIOS protocols. TCP/IP is useful if the remote workstation will run SNMP front-end applications. Microsoft's RAS supports X.25, a packet-network standard, and ISDN, in addition to its standard modem support. The initial version supports up to 64 remote workstation connections per server, using multiport serial adapters; one or two connections are supported using standard PC serial ports. Hardware-based data compression, found on most high-speed modems, is supported, or the optional software-based data compression can be used.

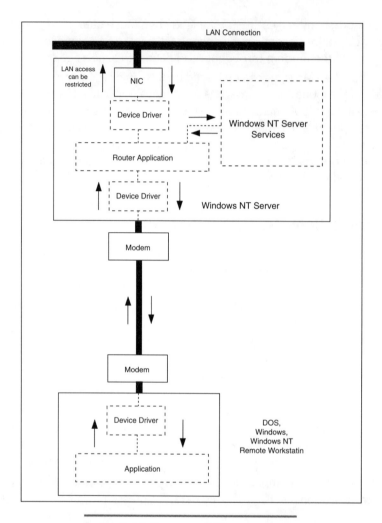

FIGURE 3.14 MICROSOFT RAS ARCHITECTURE.

RAS uses Windows NT Server's security system. It requires the remote workstation to authenticate the user, using the normal name-and-password combination when the connection is initiated. The user is also logged in at this time. The initial connection handshake procedure uses encryption (encoding that requires the proper key for decoding), which makes it very difficult for someone to figure out how to log on using your name and password, even if a person monitoring the connection can see what is being sent between modems. RAS also supports callbacks. A callback can be set up for specific users or for all remote users. The initial call from a remote user initiates the authentication process. The server then hangs up and calls the remote workstation back; the connection is then restored. This type of procedure forces the user to be at a specific location.

Figure 3.15 shows the RAS dial-in screen on the remote workstation. It is easy to use, and Windows NT Server supports all versions of Windows and Windows NT remote workstations. Remote management is possible. Like the security, the RAS tracking support is provided by Windows NT Server for user auditing.

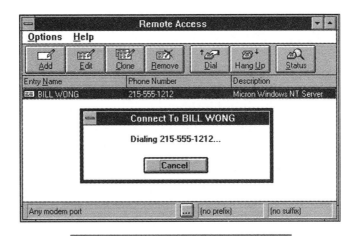

FIGURE 3.15 MICROSOFT RAS DIAL-IN SCREEN.

RAS does not impose a lot of overhead on the server, although putting 30 or 40 modems on one server can start to impact on the server's overall performance. Windows NT's excellent multitasking support lets a server provide a number of services in addition to acting as a communications server. Windows NT also supports multiple processors (with the proper hardware), which allows a server to be upgraded if one of the programs, such as RAS, starts to impose too much load on the server.

Novell Net Connect

Novell's Net Connect is similar to Microsoft's RAS for Windows NT Server. Both run on the file server and provide communications support to remote workstations. Net Connect also provides dial-out support, including modem pooling. The dial-out feature includes support for Novell's NetWare Access Services (NAS), NetWare Asynchronous Services Interface (NASI), and the DOS INT 14 redirector. The latter is a low-level serial port interface for IBM PCs running DOS and Windows. Some communications programs support NASI, but almost all support INT 14.

Net Connect supports modem pooling for dial-out use. Up to 64 ports can be split among dial-in and dial-out use. Novell calls a remote workstation a NetWare Remote Node (NRN). NRNs can be DOS, Windows, OS/2, or Macintosh workstations.

Net Connect is a NetWare Loadable Module (NLM) that runs on a NetWare 3.x or 4.x file server. Net Connect's architecture is shown in Figure 3.16. The Remote Node Service (RNS) provides remote workstation (NRN) support for DOS, Windows, and OS/2 workstations. Macintosh remote workstation support is provided by the AppleTalk Remote Access Service (ARAS), which provides dial-in support using Apple's AppleTalk Remote Access software.

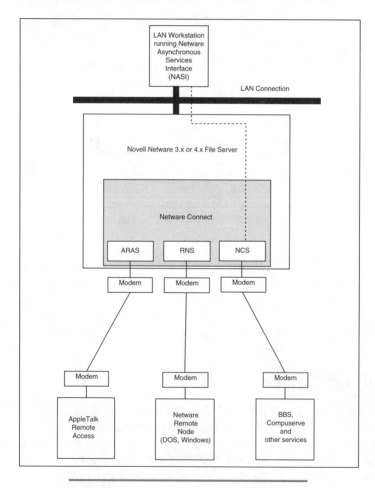

FIGURE 3.16 NOVELL NET CONNECT ARCHITECTURE.

Net Connect supports callback using both fixed and user-supplied numbers; the latter works like the normal callback, but the users supply their current modem phone number. Thus Net Connect can track where a user is calling from while still allowing users to call from different locations. Net Connect uses NetWare's user names and passwords, and the Net Connect manager can restrict service to particular ports. An optional audit trail lets the manager track overall usage. Net Connect supports SNMP and the NetWare Management System (NMS) for remote management. Net Connect supports the standard PC serial ports or a multiport serial adapter. Modem support is standard, as is X.25, as your serial ports are hooked into a public or private packet network.

Although Net Connect is available from Novell, it is only one of many remote workstation support products available for Novell's popular NetWare 3.x and 4.x networks. Artisoft's Central Station II and Xylogics ANNEX line are two other products supporting NetWare.

Artisoft's LANtastic Z and Central Station II

Novell's NetWare may be the most popular server-based network operating system, but Artisoft's LANtastic is one of the most popular peer-to-peer network operating systems. Server based networks require at least one dedicated server, usually a file server. Peer-to-peer networks allow client workstations to be servers which share client resources such as disks and printers. Communications servers that act as NETBIOS pass-through servers for remote workstations can usually support LANtastic. In lieu of a communications server, you can check out two basic remote workstation products from Artisoft. LANtastic Z is a software product that even works with a standalone PC LANtastic server; Artisoft's Central Station II is a hardware product that comes in both a LANtastic and Novell NetWare versions. LANtastic Z and Central Station II are designed to be low-cost low-line-count solutions that fit with LANtastic's typical installation: the small to medium workgroup network.

LANtastic Z, in its simplest form, is a two-workstation network with a single modem connection between the two (see Figure 3.17). The LANtastic Z package includes a two-workstation LANtastic license. LANtastic is a peer-to-peer network operating system, so this network configuration lets either workstation access services on the other. LANtastic works with DOS and Windows workstations.

Although LANtastic Z is designed for a simple PC-to-PC connection, it also works if one of the workstations is also a LANtastic server on the LAN. LANtastic Z does not provide bridging support, so the remote workstation can only access services on the server. This is often sufficient because LAN users can also access the server. If the LANtastic Z server is also a post office for the LAN, then the remote user can send and receive mail using LANtastic's standard mail service. The remote workstation can use printers on other workstations, but only if the server itself is using remote printers. In this case, the remote workstation still prints to a print queue on the server.

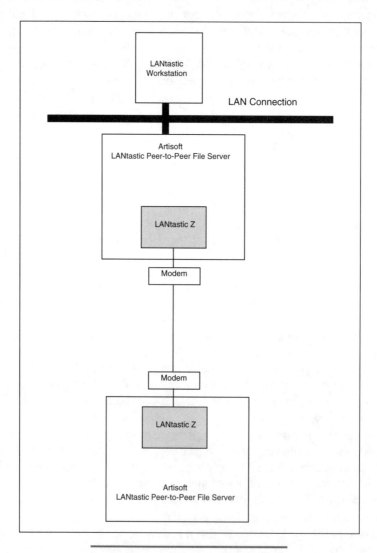

Figure 3.17 LANtastic Z architecture.

LANtastic Z uses LANtastic's security support. LANtastic Z does not scale well. It is designed to provide access to a single remote workstation. Multiple workstations can call into multiple LANtastic Z servers, but they do not share unrestricted access to the network. For this type of access there is Artisoft's Central Station II.

Central Station II is a box slightly larger than an external modem. It is actually a multipurpose server; Central Station II has two serial ports, two parallel ports, an Ethernet adapter, and a control port. The control port can be plugged into the parallel port of a PC, which can control the Central Station II, print, or access the network using Central Station II's Ethernet port. Central Station II is both a print server and a remote workstation server. Figure 3.18 shows Central Station II's architecture. Figure 3.19 shows Central Station II. The print server uses print queues on LANtastic servers (the NetWare version supports them on Novell NetWare servers). The printers can be attached to parallel ports or serial ports. If a PC is attached to the control port, it can print directly to one of the attached printers without going through the print queue mechanism, with Central Station II coordinating the two. The PC can also print to a print queue, which may be printing via the Central Station II.

Serial ports not used for printing can be attached to modems to provide remote workstation support. One or two remote workstations can be supported by one Central Station II. Multiple Central Stations can be used to provide remote workstation support on the same network.

The Ethernet access via the parallel control port is a handy way for a laptop user to gain access to the LAN when in the office. The control port can also be used with a desktop PC, but the parallel port interface is slower and has more overhead than a normal Ethernet adapter. This versatility makes Central Station II an ideal choice for mobile users who also stop by the office.

Central Station II uses the network operating system's security and provides the basic network interface support. Although it theoretically provides LAN protocol-level support, you should only count on support for the specified network operating system. I tried using the control port with a laptop running Personal NetWare without success. It turns out that the NetWare version of Central Station II works just fine with the other Novell networks.

LANtastic is usually found on networks with ten to twenty workstations, so support for one or two remote workstations is often sufficient. Other communications server products should be considered if more serial lines are needed.

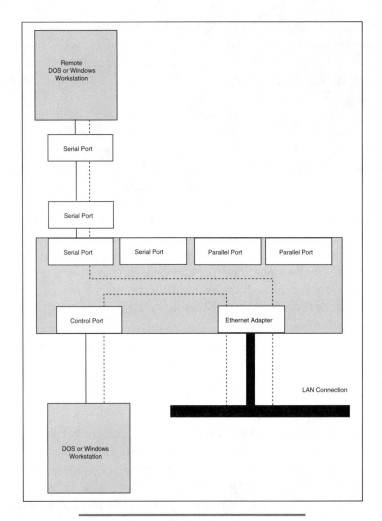

FIGURE 3.18 CENTRAL STATION II ARCHITECTURE.

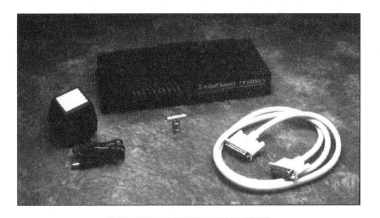

FIGURE 3.19 CENTRAL STATION II.

LAN Distance

LAN Distance (LD) provides software support for remote workstations. LD uses a standard PC to implement a communications server for one or more remote workstations. The standard PC serial ports or multiline serial adapters can be used in conjunction with modems, ISDN, or X.25 networks.

LD works and operates like a conventional standalone communications server. LD provides transparent protocol support using standard protocols, including TCP/IP, IPX, and NETBIOS. LD uses a standard device driver on the remote workstation, so LD can work with a number of different network operating systems. Protocol-level communications servers, like LD, provide access to a variety of network operating systems including Novell NetWare, IBM LANSERVER, and Microsoft Windows NT Server, as well as to protocol-level services such as SNMP.

LD's remote workstation dial-in support should be familiar by now. Network security is provided by the network operating system in addition to LD's connection security. LD supports the conventional callback and password security available with other communications servers. Remote workstation operation with LD is similar to other remote workstation implementations. LD workstation support is installed as a network device driver, and a support program is used to initiate and terminate a connection.

Software-based communications servers like LD offer flexibility over dedicated communications servers. You can make use of existing equipment, and standard PCs tend to be less expensive than customized equipment. On the other hand, multiline communications servers have been optimized for that job. Addition of adapters and modems is typically easier, because the hardware is specific to the communications server, and the matching support software is already configured to handle the added hardware. LD, on the other hand, works with a variety of hardware. Getting a specific piece of hardware, such as a multiline serial adapter, to work with LD takes a bit of work to install and configure.

One advantage of using a software-based product like LD is that new options are easier to add. Ethernet and Token Ring adapters are common on communications servers, but what happens if you need to use a different technology to attach the server to the network? 100-MHz Ethernet and ATM are just two technologies that are becoming more popular; LD works more easily with these new technologies than do dedicated communications servers.

From the user's point of view, there is essentially no difference between using a dedicated communications server and using LD. The dial-in programs for most remote workstations are functionally identical. Once the connection is made, the remote workstation operates the same regardless of the underlying support. In fact, the network operating system is more invasive than the remote workstation support. The difference is more important to the network manager. As such, security, management tools, and expandability become important concerns when you are considering remote workstation support. LD fares well in comparison with hardware approaches, as long as the network manager wants to deal with making choices on which hardware to use and the handling of the software.

CHAPTER 4

REMOTE CONTROL PROGRAMS

Remote control programs let one PC, the *client*, control another, the *host*. The client's screen shows the same thing as the host's screen. Type on the client's keyboard or use the client's mouse, and the actions are sent to the host, which reacts as if the same actions were performed using its keyboard or mouse. Figure 4.1 shows the client and host screen. Yes, they are the same.

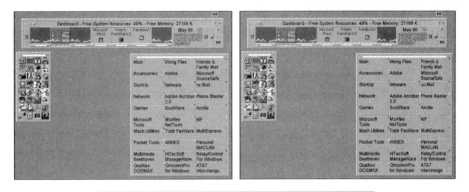

FIGURE 4.1 REMOTE CONTROL CLIENT AND HOST SCREENS.

Remote Control Programs

If the host PC is a local LAN workstation, then the client has indirect access to the LAN. The host PC runs the applications the remote user sees and interacts with. Need to edit a document on the LAN? Start up a word processor on the host PC and access the document directly. But how do you get the document to your client PC? Most remote control programs provide a file-management program that can copy files between the client and host PCs. More sophisticated remote control programs can even make the client's disk drives available to the host and vice versa. Any application running on the host can then copy or save a file directly onto the client's disk. Figure 4.2 shows some of the remote control options. Remote control programs can be used to access standalone PC, and they are also a good way to remotely access a LAN. Users familiar with programs on the LAN will be able to use a remote control host, because it runs these same programs.

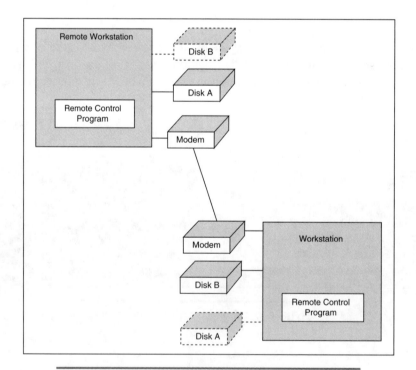

Figure 4.2 Remote control architecture with shared disks.

The host PC must be running the remote control host program before a connection can be made; it sets the modem up to accept a call when it starts and then waits for it. An unattended host PC normally starts the remote control host program as part of its boot sequence; a host PC that is attached to a LAN may or may not load the network software. The remote workstation runs the matching remote control client program. The remote user selects or enters the phone number for the host PC, and the program initiates the call. Figure 4.3 shows a sample call initiation screen.

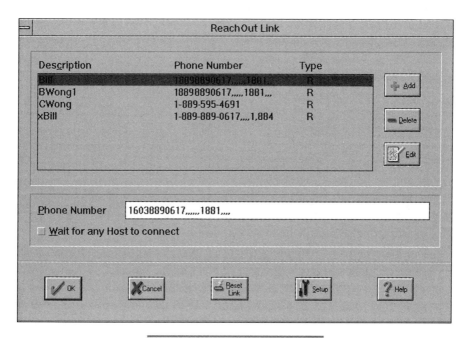

FIGURE 4.3 SAMPLE DIAL-IN SCREEN.

After a connection is made between the remote and host PCs the remote control software synchronizes the remote client's screen with the host PC's screen. At this point the user at the remote workstation can type or use the mouse, and the keystrokes and mouse movements are sent to the host PC, which reacts to them as if they were performed using the host's own keyboard or mouse (interestingly enough, the host does not *need* a keyboard, mouse, or even a monitor for a remote control program to work). In any case, the remote user can now log onto the LAN using the normal network operating system (NOS) support programs. From the remote user's point of view, the login procedure appears to be occurring on his or her machine; in fact, it is occurring on the host PC, which can lead to some occasional misunderstandings. For example, looking for a file on the remote workstation's own hard disk or floppy disk doesn't work, at least not the same way it does when the program is running on the host PC; what actually happens is that the host's hard or floppy disk is used. This problem aside, the normal operation of a LAN workstation is presented to the remote user, who can log off the network and use the host PC as a standalone workstation if necessary.

A remotely controlled host PC can do something that is not possible with other remote LAN access methods: it can continue working even after the remote workstation has terminated a connection. For example, a remote user calls into a host workstation on the LAN. After logging in he or she starts up a tape backup program, possibly using a tape unit on the host workstation. The backup could be of the host workstation, the network server or another workstation depending on the capability of the backup program. The backup procedure takes an hour to complete, but the remote user does not have to stay connected for the entire period; after making sure the operation is being performed, the user can break the connection and let the host complete the operation. Later, the user can call in and check the status of the operation. Of course, the user cannot put a tape into a tape drive from the remote workstation, but that can be done before the user leaves the office, or someone else at the host workstation's location could do it.

The main point to remember when using remote control software is that applications actually run on the *host*, not on the remote workstation. Many remote control programs let the host PC access the remote PC's disk drives, but they are defined as different drives. For example, on a DOS PC the hard disk is normally drive **C:**. The host's hard drive will also be drive **C:,** but the remote workstation's drive **C:** may appear as drive **F:** to the application running on the host PC.

Although remote users essentially use their remote workstations as if they were attached directly to the LAN, they will notice a difference in response time when using applications running on the host PC. Character-mode screens update more quickly than graphic screens because there is less data to be sent. The remote control software attempts to keep the remote PC's screen as close to the host PC's screen as possible. Changes that occur at the host PC are then sent to the remote client, so there is at least some delay before the remote user sees the changes. For many operations, the delay makes little difference, but the delay can be disconcerting for interactive operations. For example, to move to the left in a word processor you normally press the **left arrow** key. Luckily, most word processors and remote control programs can accept multiple keystrokes before the initial keystroke is processed. You can move to the left by quickly pressing the **left arrow** key many times. A PC is normally fast enough to keep up with your typing regardless of how fast you type, but mix in a remote control program and a pair of modems and the delay becomes noticeable; this is partly due to the remote control software's attempting to keep the screen updated each time you type a character. The effect is often a cursor that jumps to its final position, or typed text may appear suddenly on the remote workstation's screen. If you placed the remote workstation next to the host PC you would see that the host PC's screen reacts as you would expect it to. In many ways, it is like watching a film, but only seeing every other frame: you can see what is going on but the action is not smooth.

There are actually two types of screen update modes: synchronous and asynchronous. The *synchronous* mode updates the remote workstation's screen as each change occurs, so you see everything that happens on the host's screen. The *asynchronous* mode sends changes in batches and only sends the latest screen contents. For example, assume that text is scrolling on the host, so a batch of screen changes is sent to the remote workstation. By the time the batch of changes is sent, the screen has changed again, so another new batch is sent, which reflects the current contents of the screen. A particular line on the screen may have changed many times between the first and second batches of changes, but only two copies of the line are sent. Asynchronous mode is often preferred since it provides a faster response time, and a user typically wants to see the end result of an action. Synchronous mode is desirable if a user must see everything that is presented on the screen.

In many ways, access to a LAN by a remote control program is similar to the remote workstation support described in Chapter 3. The two are also very different, however, and so the choice of which to use is not always easy to make. For example, both use NOS security, but it is possible to accidentally bypass this security using a remote control program. Assume, for the moment, that someone else called into a remote control host on the LAN and logged into the network. He or she accidentally break the connection to the remote control host without logging off. You then call in to the same host, and lo and behold, you are logged onto the LAN using someone else's user name. You could change that person's password, copy files, and do all sorts of things you probably should not be able to do. Figure 4.4 shows this scenario in graphic detail.

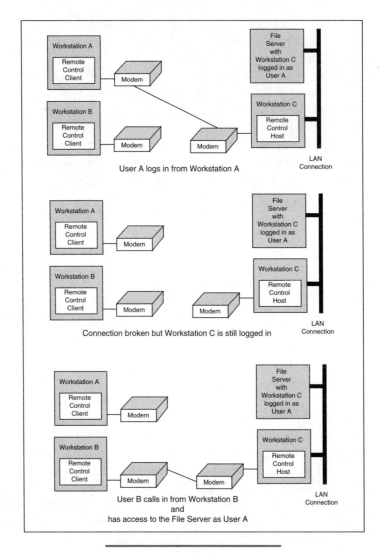

FIGURE 4.4 LOGIN SECURITY BREACH.

Before you go into panic mode and toss out remote control LAN access systems you should know that most remote control programs provide options to prevent this situation. Like network operating system security, remote control program security is only as good as the features you enable and maintain, but there will be more on security later in the chapter.

Remote control programs normally require a dedicated PC at both ends, although there is a special case where a single PC can host multiple clients. The multiple-client host is normally a multitasking operating system like IBM's OS/2, and the clients are single-screen character-mode DOS sessions; hosting multiple graphical user interface (GUI) environments on a single PC is normally impractical. One way to lower the cost of the host workstation is to remove the keyboard, mouse, and monitor. In fact, the entire workstation can be eliminated except for the processor, memory, network interface, and some support logic. Some companies have done just that, placing one or even two PCs on an adapter board that plugs into a file server. A modem plugs into the card or a modem connection is made through a *modem pool* (a group of dedicated modems so the host PC can accept calls from remote workstations. The PC-on-a-card is used specifically for remote control, and it does so at a significantly lower cost compared to a dedicated PC while maintaining a high degree of hardware compatibility.

One of the major issues in selecting remote control programs for LAN use is the operating systems and operating environments to be used. Remote control programs are usually not specific to a LAN's network operating system, but they *are* specific to the operating system and operating environment of both the host and the remote workstation. In many cases the two match, but there are many products available that support different operating systems and environments on the host and remote workstation. In fact, some even support different kinds of workstations at either end of the connection, such as a Macintosh remote workstation and a host DOS PC. The most popular platforms for remote control programs are DOS and Microsoft Windows. Remote control programs exist for almost any environment including OS/2, Windows NT, and UNIX, but the choices are fewer. The operating environment is important when you consider the applications a user wants to run. If the primary application runs on UNIX, then a UNIX remote control host is needed.

Security is the other major issue associated with remote control systems. Like other remote LAN access methods, remote control programs offer their own name-and-password based security systems, and advanced security support, like *modem callback*, is often a standard part of a product. Modem callback works like this. You call the modem. It answers and prompts for a password. It looks up the password to find the matching phone number. The modem hangs up the phone and calls the phone number. This should be the number the original call was made from. The initial calling modem then answers the call and the connection is maintained. Host workstations on a LAN can also make use of the NOS security, but remote control have their own set of unique security-related problems. For example, *Trojan Horse* programs left running on a host PC can save another user's network name and password, without the user even knowing the program is running. This information can later be used without the legitimate user's knowledge or consent. Later sections in this chapter address security issues in more detail.

Remote control systems work better with lower-speed modems than many other remote LAN access methods, because applications on the host PC work directly with the LAN-based services at LAN speeds, not modem speeds. What is impractical with a remote LAN workstation, described in Chapter 3, is practical with a remote control client. For example, you would not want to load a word processor from a file server using a remote LAN workstation, because most word processing programs are large, and moving them across a modem connection can take quite a bit of time. On the other hand, loading the same program onto a remote host workstation from the file server takes seconds, because the data is sent at local LAN speeds. The remote client's screen is updated to reflect the newly loaded word processor, but the update requires significantly less data than the entire word processor program file. Likewise, loading a document from the file server takes less time using the host workstation.

Remote control programs are practical with 2,400-baud modems, but faster 14,400 baud V.32bis or 28,800-baud V.34 modems are obviously better. The main practical difference between slower modems and faster modems is the speed of screen update at the remote workstation; the modem's speed does not have a major effect on the speed of the application running on the host.

Remote LAN access using a remote control program has another major benefit for laptop users. Although laptops are becoming more powerful, a powerful desktop PC is still a lot cheaper so most laptops will be less capable (powerful) than the host which is usually a desktop PC. Resource requirements at the client end of a remote control configuration are relatively low. The client PC only needs to update the display, handle the keyboard and mouse input, and manage the modem. There is no requirement that the client and host have the same power or hardware configuration. In fact, they are typically very different.

Remote control programs are an economical solution when the number of telephone lines is small because a PC is required to support each line. Remote LAN access using remote control programs becomes more difficult to manage and maintain when the number of lines gets large; just imagine how much room is required for 100 PCs and modems.

Remote control programs are a powerful remote LAN access mechanism. Like the remote workstation support approach presented in Chapter 3, remote control programs provide complete access to the LAN, which can be both beneficial and a bit scary when the security implications are considered. Remote control programs are particularly useful to LAN users because the same applications are run when the user sits either in front of a local LAN workstation or at a remote client keyboard.

REMOTE CONTROL PROGRAMS: A USER'S VIEW

A remote control program user's view of the world is an application on a host workstation. Once a connection is made, there are two modes of operation: interacting with the host workstation's applications and specialized functions. Interaction with the host workstation is through the standard devices: the monitor, the keyboard, and the mouse. There is typically a slight additional delay between user input and updating the display, dependent on the speed of the connection. This delay is noticeable but not usually annoying. Most remote control programs provide a number of other specialized functions, such as file transfers and a *chat mode*. Chat mode lets the host PC user and the remote PC user type messages to each other. Figure 4.5 shows the utility window for Ocean Isle's Reachout. It integrates access to the connection control with other features such as an address book and security management. Most functions can be accessed during a connection.

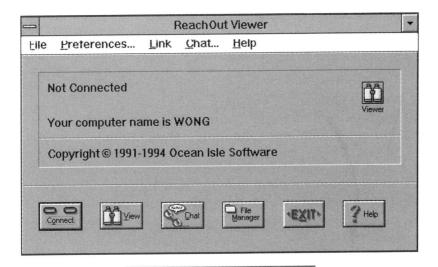

FIGURE 4.5 REACHOUT UTILITY WINDOW.

A connection is typically initiated by selecting an address-book entry. The connection can be initiated from the host or the client workstation. The workstation at the other end must be running the remote control software and it must be waiting for a call. A client's address book usually contains one or more entries. Each entry contains a name, password, and phone number. The host's address book is organized in the same fashion, but the phone number can be omitted (or it contains the phone number of the client). The phone number is required at the host's end if it initiates the call, or if *modem callback* is enabled. The name and password are exchanged by the remote control software after the phone number is dialed and a connection is made between modems. Depending on the product and its configuration, the initial connection is followed by a utility/status window on the host's screen. The latter is available from the former via a keystroke or menu selection. Getting access to the host's LAN is now a simple matter of running the login program; of course, the host computer can also be operated without logging onto the LAN.

Programs can now be run on the host, with normal access to LAN services. The host's drives keep the same designation that a host user would see. Some remote control programs allow the client's local drives to be assigned to drives that the host's applications can use. The drive designations for the client drives will differ from both the host and the network drives. The difference can initially be confusing, but regular remote control users get used to working this way. Remote control programs that do not support this re-mapping feature force you to use the remote control program's file transfer programs.

Remote control programs allow file transfers between the host and client. They are typically implemented using an interactive file-management application like the one shown in Figure 4.6. One window shows local files and the other shows host files. File-management operations like **Copy**, **Move**, **Delete** and **Create Directory** are available from menus or function keys. Drag-and-drop and multiple-selection operations are typical features. File transfers can often be queued and performed in the background; background transfers let the remote control program use the connection when it is not being used to send keystrokes to the host or screen update information to the remote workstation. Priority is given to screen updates and keyboard and mouse input during background file transfers so there is no degradation in application response time.

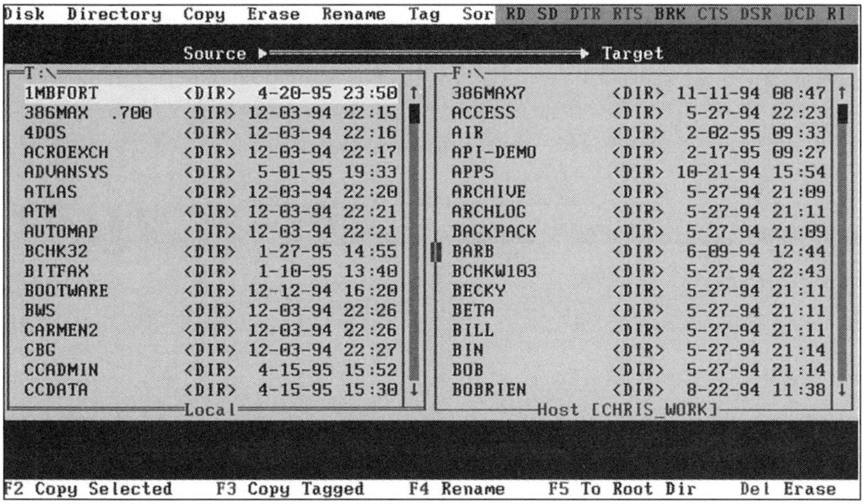

```
Disk   Directory   Copy   Erase   Rename   Tag   Sor RD SD DTR RTS BRK CTS DSR DCD RI

                    Source ▶════════════════════▶ Target
  ┌T:\─────────────────────────────────┐  ┌F:\─────────────────────────────────┐
  │ 1MBFORT        <DIR>  4-20-95 23:50│↑│ │ 386MAX7        <DIR> 11-11-94 08:47│↑│
  │ 386MAX  .700   <DIR> 12-03-94 22:15│▓│ │ ACCESS         <DIR>  5-27-94 22:23│▓│
  │ 4DOS           <DIR> 12-03-94 22:16│ │ │ AIR            <DIR>  2-02-95 09:33│ │
  │ ACROEXCH       <DIR> 12-03-94 22:17│ │ │ API-DEMO       <DIR>  2-17-95 09:27│ │
  │ ADVANSYS       <DIR>  5-01-95 19:33│ │ │ APPS           <DIR> 10-21-94 15:54│ │
  │ ATLAS          <DIR> 12-03-94 22:20│ │ │ ARCHIVE        <DIR>  5-27-94 21:09│ │
  │ ATM            <DIR> 12-03-94 22:21│ │ │ ARCHLOG        <DIR>  5-27-94 21:11│ │
  │ AUTOMAP        <DIR> 12-03-94 22:21│ │ │ BACKPACK       <DIR>  5-27-94 21:09│ │
  │ BCHK32         <DIR>  1-27-95 14:55│▐│ │ BARB           <DIR>  6-09-94 12:44│ │
  │ BITFAX         <DIR>  1-10-95 13:40│ │ │ BCHKW103       <DIR>  5-27-94 22:43│ │
  │ BOOTWARE       <DIR> 12-12-94 16:20│ │ │ BECKY          <DIR>  5-27-94 21:11│ │
  │ BWS            <DIR> 12-03-94 22:26│ │ │ BETA           <DIR>  5-27-94 21:11│ │
  │ CARMEN2        <DIR> 12-03-94 22:26│ │ │ BILL           <DIR>  5-27-94 21:11│ │
  │ CBG            <DIR> 12-03-94 22:27│ │ │ BIN            <DIR>  5-27-94 21:14│ │
  │ CCADMIN        <DIR>  4-15-95 15:52│ │ │ BOB            <DIR>  5-27-94 21:14│ │
  │ CCDATA         <DIR>  4-15-95 15:30│↓│ │ BOBRIEN        <DIR>  8-22-94 11:38│↓│
  └─────────Local──────────────────────┘  └──────────Host [CHRIS_WORK]──────────┘

 F2 Copy Selected   F3 Copy Tagged    F4 Rename   F5 To Root Dir   Del Erase
```

FIGURE 4.6 FILE MANAGER SCREEN.

File-transfer support is often implemented as a command-line-initiated program, which allows the use of batch files to automate common operations. PC DOS uses a command line interface. You type commands or program names to execute commands and run programs. Often the commands have similar names and syntax to the standard operating system's counterparts, such as **Copy** and **Rcopy** or **Del** and **Rdel**.

The other major feature found in most remote control programs is chat mode. *Chat mode*, shown in Figure 4.7, lets a user on the client workstation interact with a user at the host workstation. The chat window typically consists of a conversation subpane and an entry pane. You type into the entry pane, and the text is displayed in the conversation pane on both workstations once the line is complete. The chat window is part of the remote control program, so it does not interfere with the host application. Chat mode is handy if problems arise that require a fix at the host end. For example, running a tape backup program on the host is sometimes useful, but only if a tape is in the tape drive. The person who puts the tape into the drive does not need to know how to run the backup program because the person running the client workstation can do that, but only the person at the host workstation can actually put the tape into the drive.

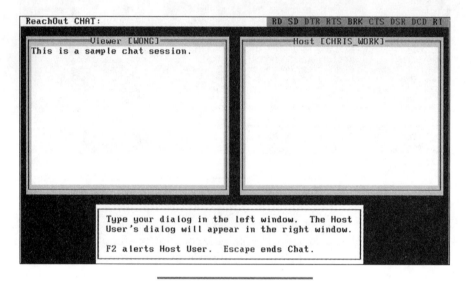

FIGURE 4.7 CHAT MODE SCREEN.

For the most part, remote interaction with the host application and with the utility window is all a user will do, but there is more to using a remote control program than one initially sees. The host continues to run its applications regardless of whether there is a remote connection. Some remote control programs can be set up to reboot for security reasons if a connection is broken; more on this later. The more important issue is that the initial connection is made some time *after* the host workstation boots and loads the remote control program. In fact, it is possible for a user to call into the host workstation, start an application, and break the connection, while allowing the application to continue to run. The user can call in later to see how the application is working. The prior example involving a tape backup operation is one use for this unattended mode of operation.

Unfortunately, a problem can occur if the breaking of a connection is accidental, or if a second remote workstation user makes a connection between the time a remote user starts an operation and when he or she calls in again to check the status of the operation. In this latter case, the second user will find him or herself with a screen from the application started by the first user, and may, perhaps inadvertently, abort the operation, much to the chagrin of the first user. Some remote control programs can prevent secondary users from gaining access to the host after an initial user has reserved access, but most of them simply allow access by any user with a valid name and password. Security and privacy are two aspects of this problem. Security is a problem because the first user provides uncontrolled access to running applications and data to the second user. Privacy is a problem because the second user gets to see what the first user was working on.

A similar problem exists when the host workstation is located in a spot accessible by other people. Some remote control programs have the ability to lock out the host's keyboard and mouse and some can even blank the screen. Unfortunately, the remote user cannot actually verify any of this without having someone sitting in front of the host workstation. Also, most people set up remote hosts so that the host's screen, keyboard, and mouse are enabled. A person at the host workstation can watch you create a confidential memo or do work on the payroll without your knowledge.

Another problem remote users can encounter is the occasional system crash. People tend to use reliable applications, but occasionally they fail. The remote control program may not lock up and the remote user can cause the host workstation to reboot. The host remote control program may not lock up when the application does because it communicates with the remote workstation using serial port interrupts that are not usually disabled when an application fails. Unfortunately, often both the remote control program and the host application lock up, and someone must reset the workstation manually. There are some power control devices that monitor the modem line, which will reset the workstation when the connection is broken.

One interesting aspect of remote control programs is their ability to use dissimilar hardware and software at either end. Obviously items such as modems, the amount of memory, and hard disk capacity can differ, but it is even possible for screen resolution and processors to be different; one of the more extreme cases is an Apple Macintosh client controlling an IBM PC-compatible host. The more conventional environment has similar hardware workstation characteristics at both ends. Some remote control programs can perform screen-resolution and color-depth translation. For example, the host may be running in standard VGA mode, 640 by 480 pixels with 16 colors, while the client may be running in a SuperVGA mode like 800 by 600 with 256 colors. Some remote control programs show the smaller VGA screen in the upper-left corner of the client or within a window of the with the same height and width in pixels as the host, while other programs scale the window to the full screen. Both map the smaller color palette to the larger color palette. Going in the other direction is a bit more difficult, but possible; showing a larger screen resolution on a smaller screen resolution can be done by scaling, or presenting the screen with scroll bars and showing only what the client screen is capable of showing at one time. Mapping a larger number of colors to a smaller palette normally results in a loss of information, but often the results are acceptable. A performance penalty is incurred by this translation, which can add to the screen-update delay encountered by remote control programs.

Workstations that run DOS and Microsoft Windows must address the difference in screen handling. Many client applications operate only in one environment or the other but support both environments on the host. Some remote control products only support character-mode DOS operation, while others support various graphic modes under DOS. Typically a DOS client can be used to control a DOS or Windows host.

Remote control access to a host workstation on a LAN can be seductive. Your remote client looks and acts like it was connected to the LAN. Even the applications that are run on the host run at full speed. The added delay between keystroke and screen update is enough to help you remember that you are not really there. As long as you remember that this is the case, you can remember to be careful about what you type. Remote control access to the LAN will be the preference for any user who must access and manipulate medium to large amounts of data on the LAN. In one sense, it is a form of universal client/server computing. In this case the client is the remote workstation and the server is the host workstation.

REMOTE CONTROL PROGRAMS: A LAN MANAGER'S VIEW

WARNING

Stop! Read this: If you do not want to provide unrestricted remote LAN access to all network services, read this section carefully and read the documentation to any product that you consider for providing remote control programs support. A remote control programs controls a local workstation that has access to the LAN. Although most network operating systems provide security measures that can restrict general access, they often allow some access without using the security measures. The bottom line: beware, be careful, be smart.

With that warning in mind, considering and implementing remote control program support is a relatively straightforward but tedious process. Most remote control programs are designed for use on one host that supports one remote workstation at a time. They are set up on a particular host workstation and managed from that workstation. Some remote control products are moving toward network-based management, but single-workstation orientation is still the norm. This is not to say that multiple host-workstations on a LAN are impractical or undesirable. On the contrary, it is easy to set up multiple host-workstations; it is just difficult to manage and monitor them. If you plan to have more than one or two remote workstations, then you will want to check out a product's LAN-administration support in greater detail, if it exists.

There are three primary items to manage on a remote control host: the address book, the hardware, and the access log. The address book, which may have different names depending on the product, lets the remote control host program know who is allowed to call into the host. Minimally, an address book entry has a user name and password. The client's address-book has a matching entry that is used to make a connection. The host's address-book entry often has a number of other attributes associated with it, to control the security and services to be provided by the host to the remote client.

The second management item is the hardware itself. Remote workstation support, covered in Chapter 3, at the communications server typically allows a connection to be broken or reset by the LAN manager, using a management program on another LAN workstation. Most remote control programs do not support this type of operation, which means that manual intervention is often required to clear a workstation that is *locked up* or to break a connection with an errant user. Two alternatives exist that provide the same service, although indirectly. The first is to use a remote power-control system that is accessible through the LAN or is attached directly to the LAN manager's workstation. These power-control systems let a PC turn power on and off. A host-workstation plugged into one of these power-control systems can be reset by turning off its power. It is not an elegant solution, but it works. The other alternative is to use network-based modem pools to support the host-client connection. The modem-pool-management software can then be used to break connections. This solution is more effective, but it is more expensive to implement unless the modem pool is already in use. The incremental cost to add modems to a modem pool is relatively low, but the initial cost tends to be rather high.

The final management item is the access log. Most remote control programs can keep an optional access log. The details vary from user name and connection times, to the number and name of the files transferred and accessed and the programs used. The access log also tracks invalid accesses, which can help if someone is trying to break into your LAN.

LAN-based management of host workstations can be done if the various support files, such as the address book and log, are placed on a network file server; the problem is that these files can only be accessed when the host workstation has access to the LAN. Access may be limited, and the host's remote control support program can often be set up to prevent access to these files by the client. Unfortunately, this level of LAN access may not meet the security requirements of some networks. The level of security provided by a remote control host is a major concern to network managers. Knowing the capabilities of a particular product and the kinds of problems and security breaches that can occur will help in determining whether a particular product is suitable, whether remote control access should be used as a remote LAN access method, and how to prevent problems from occurring.

Some remote control products provide minimal security support, while others provide varying degrees of support. Name-and-password matching and call-back modem support are two methods that have already been mentioned; they are supported by most products. Other security mechanisms include the ability to limit access to local drives and directories to limit the use of host hardware such as printer ports, and to control reboot options and file-transfer rights. Some of these features are similar to those provided by the LAN's network operating system, but they are applied to the host workstation, which a network operating system does not normally protect. Network resources are normally protected by the network operating system's security, which is usually implemented independent of the remote control program.

The ability to limit an application's access to the host's drives and directories is normally implemented in a fashion similar to that of a network operating system. A user, based on the user name in the address book, is given access to local drives and directories by the host workstation's manager. One user may have access to some directories but not others; directories that contain the remote control program's support files are normally off-limits. Unfortunately, the mechanism that prevents a remote user from accessing the protected files and directories is not as airtight as a network file server, because the remote control program providing the security is running on the host workstation, not a file server. It is possible to bypass this security, but it requires a technically sophisticated user and program to do so. Preventing access to debugger programs and preventing the ability to download programs from the client will make this type of security breach much more difficult to achieve. Limiting user access to host hardware is also important.

Third-party security programs do exist that can provide more controlled access to local files and directories. These programs actually store the files and directories in an encrypted (encoded) form. Users must supply a name and password to allow the files to be decrypted (decoded) only when accessed by an application. Bypassing the security software will not give you access to other data, because you do not have the necessary name and password.

Reboot options are available with many remote control programs. The remote control program can be set up to reboot when a user terminates a connection or if the connection is lost by accident. The options are normally set by the host's manager, but often a user will have the capability of changing the options remotely and temporarily. Reboot support is one way of preventing the use of Trojan Horse programs.

A Trojan Horse program (see Figure 4.8) is one that fools you into thinking another program is running. Often the Trojan Horse program runs at the same time as an application. It captures keyboard and mouse input, records it, and then sends it on to the application so you think you are interacting only with that application. Trojan Horse programs are typically used to record user names and passwords which are saved in hidden files until the owner of the Trojan Horse program picks them up. Trojan Horse programs are a particular problem with remote control host systems, because the typical user is used to calling into a host workstation that is already running; unfortunately he or she cannot tell *what* programs are already running or who may have replaced existing programs. Preventing the download of application programs can help prevent the latter; rebooting the machine after each connection prevents the former. Trojan Horse programs can be hard to detect if users have the ability to run programs from the client's disk drives. In this case the user could run the program Trojan Horse and then break the connection. The next user to call in would use the host while the Trojan Horse program was running.

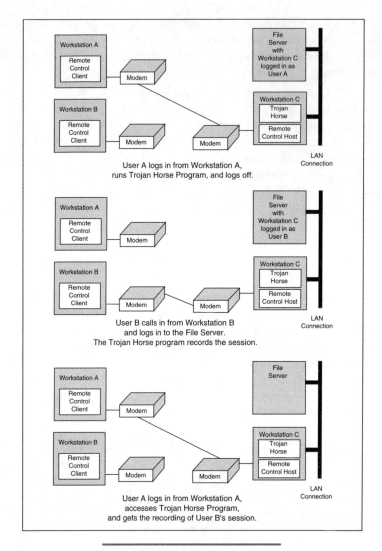

FIGURE 4.8 TROJAN HORSE DIAGRAM

As you might have guessed, controlling file-transfer rights is one way to prevent Trojan Horse programs from being introduced. Preventing the ability to run programs from the client's drives is another way. Preventing the copying or movement of files from the client's drives to specific directories on the host or LAN is another. *Selective copying* lets programs and files be copied to directories where the files can be verified by other parties before they are made available for general use.

Remote control programs can be hard to manage simply because they are so easy to install. Almost any user can set up a LAN workstation as a remote control host. Unfortunately, most users do not consider the security and management implications that are often paramount to network managers. Having a company policy that prevents unauthorized installation of software on LAN workstations will help. Automatic workstation software auditing will also help.

If you plan on supporting a large number of remote control hosts, then specialized hardware can prove economical and more secure than putting a dozen full-blown PCs in a room. The alternative is to use a PC on an adapter board. This type of board typically plugs into an IBM PC-compatible workstation. Multiple boards can be plugged into one workstation. The workstation's peripheral bus, such as the ISA, RISA or PCI bus, is used as an internal local area network. The workstation has its own network interface card (NIC), and the PC boards can work with the workstation to use this NIC to access the LAN. Each PC card contains most of the circuitry found in a typical workstation, including a processor, memory, and a video adapter, but it does not have the typical peripherals such as a monitor and keyboard. Often the main workstation's peripherals can be logically connected to a particular PC board for debugging or status purposes. The PC cards often have a serial port, which can use a modem for a connection with a remote client.

Remote control workstation support is often the only suitable choice for some remote users. Many applications use significant amounts of LAN-based data to operate. Remote workstations, discussed in chapter 3, do not work well in this instance, and other remote LAN access methods do not provide the proper access to the necessary data or services. Unfortunately, remote control host workstations are difficult to manage and are potential security risks, more so than most other remote LAN access methods. Remote control programs are usually more suitable for use by those company employees who have a strong reason to maintain security. Regardless of the remote user population, it is important to use security measures available through the remote control program or external means. Rebooting when a connection is broken is preferable. You can use a remote power control device that monitors the phone line attached to a modem. The remote power control device can restart the PC after the connection has been broken.

If security is a major issue but you must support a wide variety of users with different security levels, then consider using different hosts for different users. The remote control hosts can be configured to provide access to only a small set of users. Other mechanisms can then be used to limit access to the LAN. For example, many NOSes can limit which workstations a user can log in from. Some can even limit the day and time. Low-security host workstations can be limited to matching users; high-security host workstations may have different reboot options enabled.

Careful installation and subsequent management of remote control hosts will make their use more secure. Thorough training of remote users is also important for both security and general operation.

What are Remote Control Programs and How do They Work?

The basic concept of remote LAN access using remote control programs was presented at the beginning of this chapter; in this section we look at the various ways remote control program support is actually implemented.

Remote control programs consist of two parts: one on the host workstation and one on the client workstation. Some remote control programs integrate these two parts into one program, while others allow both to run on one workstation at the same time so it can act as both a host and a client. The latter is useful if you want to control one host from another, as when a host on the LAN may have special characteristics, such as access to a mainframe, or when it may have a tape drive for performing network backups. A client workstation on the LAN can be used to control the workstation. For example you are using a remote client that can call into the LAN but not directly into this host, so the host you *do* call into acts as a host for your remote client and runs the client software as an application to control the other host.

Host remote control software can be implemented as a device driver (a resident program that supports a device like a serial port), a terminate-and-stay-resident program (TSR, a program that sits in memory ready to run; it is found in DOS environments), or as an application. The last is possible when the host environment is running a multitasking operating system, such as IBM's OS/2. In all cases, the host software runs in the background and is effectively hidden from the host's user. Special key combinations or running a support program will bring up the utility window that can be used to change the host's configuration. The host software sets up the modem to wait for an incoming call; when it comes in, the host software works with the client software to verify the name and password of the client's user. After a connection is terminated, the host software either resets the modem and waits for another call or resets the PC. The host software has intimate knowledge about the operating system and hardware that it is running on, so it can access the video signal and emulate keyboard and mouse operation when a connection is active.

The client remote control software is typically an application, although some products implement the DOS client as a TSR program. The client software needs to know what video, keyboard, and mouse are installed, but its integration with the client's operating system is as a typical application. Keyboard and mouse input is sent to the host, and the screen is updated based on the information sent from the host.

The client and host may also interact to support exchange of information related to other devices. For example, some products allow printer output from the host's application to be routed to a printer attached to the client. Some products also allow the client's files and directories to be available to the host's application. Most products also include other support programs for security and address-book manipulation, as well as host and client support. File-management programs are often provided as separate programs.

Remote control program support can be divided into three types, based on the display mode of the host: character mode, graphics mode, or graphical-environment mode. *Character mode* is a text screen typically used with DOS hosts. The screen size is typically 25 lines by 80 columns, although other configurations are possible and some remote control programs support these other possibilities. The text can have limited attributes including colors, highlighting, and blinking. *Graphics mode* allows direct screen manipulation by applications. Applications have unrestricted access to the video support, and the remote control program must monitor the screen and/or the hardware to sense when a particular area of the screen changes. *Graphical environment*, such as Microsoft Windows, force applications to use a specific application programming interface (API) to manipulate the screen. Applications are not allowed to access the screen directly as they can in graphics mode. Remote control programs take advantage of this API to track how applications manipulate the screen, instead of using the more basic graphics-mode support. For example, a graphical environment can typically load a bitmap or icon from a file and use it repeatedly; in graphics mode, a remote control program would see the change made by an application that drew the bitmap or icon in the display memory and then send this information to the client for subsequent updates on the client's screen. With graphical environment support the host sends the bitmap or icon to the client, which keeps it in a cache. The host then references that item when it sends screen-update information to the client. This results in significant bandwidth savings, because the reference is typically a smaller piece of information than the bitmap or icon. Similar savings can be gained when the application uses drawing functions in the API, such as moving portions of the screen or drawing stock objects such as lines and rectangles.

All three modes can operate synchronously or asynchronously. *Synchronous operation* causes the host to send all screen operations to the client. The client's screen gets updated in the same sequence, although the rate of update may differ due to the delay in sending the information from the host to the client. The processing speed of the host may be significantly different that of the client, which itself may cause a difference in the appearance of information on the client's screen. Synchronous operation may also slow down the host. Update information is normally queued on both the host and client sides; it is queued at the host until it can be sent to the client, and it is queued at the client to await processing. The host stops the application's update of the screen if host's queue is filled.

Asynchronous operation deals with the host queue in a different fashion. The host's remote control program does not queue all changes; instead, it sends the current update information and then looks to see which changes have occurred. It compares a snapshot of the state of the screen for the last update with the current state. It then sends the differences to the client, making the current state the new snapshot. Many changes may be made to the screen between snapshots, but the largest difference is a change of the entire screen. If this occurs more than once, the asynchronous operating mode sends only one new screen—while a synchronous operating mode would send each screen change. In theory, the worst-case asynchronous operating mode information matches the synchronous operating mode.

Asynchronous operation is not always desirable. Often what you *don't* see during asynchronous can be important. For example, if you are playing a game (hey, it happens) then a briefly flashing status word may not appear on the client's screen. Asynchronous operation is suitable for character mode and graphics mode, but *not* for a graphical-environment mode. The last must operate in a synchronous mode because only graphical API operations made by an application are sent. Asynchronous mode only works if snapshots can be taken. Some operations can be optimized with graphical environments.

The host and client operating systems and operating environments do not have to match; in fact, they often do not. Likewise, the processing power of the host and client can differ significantly. The only thing that needs to match is the communications protocol used over the client-to-host connection. The simplest case is matching character-mode environments. Matching modes, the same mode on both the host and remote workstations, for graphics and graphical environments is also typical. The other typical match is a graphical environment on the remote workstation and a graphical environment on the host such as Microsoft

Windows.. In this case, the client essentially emulates the graphical environment's video support.

Remote control software operation is logically simple: show the host's screen on the client's monitor and echo the client's keyboard and mouse input to the host screen. Sounds simple, but it is a technical challenge. Luckily remote control software vendors make it simple to do.

WHY USE REMOTE CONTROL PROGRAMS FOR REMOTE LAN ACCESS?

Remote control programs have a number of advantages and disadvantages when they are used for remote LAN access. The following list summarizes these.

Advantages

Applications have direct access to LAN resources

Access to LAN protocols

Simple user interface

Require no user interaction to access resources

Ability to continue with application if the connection accidentally is broken

Ability to run applications when deliberately disconnected by the user

Disadvantages

Telephone time not minimized

Manual connect/disconnect

Compatibility with applications

Difficult management

Possible security problems

On the plus side, remote control LAN access lets host applications directly access LAN resources at LAN speeds; applications can run as quickly as they do on any other LAN workstation. Other remote LAN access methods do not have this advantage, which is why the remote control method is popular. It also means that the applications do not have to be on the remote client. This speeds up loading of the application, and it keeps application management a LAN-based operation. A variety of products exist to manage LAN-based applications.

Host applications also have access to LAN protocols, since the host workstation is really no different from any other LAN workstation. Network management applications that directly use LAN protocols work equally well on a host workstation or on any other LAN workstation.

The remote control program's client interface is relatively easy to use. Making a connection is straightforward, and once connected the user works as if he or she were on a locally connected LAN workstation. No user interaction is required to access such LAN services and resources, since the host workstation already has such access. Of course, those services and resources a particular user can access will be based on that user's security clearances.

Remote control programs have the unique ability to let an application run on the host even if the client is not connected to it; the termination of the connection can be accidental or deliberate. In the case of accidental termination, this feature allows a remote user to continue where he or she left off—all the user has to do is log on again. In fact deliberate disconnection is often used to allow a long operation to proceed unattended. Unfortunately, allowing the host to continue operation while a connection does not exist is both an advantage and a disadvantage. The disadvantage is due to the possibility of a security breach, as discussed earlier in this chapter.

On the minus side, the remote control program LAN access method does not implicitly minimize telephone connect time, although it is possible to automate many operations using batch files or other programming mechanisms. Likewise, remote control programs often allow the remote user to start up an application and break the connection, while still allowing the application to operate; in this case, the method is actually more efficient with its telephone connect time than other methods.

Manual connect and disconnect operations are often augmented by timeout options not always found with other remote LAN access methods. The host or remote workstation can be programmed to break the connection after a specified amount of time occurs with no user input or screen updates. Manual connection operations can be tedious, and typically, remote users must also log onto the LAN after the client-and-host-workstation connection is made.

Compatibility between the remote control programs and host applications is not guaranteed; often compatibility must be determined by trial and error. Also, some client/host/application combinations may work, but changing one of the elements may cause a problem. A remote control product's compatibility with various combinations is always improving, but do *not* assume that all combinations will work just because the product is designed to work with your client and host's hardware and software.

Limited network management for most remote control programs is a definite minus for installations, requiring a large number of host workstations. Network management of remote control hosts is possible if the remote control programs include this support. Unfortunately, most do not include any of this support. Keeping all the workstations in a single room can make the job easier. Likewise, providing remote control program access through the LAN can make a LAN manager's job do-able from any workstation on the LAN, but it does not eliminate the need to manage each station individually.

If you liked all the advantages of remote control LAN access and have made it this far through all the disadvantages, then it is time to address the most critical disadvantage: possible security problems. It is possible to implement relatively secure remote control LAN access policies and procedures, but it must be done carefully and explicitly. Most default product installations will *not* provide the level of security most companies can afford to live with. Accidental and deliberate security breaches must be taken into account by the LAN managers who install, manage, and audit remote control hosts.

Remote control products provide a unique approach to remote LAN access; in many cases it is the only viable solution. Unfortunately, it is not always the most desirable choice. Determining whether remote control programs are appropriate for your LAN will depend on whether the advantages outweigh the disadvantages based on your company's needs.

REMOTE CONTROL PROGRAMS: CONSIDERATIONS FOR REMOTE LAN ACCESS

There are a number of basic considerations that need to be examined before a remote control programs should be implemented. These considerations can help determine if remote control programs are suitable, practical, and desirable. If your requirements differ from these considerations then other remote LAN access methods may be more suitable. The following is a list of considerations we will examine in more detail.

- ✧   Access to LAN users (yes)
- ✧   Access to LAN services (yes)
- ✧   Ease of use by remote users (good)
- ✧   Network operating system (not important)

✧ Network protocol (not important)

✧ Telephone time (high)

✧ Number of simultaneous active lines (high)

✧ Performance (good)

✧ Scalability (good)

✧ Hardware requirements (variable)

✧ Client licensing (variable)

✧ Cost (variable)

✧ Adding users (manual)

✧ General maintenance (minimal)

✧ Security (LAN security and host security)

✧ Auditing (varies)

✧ Automation (possible)

Remote control programs provide access to LAN applications and services in the same fashion as a LAN workstation, because a remote control host on the LAN *is* a LAN workstation. More importantly, remote control hosts have access to LAN services at local LAN access speeds. The client-to-host connection speed is not a direct limitation.

General operation by the remote user is good, compared to other remote LAN access methods. LAN access is done using conventional network operating system support programs. The NOS and its supported network protocol are unimportant in the selection of the remote control program. Some remote control programs can use the LAN as the connection between host and client, in which case the network operating system and network protocol are important, but for our remote LAN access purposes it is not.

Telephone usage tends to be comparatively high for remote control programs, which is true for any remote LAN access method that has a user directly involved during the connection. Short connections are possible, especially if the user is adept at typing and at running applications on the host. Connections as short as a couple of minutes are possible. Connection time tends to be longer when users must perform interactive operations, such as typing a mail message.

The number of simultaneous active lines can be high, but there must be a matching number of workstations and modems. A large number of host workstations can make management difficult. There are two special cases that can reduce their number. The first uses a multitasking operating system like OS/2 or UNIX. Each incoming call is allocated a host task, which manages a virtual screen. The remote control host program then uses the virtual screen as if it were a normal workstation's screen. This approach has typically been applied to character-mode applications. The second case uses a single workstation with multiple PCs on a card. Each card is connected to an incoming telephone line. The remote control host software runs on each card. There is no difference in the software running on each card, other than the network device driver and possibly the hard disk driver. The difference between these drivers and those on a workstation is that he card drivers forward operations to the master workstation, while the standard drivers manage the hardware directly.

Application and screen performance with remote control software is good, which is the primary reason for choosing it as a remote LAN access method. Applications run at their normal speed. Access to LAN services is the same as from any other workstation on the LAN. Screen updates on the client are delayed and may be slower than on the host alone. In general, though, screen updates are adequate for most users.

Remote control systems scale well, or at least linearly, in terms of hardware and software requirements; add a new host workstation to support a new incoming line. Unfortunately, their management does not scale as well—most remote control programs are designed for a single host, and so are the management tools.

Hardware requirements vary, depending on the implementation used and the computing power required by the host. The standard implementation consists of a workstation with a modem plus a telephone line. One alternative is to use a modem in a modem pool.

Client and host licensing varies from product to product and vendor to vendor. The least-expensive alternative is based on a single host with unlimited usage for the client software. A more expensive alternative has a license for each host and each client. A single host-and-client pair typically cost the same regardless of the licensing approach, but large installations with many remote users will have varying costs depending on the product chosen.

Overall costs vary depending on the hardware and software costs, which also vary. A single installation can be relatively inexpensive if the hardware is already available. Often an un- or underused PC will suffice as a host.

Adding new users is a manual task for most remote control products. Unfortunately, it is often difficult to add a new user when there are multiple hosts.

In this case, the modems are often connected to a single phone number that automatically switches to an unused modem. This configuration means that a remote user's client may wind up connected to a different host workstation each time. To allow this to happen, each host must be set up to accept a call from any user, so the address book on each host must match.

General maintenance is minimal once the hardware and software are set up. Typical support entails resetting a host when it locks up. Remote power-management hardware can make this job easier if you have multiple hosts.

Remote control program security is a mix of host and LAN security. Typically the two are independent—LAN security controls LAN services, while host security controls access to the host workstation. Remote control programs provide most of the security features found in other remote LAN access methods, including required name and password for initial access, limitations on operations, and access to services on both the host and the LAN based on this information. There are two aspects of security that will have a major impact on whether remote control programs are a suitable choice for remote LAN access. The first is that the host workstation has essentially complete access to the LAN. LAN access is controlled by the network operating system, and it is secure if the security cannot be bypassed. This brings up the second aspect of remote control program security: host operation when a connection is not active. This is actually a feature that allows users to start an application, break the connection, allow the application to run, and reconnect later to see how the application has performed. A variety of tasks can be performed in this unattended fashion. Unfortunately, another user can make a connection after a deliberate or accidental disconnect. Some products allow the host to be automatically reset when this occurs, while others prevent a new user from accessing the host while the initial user has *control* of the host. In any case, a breach of security occurs if a second user gains control of the host while the initial user's security clearance is in effect. For example, the initial user calls into the host, makes a connection, and then logs into the LAN. The connection is broken and the second user calls in and makes a connection. The second user now has access to the LAN as if he or she were the first user. Passwords can be changed and files manipulated without the knowledge of the initial user.

Other security bypass mechanisms can be used by users intent on mischief or sabotage. Trojan Horse programs can be left running on the host to copy a subsequent user's LAN name and password or other valuable information. Trojan Horse programs are a kind of mix between a computer virus program and the remote control program, because they operate in the background, hidden from detection by the remote user, and they monitor the screen, mouse, and keyboard. Often they simply store this information in a hidden file, which can be picked up at a later time.

Many of these possible security problems can be eliminated by proper configuration, the education of remote users, and regular auditing of the host's operation, but these issues must be addressed when looking at a particular remote control product. Host security is important because of the power of the host computer and the access it has to the LAN.

Audit support varies from product to product. Many products provide none while others go to the other extreme. In the latter case, user login time is allocated to application usage, file transfers, and almost any other detail you can think of. Unfortunately, audit support is often designed for a single installation; each host will have its own audit trail. Merging audit files from multiple hosts may not be possible.

Remote control programs support automation through applications that run on the host or through custom scripts that run on the client. The latter ability is available with some remote control products, but not all; some provide this feature as a separate product. Using automation on the host provides one of the most flexible solutions of all remote LAN access methods, because the number of tools is so large. Programming languages, batch files, and application macros are all suitable tools for automating all sorts of tasks.

There is a lot to consider when looking at remote control programs for remote LAN access. They provide a high level of access to both the host and the LAN, but you must take a look at the security issues. Security may be the most important reason you must consider before using remote control programs for remote LAN access.

SOME EXAMPLES OF REMOTE CONTROL PROGRAMS

Remote control programs come in a variety of implementations, most use the same technology but some have unique features, such as the ability to use communications servers as gateways to host workstations on the LAN. Others allow different host and client operating systems and environments.

The products we examine will include Ocean Isle's Reachout and Triton System's CO/Session. Triton also sells an add-on product to CO/Session called Session/XL. Session/XL is a scripting language that operates at the client end and is specifically for automating data transfers between systems. These products are designed to run on DOS and Windows client and host workstations. They should work with just about any network operating system.

There are dozens of remote control programs available from different vendors. Most are designed to work with DOS and Windows client and host workstations, but there are also many good products designed for Microsoft's Windows NT, IBM's OS/2, and Apple's Macintosh, as well as UNIX systems. The choices are fewer, but the quality and performance are often as good—and occasionally better.

Luckily, trying out a remote control program is a relatively inexpensive proposition, at least for a single pair of workstations. The workstations and modems are usually already installed, so all that is required is the remote control software.

Ocean Isle's Reachout

Ocean Isle's Reachout is your typical remote control program. It is licensed on a per-user basics but the package includes both the host and client software. A single host workstation can support multiple clients, but each client must be licensed individually. DOS and Windows are supported at both the client and host ends.

Figure 4.9 shows Reachout's architecture. Reachout supports modem as well as LAN connections. It allows a host to act as a LAN client. Modems in a LAN-based modem pool can be used by either the client or the host. Reachout also supports remote access of the client's drives by the host and the host's drives by the client. The latter makes sense only when running Windows, because an application cannot be running while the DOS version of the client is running. A DOS client can be used to control the host in DOS or Windows, and you can readily switch between the two during a single session.

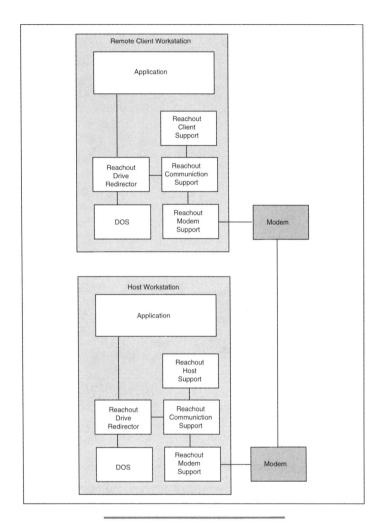

FIGURE 4.9 REACHOUT ARCHITECTURE.

Reachout's documentation is very good. It even includes tips such as making the client and hosts background color different when running under Windows; this allows you to see the difference and know whether you are viewing the client screen or the host screen. Switching between the two is done by clicking on the appropriate button or using a hot-key sequence, so the switch can occur very rapidly. Operating the client and host at difference resolutions also helps, because then the client screen shows the host screen within a window. For example, the host can operate with a screen resolution of 640 by 480, while the client operates at 1024 by 768 or 800 by 600.

Figure 4.10 shows the DOS and Windows utility screen that is initially presented. General maintenance and connection initiation can be performed from this screen. The DOS version can be accessed using a hot-key combination at the client after a connection is made. The Windows version remains as a running application, which can be selected like any other Windows application. Reachout calls its client the *Viewer*. Under Windows, a client controlling a DOS host can show the host's screen in a window so it looks almost like another application (see Figure 4.11.)

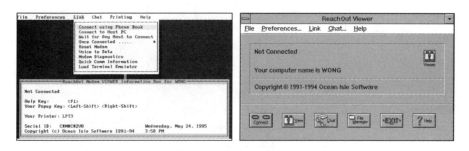

Figure 4.10A+B Reachout DOS and Windows utility screen.

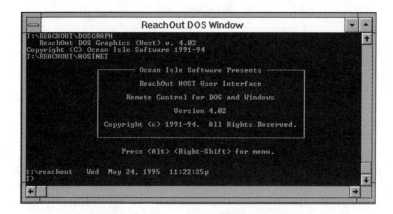

Figure 4.11 Reachout DOS host screen under Windows.

Reachout's Windows File Manager, shown in Figure 4.12, is available from the utility screen. It is similar in design and operation to the Windows File Manager application, but Reachout's version knows about the host's drives. Any Windows manager application, such as the Windows File Manager or Symantec's Norton Utilities for Windows, can be used on either the client or host to copy and move files if Reachout's remote access (RA) feature is enabled. RA lets the host see the client's drives and the client see the host's drives, or either direction can be enabled individually. The advantage of using the Reachout File Manager is that it will make a time estimate for files to be transferred between systems, which can be handy if you want to abort a large transfer once you see how long it might take.

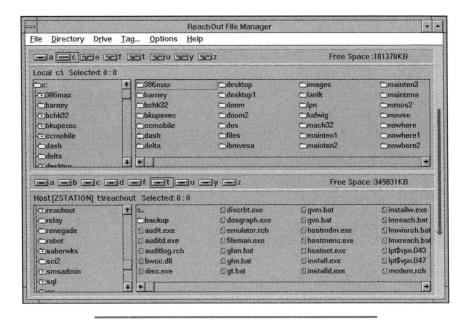

FIGURE 4.12 REACHOUT WINDOWS FILE MANAGER SCREEN.

Reachout supports a chat window, which is shown in Figure 4.13. The top pane shows what the host user types, while the bottom pane shows what you type. Characters are echoed at either end as they are typed. There will be no conflict between users since each has his or her own typing area. Chat mode can be invoked at either end at any time during a connection, and the menu (not shown) has an option for an audible alert at the other end. Reachout does not record the chat session, although some remote control products do. Chat mode is useful when you are trying to find things on the host workstation or if you need to ask the user at the host to perform some function that the remote user would otherwise do his- or herself such as putting a tape into the tape drive.

FIGURE 4.13 Reachout Windows chat screen.

Reachout's security is extensive, although not exhaustive. Figure 4.14 shows the supervisor's security screen. Reachout has supervisor and user security levels. A user on a client workstation has security access based on his or her individual security settings in the host's address book and the supervisor settings. The supervisor settings override the individual settings.

Reachout includes a number of security features. The password file is encrypted and kept off-limits from the client's user and host applications. User-specified files and directories can also be hidden. For example, protecting **AUTOEXEC.BAT** and **CONFIG.SYS** can prevent accidental changes that might prevent the host from rebooting properly. Client file access can also be restricted to the Reachout File Manager. This essentially turns off RA support. In fact, this support can be disabled for either direction individually.

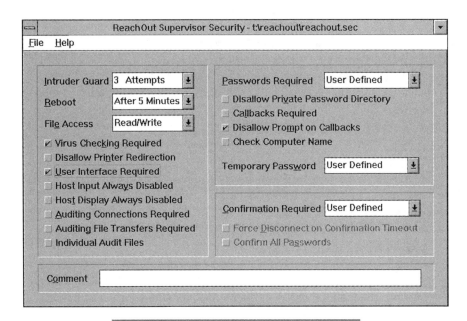

FIGURE 4.14 REACHOUT WINDOWS SECURITY SCREEN.

Reachout's *intruder guard* option is actually an invalid-connection-attempt counter. When it is enabled, Reachout will lock out all access if too many attempts are made to connect without a valid connection. It can only be reset at the host. The intruder guard is useful in preventing people from trying to guess passwords. It can also be an annoying feature, if its count is set too low, when someone forgets his or her password. Unfortunately, the feature locks out *all* other users if too many invalid attempts are made.

Reachout can be set to reboot whenever a connection is broken. A client user can also request a reboot when a connection is terminated. The host display, keyboard, and mouse can be individually disabled. Disabling the display prevents someone from watching you type a confidential memo or examining the payroll spreadsheet. Preventing input from the host prevents accidental interruption of input by the client. It is difficult to type when two people are controlling the keyboard. These options can also be enabled and disabled while a connection is in progress.

Reachout supports *modem callback*. A supervisor can also require callbacks or use them selectively. Callback mode can request a callback phone number, or it can be restricted to one in the address book. Password confirmation can be required, which means the client's user must actually type in the password before a connection is started. A temporary password can also be set up so a manager can let a user call in without permanently adding his or her name to the address book. A temporary connection is handy, where the manager watches the host to visually approve the remote user's operations. Of course, the manager may also want to prevent host keyboard-and-mouse lockout and host screen blanking.

Reachout supports a wide variety of modems, and custom modem setups can be created. It includes modem diagnostic support, which is very useful for troubleshooting a new modem or when problems are encountered with an existing modem. The diagnostics can be used at both the client and the host.

Reachout includes a terminal-emulation mode, which can be used with bulletin board systems and commercial services. It is not designed for use with the Reachout host, and you cannot call into a Reachout host using a terminal-emulation program. The feature is simply easy to include, and it is handy to have a single communications program. You will find this feature in many remote control products, but it often goes unused because users are only interested in the remote connection support.

Reachout represents the typical remote control product. It is ideal for remote LAN access. Ocean Isle sells a version of Reachout that works on a LAN as well; in this case the client and host are both on the LAN, which is used for the connection. The interface for both versions is identical.

Triton System's CO/Session

Triton Technologies sells a number of software communications products, including CO/Session and Session/XL. CO/Session is the remote control program. DOS and Windows versions are available. Modem and LAN communication products are available. Session/XL is a client-based scripting language that works with CO/Session hosts. CO/Session ACS is another product sold by Triton Technologies. CO/Session ACS is a modem-pool program that is compatible with CO/Session and Session/XL.

CO/Session's remote control architecture, shown in Figure 4.15, is similar to most remote control programs. CO/Session ACS can be used to provide modem support to CO/Session. ACS can also be used with many other modem-based remote control programs. The CO/Session host works with a CO/Session client or with Session/XL running on a client, but not both at the same time. The CO/Session DOS client differs from many other remote control programs because the CO/Session DOS client is a TSR program. The client software can stay in the background until it is needed. It is brought up using a hot-key combination. You can have an application running on the client and still make a connection with a host workstation.

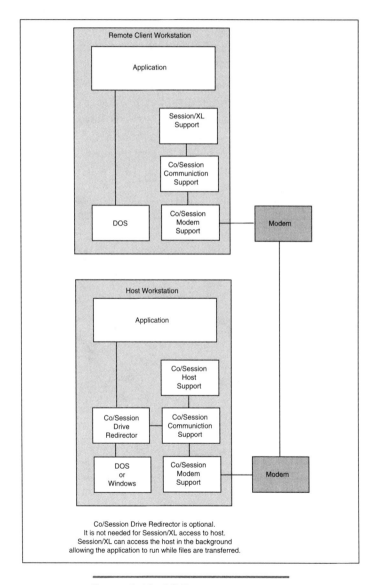

FIGURE 4.15 CO/SESSION ARCHITECTURE.

CO/Session's DOS host version can operate in a multitasking environment like DESQview or OS/2. Multiple sessions can be supported on a single machine, providing support for multiple hosts. CO/Session also supports voice-to-data and data-to-voice switching. This allows a single telephone line to be used for voice and data, but only one at a time. In a remote LAN access environment, this feature can be useful if a user at the host end needs to talk to the user at the client end. A set of screens walk both sides through the mode change, including telling them when to pick up the telephone.

CO/Session's DOS and Windows utility screens, shown in Figure 4.16, are similar to other remote control programs. They provide access to maintenance and connection options. CO/Session's setup screens have quite a number of options, which lets you customize CO/Session's connected operation. CO/Session supports synchronous and asynchronous screen updates. CO/Session connections can be initiated from either the host or the client workstation.

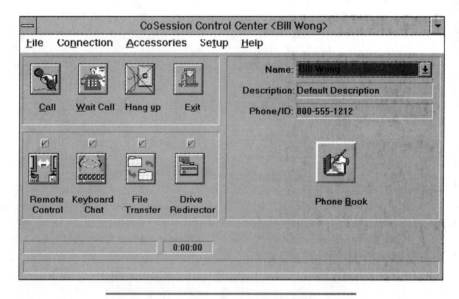

FIGURE 4.16 CO/SESSION WINDOWS UTILITY SCREEN.

CO/Session's file manager works like most other remote control program's file managers but CO/Session's file transfers can operate in the background at the host end (see Figure 4.17). This means the host application can continue operating while the file transfer occurs. Background transfers are handy if someone else is using the host workstation. This feature is actually even more useful with Session/XL, because the CO/Session client must wait until the transfer is completed before it can be used to control the host, but Session/XL's background host operation lets a client-based script make a file transfer transfer files through a host workstation without interrupting operations on the host. CO/Session also supports a DOS program on the host, which can copy files between the host and client.

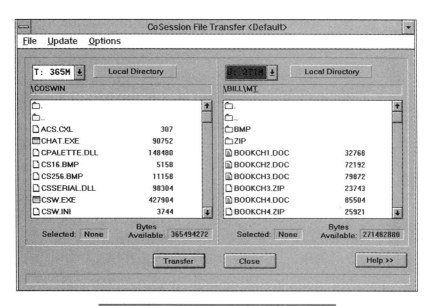

FIGURE 4.17 CO/SESSION FILE-TRANSFER SCREEN.

CO/Session has a typical chat mode. The chat screen, shown in Figure 4.18, has a local pane (top) and a remote pane (bottom). Like most remote control programs, the chat mode is limited. There is no recording capability and once text scrolls off the top of the pane it is lost, so don't type too fast.

FIGURE 4.18 CO/SESSION CHAT SCREEN.

CO/Session's security screen, shown in Figure 4.19, lets you disable password protection (not a great idea for remote LAN access), control reboot options, restrict access to directories, and enable unattended access. CO/Session's reboot options are rather flexible. The host can reboot itself: every time a connection is terminated; only when the session is terminated abnormally; only when it is terminated normally, or the host never automatically reboots. Automatically rebooting after an abnormal termination is one way to prevent someone else from calling in after you are finished using the host and gaining access to the LAN using your network account. Rebooting after normal termination lets you call back after an abnormal termination to continue with your session. Unfortunately, CO/Session will also let in any valid user, which may not be desirable. Rebooting after every connection is terminated is the safest way to operate.

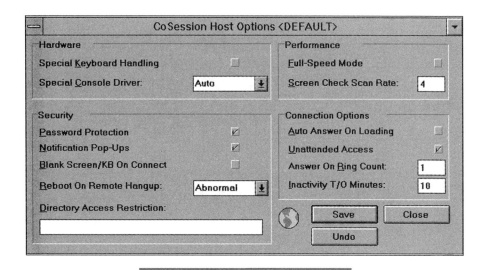

FIGURE 4.19 CO/SESSION SECURITY SCREEN.

Although the CO/Session program is similar to other remote control programs, Session/XL may swing the choice of remote control programs toward Triton's products. Figure 4.20 shows Session/XL's architecture. It operates with a CO/Session host. No special configuration is required at the host end. A CO/Session host can accept calls from both CO/Session clients and Session/XL clients.

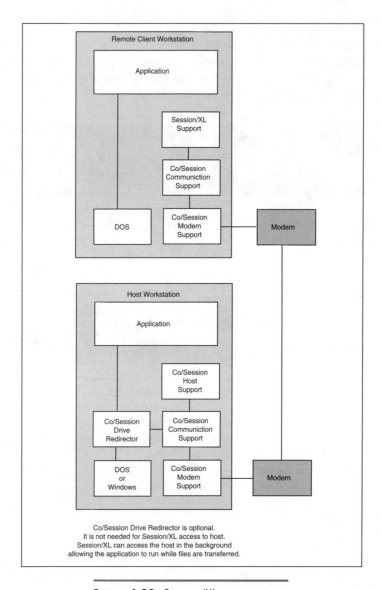

Figure 4.20 Session/XL architecture.

Session/XL clients are driven by a Session/XL script. The script language is similar to the DOS batch language and is capable of calling multiple hosts sequentially. It can copy, move and delete files. It can even manipulate address books.

Session/XL scripts can distribute files, pick up files, and keep files in sync. The scripts are even capable of displaying menus and dialog boxes, so a user at the client end can interact with the scripts. A user at the client workstation could start up a Session/XL script and wait for it to call and check out the host; the script could then present the status of the host files and let the user choose from a set of options. The script could then continue on its merry way unattended. Figure 4.21 shows a sample script, including comments.

```
Sample Session/XL Script

; Comments can be used liberally
;
; A INPUT.DATA contains a list of location and file
; name pairs. The script calls each location and
; copies the specified file to the location's disk (R!).
; Status is reported in OUTPUT.DAT.

          OPEN input.dat R %rfh1
          IF ERROR : GOTO _err
          OPEN output.dat W %wfh1
          IF ERROR : GOTO _err
_loop:
          READ %rfh1 %location
          IF NOT %location : GOTO _end
          READ %rfh1 %file
          IF NOT %file : GOTO _end
          CALL %location
          IF ERROR : GOTO _err
          COPY %file R!%file
          WRITE %wfh1 "%file copied to %location"
          DISCONNECT
          GOTO _loop

_end:
          WRITE %wfh1 "All locations called"
          CLOSE %rfh1
          CLOSE %wfh1
          EXIT

_err:
          PRINT "Fatal Error %ERROR"
          EXIT
```

FIGURE 4.21 SESSION/XL SCRIPT.

Batch files on the host can often perform many of the operations that Session/XL, can but the former must be initiated by the user on the client system. Session/XL scripts can also run applications and batch files on the host, and Session/XL scripts can themselves initiate operations once the script is started. Session/XL scripts are just as useful for polling standalone workstations and workstations attached to a LAN. In fact, polling branch office LANs is an excellent application for Session/XL.

Triton's products provide a number of useful features, some of which are not found in comparable products. Session/XL's features may be just what you need in your automation toolkit. If you don't need this kind of toolkit, then features in other remote control products may make them more desirable.

CHAPTER 5

NETWORK-BASED BULLETIN BOARD SYSTEMS

If you have not heard about bulletin board systems (BBSes) then you have probably been completely distracted by the Internet. Where the Internet spans the world, a BBS typically runs on a single workstation. This is not to say that a BBS cannot be well-connected; put a BBS on a LAN workstation, and it can connect LAN users with the outside world. Some BBS programs can also connect with other BBS systems and even the Internet.

BULLETIN BOARD SYSTEMS (BBSES)

Remote users connect to a BBS using a modem and a terminal-emulation program. Some BBS products support or require a custom communications application on the remote workstation. A BBS can provide a variety of services. A basic BBS typically provides basic mail support along with a file repository service where files can be uploaded and downloaded, while a more advanced BBS may provide database services. Some BBS products that run on LANs provide access from LAN workstations, but it is possible to make effective use of a BBS on a LAN even without this support. File storage can be done on a LAN file server.

A BBS has a number of features that other remote LAN access methods do not. For me, a BBS is more open to accepting new users. Many let new users call in without prior approval and allow them to select their own user name and password. The ability of most BBS products to be accessed using any terminal-emulation program means a remote user does not have to be given any special software prior to accessing the BBS. Terminal-emulation programs run on almost any workstation, from an Apple Macintosh to a UNIX workstation. Many operating systems or environments, such as Microsoft Windows and IBM's OS/2 Warp, are bundled with basic terminal-emulation programs. This variety of clients make a BBS a universal host.

A typical remote-access session goes as follows. The remote user starts up the terminal emulation program. Most programs have a limited address book or allow a phone number to be entered to place a call. The terminal-emulation program calls the BBS. The BBS modem answers and the BBS sends back a text prompt. The prompt normally includes the name of the BBS and other introductory text followed by a request for the user's name. The remote user types his or her name. The BBS then requests a password (if passwords are required). The user enters the password and the BBS verifies the user's name and password. An error response is given if the name and password are not in the BBS's user database; otherwise, the user is greeted with additional introductory text followed by a menu of options. The BBS then waits for the user to enter a menu selection. Every BBS is different. The menu items and the menu structure can be customized on most BBS products, and most BBS system operators, or *sysops*, do just that. One option found on all BBS systems is to log off. At this point the remote user will get a message of some sort from the terminal-emulation program that indicates *carrier was lost*. Loss of carrier indicates that a connection was terminated and the modem has essentially hung up the phone. Figure 5.1 shows an abbreviated connection with a BBS. I used my own BBS so the introductory text was kept as short as possible. Note that the password is not echoed (printed) on the screen.

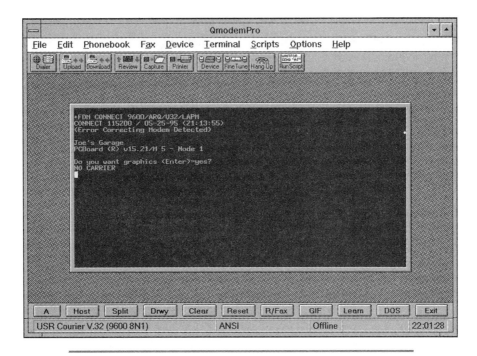

FIGURE 5.1 ABBREVIATED BBS CONNECTION USING A TERMINAL EMULATOR.

Some BBS systems can use terminal emulator programs that support special display features, such as color, fonts, and cursor positioning. The latter allows the BBS to present a screen-oriented editor for creating mail messages. Terminal emulators that do not support cursor positioning may scroll text off the screen only by adding more at the bottom, where all new text is displayed. It is crude but it works.

More sophisticated BBS systems support the Remote Imaging Protocol (RIP), a graphical communications protocol that lets the BBS present information using lines, bitmaps and color. RIP also allows input via a mouse if the terminal-emulation program supports it, and if a mouse is installed on the remote workstation. Menu selections can be made using the mouse or the keyboard. The additional overhead of sending graphic information is typically minor compared to a text-only BBS, and the results often match a resident GUI application in form and function.

Some BBS products support direct LAN access when the BBS runs on a workstation attached to a LAN. Other LAN workstations access the BBS using terminal-emulation programs that use a LAN connection instead of a modem connection. The BBS with LAN support waits for LAN workstation connections in the same fashion as for modem connections. User interaction is identical for modem and LAN connections; only the speed is different.

The same BBS features are typically available regardless of which type of terminal emulation is used. In fact, how the features operate is essentially the same; only the presentation is different. BBS features are accessed through menu selections or commands typed in by the remote user. BBS products have their own security features that can limit users access to features and data provided through the BBS. My initial discussion of BBS features is somewhat general so that the comments may be applicable to most BBS products. The actual implementation and presentation details can differ from product to product and not a BBS products implement all features discussed, but if you are trying to get a general feel for BBS features, then the discussion should be what you need. The end of the chapter addresses particular products, including more detailed discussions of their features.

A remote user can share files with LAN users and access files on the LAN through the BBS. A BBS typically has *file areas*. A file area typically is located in a directory on a hard disk accessible to the BBS. It can be a local disk or it can be a LAN file server. The local disk cannot be accessed directly by LAN workstations unless the BBS is running on a workstation that is a server in a peer-to-peer network or on a workstation running a multitasking network operating system (like IBM's LAN Server) that is also capable of running a BBS program. In this case the LAN workstations can access the local drive, if the network operating system provides access to it as a network service. A remote user can *upload* a file (send it to the BBS file area) or *download* a file (send it from the BBS file area to the remote workstation) using a file-transfer protocol such as Xmodem. LAN users can leave files for downloading by copying the files to the matching directory and can pick up files that were uploaded by copying from the matching directory. Unfortunately, there is no automatic notification to either remote users or LAN users when a file has been uploaded or downloaded. Typically an additional mail message is sent by the person performing the file transfer to the sysop for notification purposes or a perhaps a verbal telephone call is made for the same purpose.

Remote users can also leave mail messages on a BBS. The BBS typically maintains its own mail database. Some BBS products have mail gateway support as well. In this latter case, messages can be sent to LAN users through the gateway and responses can be sent back. Remote and LAN users are typically unconcerned about where a recipient picks up his or her mail because the gateway is transparent. LAN users who have access via a LAN-based terminal emulator can access the BBS mail directly. LAN users on a LAN-based BBS product without mail gateway or LAN-based terminal-emulation access will be unable to access BBS mail without calling in via a modem connection.

Remote LAN access via a BBS is typically more limited that other remote LAN access methods, but it is ideal for providing limited LAN access to users who should not have broader LAN access. Customers and clients often fit into this category.

A BBS can be used to provide support, sales, and software and data distribution. Often, remote users may not know that the BBS is actually on a LAN. Technical support or sales support staff on the LAN can interact directly and quickly with remote users. File areas can be set up to distribute support and sales literature, and tech support can even keep the latest set of device drivers there (*device drivers* are programs to run specific video cards, printers, etc.).

BBS systems are one of the few remote LAN access methods that have effective and automated new-user registration. Most other remote LAN access methods either avoid remote security options completely, or disallow access except by preregistered users. Most BBS products support a variety of automatic registration features. Minimally, new users are allowed to register the first time they call in. A BBS mail message is typically sent to the sysop, notifying the sysop of the new user. At that point the new user may be forced to log off, or he/she may be given limited access to mail and file areas. Some BBS products can even accept and verify credit-card numbers, which are then used to bill for the remote user's access time and operations performed.

Consider a network-based BBS for remote LAN access if there is a need for separately-managed security, a wide variety of remote users, or special BBS add-ons. For the latter, many BBS vendors have their own or third-party add-on products, such as credit card verification, order entry, database support and even multiplayer interactive games.

A User's View of BBSes

A user works with a BBS through a terminal-emulation program or a custom BBS-access program. Customized programs may make connections more automatic or provide transparent access to a BBS database but they accesses the BBS in a similar fashion to the plain old terminal-emulation program. We will take a look at a basic terminal-emulation program for our examples. Figure 5.2 shows the initial screen for the Microsoft Windows Terminal program. It provides all the necessary functionality to access the typical BBS.

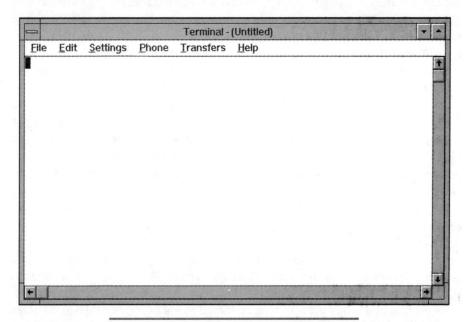

Figure 5.2 Initial MS Windows Terminal screen.

The first thing a user needs to do is set up the terminal program to call the BBS. There are two pieces of information that need to be entered. The first is the low-level communications settings. The second is the telephone number. The low-level settings are often noted as sequences like "8, 1, None." Sounds like Greek? It's actually not that bad, and once you know what the options mean and where to set them, it will be easy to set up the terminal program accordingly. The three items specify the number of data bits, the number of stop bits and the parity mode used by the serial hardware. Other remote LAN access methods use these settings, but thankfully hide them from a user. Terminal-emulation programs use these settings so the user must adjust them accordingly. The number of data bits is 7 or 8. The number of stop bits is 1, 1.5 or 2, and the parity setting can be None (no parity), Odd, or Even. You will often see settings listed as 8, 1, N or 8, N, 1 for 8 data bits, 1 stop bit and No parity.

Figure 5.3 shows what serial data looks like if you could watch the electrical signals. It is interesting to know what is going on but it is only necessary to have the matching settings for the terminal program to work with a BBS. A BBS is set up in the same fashion. A mismatch results in odd characters being received and sent, and the terminal-emulation screen will look like a bunch of junk.

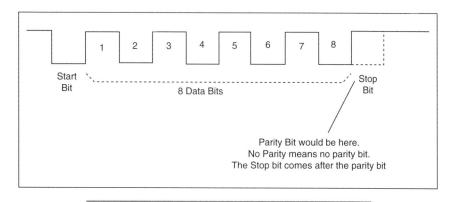

FIGURE 5.3 SERIAL PROTOCOL DRAWING SHOWING 8, 1, N.

Figure 5.4 shows the *Communications* dialog box for the Windows Terminal program. The numbers for data bits, stop bits and parity are set from this dialog box. The baud rate is also set here. The *baud rate* or data speed is another setting which is usually associated with serial communications, but most modems and terminal-emulation programs perform automatic baud-rate detection. If you set the baud rate too high, the terminal program will adjust the actual baud rate when the connection is initially made. If the BBS specifies a baud rate, then choose the that baud rate in the *Communications* dialog box. If your modem has *lower upper baud rate* then you must use the lower baud rate. For example, say a BBS has a new V.34 modem that runs at 28,800; you have a V.32 modem that has an upper limit of 9,600. The setting in the dialog box should be 9,600.

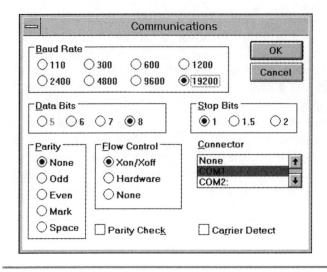

FIGURE **5.4** MS W**INDOWS** T**ERMINAL** C**OMMUNICATIONS** **DIALOG BOX.**

Now that we have these details out of the way we can try calling the BBS. Selecting the appropriate menu item initiates the call. Figure 5.5 shows a sample dialog box that indicates the program is making a call. In the terminal-emulator screen you may also see the commands sent to the modem. The **ATDT** is the part of the Hayes-compatible command set which tells the modem to dial a phone number and make a connection with the modem at the other end (Hayes is a modem company which originated the use of the AT command set used by almost every modem available today).

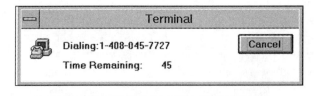

FIGURE **5.5** MS W**INDOWS** T**ERMINAL** **DIALING.**

Assuming all goes well, the BBS modem and the remote modem will literally sing their song to each other and agree on data rate and other little details, such as whether data compression is used. The modems then tell their respective workstations the agreed-upon data rate and then are ready to send data between the workstations.

The BBS normally starts sending data. If nothing happens, then try pressing the **Enter** key twice (some BBS systems wait for the user to type some characters before sending the initial prompt). Figure 5.6 shows a typical BBS prompt. It tells the name of the BBS and asks the user for his user name. It also indicates how a new user can start the automatic registration procedure. At this point you type in your user name.

FIGURE 5.6 INITIAL BBS PROMPT

New-user registration typically consists of a series of questions including your real name, address, and telephone number. You usually get to select a short user name, which could be your last name, and a password. Depending upon the BBS, you may receive full access to the all BBS features immediately, or you may have a restricted set until your identity has been verified by other means, typically a telephone call. The most restrictive case is no access at all. In this case, you have your user name and password and the sysop has been notified by BBS mail.

After the BBS verifies your user name and password, it will normally present you with any new notices that have been posted by the sysop. A typical notice includes the availability of new files, or the addition of new features. The notices are typically followed by the main menu. You may have noticed the use of the word *typically* often in this discussion so far, almost all BBS products can be customized to the point that two installations of the same product will appear completely different to a user. Our example represents what most BBS installations look like.

A Main menu, like the one shown in figure 5.7, lets you move to different menus or log off. Menu selections are often made via a single keystroke or pressing a key followed by the **Enter** key. The three menu items we are going to address are Mail, File, and Forums. All three call up additional menus for the respective operations. The Mail menu lets you read, create and send BBS mail. The File menu provides access to file areas for uploading and downloading files. The Forum menu provides access to message forums. Forums are like public mail. You can leave messages in a forum for others to read. You can respond to other messages in the forum. Users can follow related messages and add their own comments. Forums typically have a theme such as tech support, new products, or descriptions of files in a specific file area.

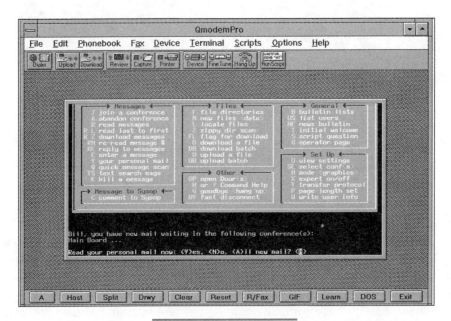

FIGURE 5.7 BBS MAIN MENU.

Now is a good time to address the two ways information is presented by a BBS. The first is line-oriented and the other is screen-oriented. *Line-oriented* text is displayed a line at a time. When the cursor is at the bottom of the page and a new line is displayed, the entire screen scrolls up and the top line is lost. Some terminal-emulation programs save lines that scroll off the top so you can view them later. *Screen-oriented* presentations are the preferred mode of operation, but they require a terminal-emulation mode capable of positioning the cursor anywhere on the screen. The trick to using a screen-oriented presentation is to set up and your terminal-emulation program to use the same terminal emulation as the BBS. Typical terminal emulations capable of supporting screen-oriented presentations include ANSI, VT-100, and VT-220. Use ANSI if the BBS and terminal-emulation program support it. Without my going into too much history or detail, just take it on faith that these screen-oriented protocols must match, just like the 8, 1, N for the communications protocol. A mismatch will result in text all over the screen. The desired terminal emulation used by the BBS is often set during a new-user registration sequence. If you use a BBS often, then checking out the terminal emulations it supports will be worth the research time.

Figure 5.8 shows a sample Mail menu. The Scan menu selection displays a list of mail which has been sent to you. List entries show just the message subject, the sender's name, and the date. This lets you quickly see what messages you may need to read right away and those which may be left till later. Mail can often be read and left in folders, which can be scanned later for reference purposes.

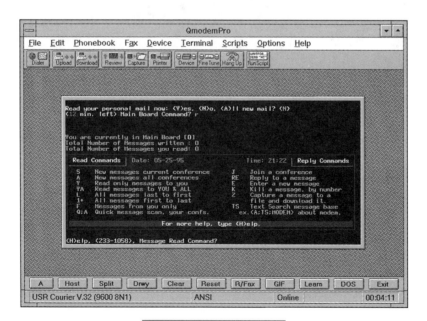

FIGURE 5.8 BBS MAIL MENU.

Figure 5.9 shows a message being created using a line oriented editor. Line-oriented editors were initially supported by BBS products, with screen-oriented editors now being the preferred type. Most users are now familiar with screen-oriented text editors but there was a time that everyone was stuck using the lowly line-oriented editor.

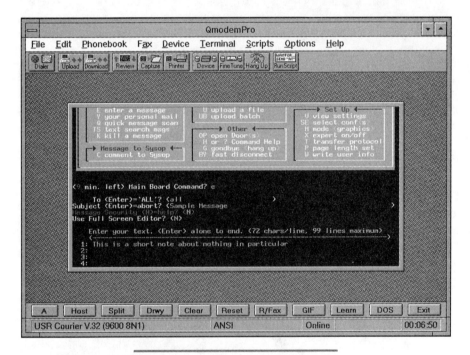

FIGURE 5.9 MAIL MESSAGE BEING CREATED.

The line-oriented editor is available with most BBS products. You can edit the text on the line you are entering but not the prior lines. Often you can only delete characters to the left of the cursor. The end of a message is often indicated by entering a blank line. Line-oriented editors are adequate, but not desirable, tools. Screen-oriented editors are not created equal. Some are as sophisticated as word processors; you can mark blocks to be deleted or copied. Others are more restrictive. These simply let you move the cursor using arrow keys, and type over text. In either case, the end result is a text message which can be read by the recipient. Once a message is completed it can be sent. Often a single file can be optionally attached to a message; this is often a good way to give a file to another user without having to upload the file into a file area. BBS mail functionality varies from product to product. Some support mailing lists, message folders and features found on dedicated mail programs. Others provide minimal mail support.

Figure 5.10 shows a sample File menu. The File menu provides access to file areas. A *file area* consists of a list of files which can be downloaded. A file area normally resides in a disk directory available to the BBS. BBS file areas are often augmented with a description for each file and download information, such as the number of times a file has been downloaded or how long a download might take. The File menu lets you select the file area to be searched or used for downloads and uploads.

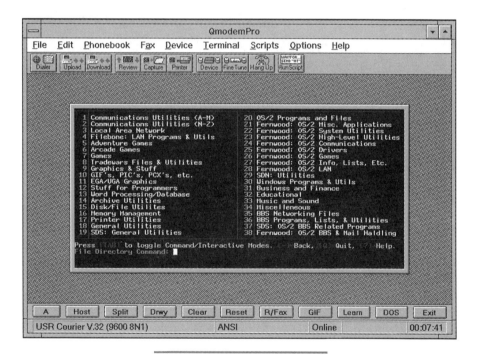

FIGURE 5.10 A SAMPLE FILE MENU.

Figure 5.11 shows a list of files in a file area. A BBS normally deals with a *current file* area. You select the current file area from a list of file areas. Note how each entry shows additional information about the associated file. The text at the bottom of the screen indicates that files can be marked. The list of marked files is used to download the files. Marking lets you scan through a large list of files for the two or three you want to download.

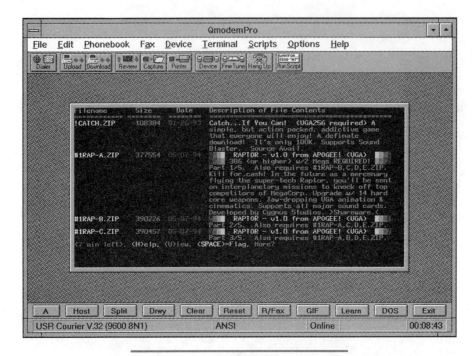

FIGURE 5.11 A LIST OF FILES IN A FILE AREA.

Figure 5.12 shows a file download menu. This menu is presented after you have selected the files to download. The list of file-transfer protocols is often extensive, and your terminal-emulation program will typically support only some of the protocols. File-transfer protocols get data from one side of a connection to the other without any errors. Some protocols send the file name while others do not (Xmodem). Some can send multiple files during a single transfer while other protocols (again, like Xmodem) send only a single file. In the latter case, multiple files are sent using multiple transfers. The preferred file-transfer protocols are Zmodem and Kermit. Both send file names, support multiple file transfers, and are efficient and robust data-transfer protocols. Ymodem is the next step down, supporting file names and multiple file transfers. Xmodem is at the bottom of the list, with no file names sent by the transfer and only a single file per transfer.

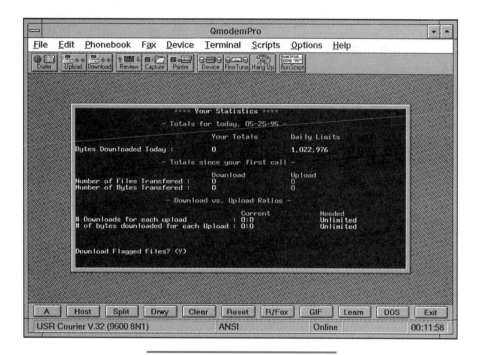

FIGURE 5.12 A FILE DOWNLOAD MENU.

Figure 5.13 shows a file name being selected for a file to be downloaded. Entering a file name is necessary for some file-transfer protocols, which do not send the file name when sending the file. In any case, the destination directory must be selected. Downloads of multiple files results in placing the files into the same directory.

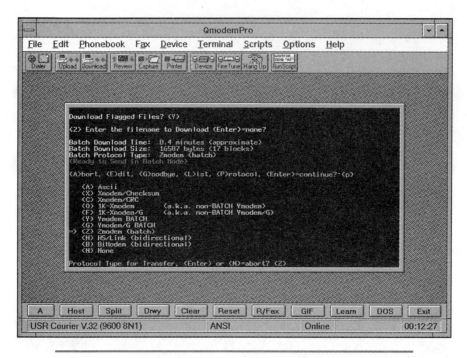

FIGURE 5.13 A FILE NAME BEING SELECTED FOR A FILE TO BE DOWNLOADED.

Figure 5.14 shows a file being downloaded from a BBS. The time estimate is handy when downloading large files. Transfers can typically be cancelled; if all else fails to stop the transfer you can always hang up the phone. File transfers often take a long time, so most BBS products will automatically log off when the transfer is complete.

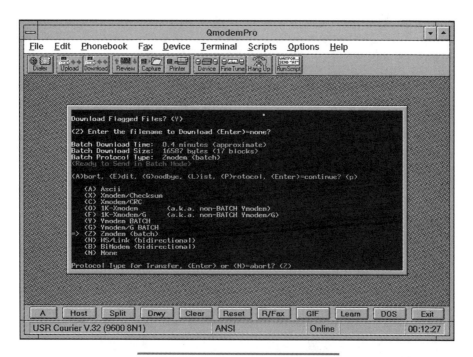

FIGURE 5.14 A FILE BEING DOWNLOADED.

Forums are to messages as file areas are to files. Forums are collections of messages for public consumption. Messages are typically linked in threads. A *thread* is a sequence of messages and responses. A typical thread might start with a question, followed by an answer, followed by a more detailed question, and so on.

Figure 5.15 shows a Forum menu. It lets you select different forums, scan messages in the currently-selected forum or leave a new message. Figure 5.16 shows a list of forum messages. You can select a message to view or respond to. Often you can select a group of messages and download the messages as a single file for viewing after you disconnect from the BBS.

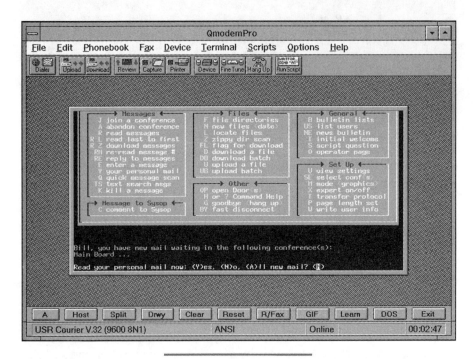

Fɪɢᴜʀᴇ 5.15 A Fᴏʀᴜᴍ ᴍᴇɴᴜ.

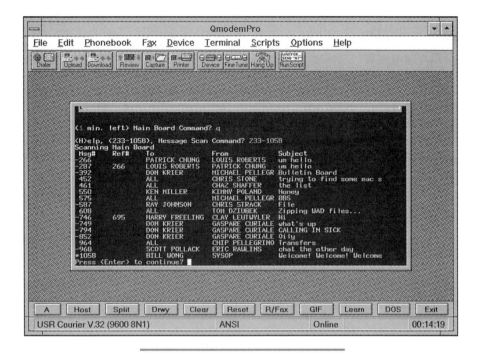

FIGURE 5.16 A LIST OF FORUM MESSAGES.

Figure 5.17 shows a sample forum message. Forum messages are created in the same fashion as mail messages. The additional item found with a forum message is the number of associated response messages. The typical way to add to a thread is to read a message and add a response message.

Figure 5.17 A sample forum message.

BBS menus are typically implemented in a tree structure, with the Main menu at the top of the tree. Each submenu normally has a way, often with a menu selection, to back up to prior menus. BBS products typically come with a number of menu configurations, but sysops are free to customize. A BBS may have three Mail menus instead of just one. For example, there might be a general Mail menu, one for tech support and another for sales. BBS menus can also lead the user to custom BBS applications. The applications can range from games, to sales, to full-text database searching. The applications will typically be a combination of menus, forms and prompts. Again, there is no standard method of presentation, and customization tends to be the norm.

One way presentation may be altered is through the use of Remote Imaging Protocol (RIP). RIP is a terminal-emulation protocol similar to, but more sophisticated than the terminal emulators that support cursor positioning mentioned earlier in this section. The terminal emulators are character-oriented, while RIP is graphically-oriented; the former can show a line of text, while the latter can draw a line. From a user's operational standpoint, there is little difference between the character-mode BBS and one using RIP. Figure 5.18 shows a RIP menu. The menu can be fancier and graphics can augment the presentation.

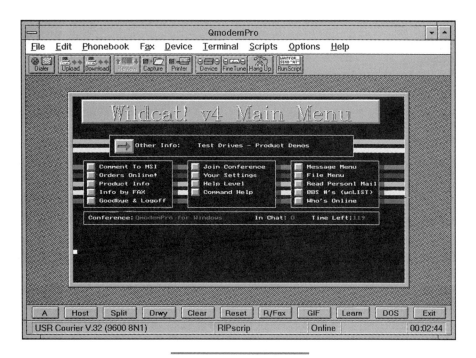

FIGURE 5.18 AN RIP MENU.

From a user's point of view, the BBS is the system being used, regardless of its connection to a LAN. Mail and file areas allow information to be shared with LAN users, but the BBS acts as a transparent gateway between remote users and LAN users.

Using a BBS is not difficult once everything is set up properly. When in doubt, try this: 8 data bits, 1 stop bit, no parity, use an ANSI or VT-100 terminal emulation, and the Zmodem file-transfer protocol.

A LAN MANAGER'S VIEW OF BBSES

A network BBS represents a unique tool for LAN managers. A network-based BBS has its own security and isolates the LAN from the remote user. The network BBS sysop, often the LAN manager, can provide as little or as much access to the LAN as he/she desires. A network-based BBS cannot provide as much access to the LAN as remote workstations and remote control programs, but such a BBS can provide access to the users and the data found on a LAN. A network-based BBS is one of the few remote LAN access methods that does not require custom software on the remote workstation. As shown in the prior section, the remote user is burdened with a more complex configuration, but this tradeoff must be balanced against the almost universal availability to a BBS client: the terminal emulation program.

A network-based BBS is also one of the few remote LAN access methods with automatic new-user management. Most remote LAN access methods either require manual new-user additions by the LAN manager or they must eliminate all security measures.

While periodic management can be minimal, the initial setup typically requires more work than other remote LAN access methods because of the customization required. A basic BBS configuration can be done in an afternoon, but a more sophisticated installation can take much longer. Often the BBS is a growing program with customizations and menu alterations done in an incremental fashion.

Network-based BBS configurations grow to be rather complex, with multiple LAN workstations running their own BBSes and with multiple phone lines connected to each BBS. Multiple-line serial adapter boards can be plugged into a workstation to handle a large number of telephone lines. Although setup and management of a large BBS configuration is more complex than a basic network-based BBS, the main difference is the amount of work, rather than the kind of work, that needs to be done.

A network-based BBS is a single point of entry for remote LAN access. It is typically managed from the workstation's console, but remote management is sometimes an option. Typical access is via modems for remote workstations, but many BBS products also support the same type of access from LAN workstations. Setting up a network-based BBS consists of the usual hardware and software installation, but this must be followed by menu customization, mail configuration, file area configuration, user configuration, and forum configuration. Other BBS options such as fax support require their own installation and configuration.

Menu customization is where most configuration time is spent. Most BBS products have one or more default menu configurations to start with, but normally the entire menu system is customizable. Initial log-in messages and bulletins must be entered before remote users call in. If you are going to provide different kinds of support from the same BBS, such as faxing documents or tech support for a variety of products, then partitioning functionality into different menus will make the BBS easier to use.

Network-based BBS mail configuration varies depending upon the support provided and used. BBS products typically have a standalone mail system which requires no significant configuration, other than making the features available from the BBS menus. Additional configuration is required if the BBS has gateway support for your LAN mail system. Novell's MHS (Message Handling System) is the most common gateway available for BBS products. MHS gateways are often available with LAN mail products that do not utilize MHS directly. Gateway configuration is required if this feature is used.

The BBS file areas must be matched to a disk directory. Different areas can be assigned to different locations. Directories can be exclusively on the workstation's hard disk, thereby isolating the files from the LAN, or the directories can be located exclusively on a network file server. In the latter case, restrictive access to the directories from the LAN can be maintained using the network operating system's security. Various combinations of directory placement and security settings can be used to prevent some network users from having access to some file areas, while providing access to others.

The initial user-list configuration will vary depending upon the use of the BBS. The LAN manager may want to manually enter users into the BBS user database, or let users log in using the automatic registration. The parameters for automatic registration will need to be set first, but these can be altered at any time. Typically any potential users that are already known will be entered initially, so their security privileges can be set accordingly. Known users might be employees or existing customers. New users might be new customers. Otherwise the LAN manager or BBS sysop will have to change the settings for a user at a later time.

Message forums are a place that users can interact as a group. Forums are the original form of groupware. Forum configuration is required if message forums are to be supported by the BBS. Forums can be added or modified after a BBS is set up. Forums can be an "infinite resource sink" if messages are continually added; sysops are often charged with cleaning up old or unnecessary messages from a forum. Many BBS products even provide automatic pruning of forum messages. Message pruning limits are often based on the number of messages, the time they have been posted, or the amount of storage used by the messages. Pruning may also be applied to file areas.

One other item which should be addressed when setting up a BBS is the audit trail. BBS products often support very detailed audit trails. Minimally, the audit trail tracks use, login, and logoff time. File transfers, forum access and almost any BBS operation can be tracked. Of course, extensive tracking can generate a great deal of information. The audit trail is typically saved in a disk file. Like message forums, the audit trail can be automatically pruned.

A BBS can grow to encompass hundreds or even thousands of users with a large number of forums and file areas. Tracking all this information can be excessive for one person. BBS products address this problem by allowing multiple sysops to manage various areas. Like sophisticated network operating systems, these BBS products can also provide different levels of security and limits for sysops. Some sysops can be given control only over specific forums or file areas, while others may have the ability to add new users or change a user's security level.

BBS management is typically done from the BBS workstation's console. Remote management is possible with some products, either through a modem connection or through the LAN. Remote control programs can be used to provide remote BBS management if the BBS itself does not support remote management.

WHAT ARE BBSES AND HOW DO THEY WORK?

A BBS is typically a multitasking program that provides shared message, data, and application services to users running remote terminals. These days the remote terminals are PCs and workstations running terminal-emulation programs, and the connections can be through modems or over a LAN.

BBS products are not limited to a particular platform or operating system, but BBS products started their popularity on CP/M (a precursor to DOS) systems with 300- and 1200-baud modems. Today DOS-based BBS products are the most popular, with V.32 and V.34 modems.

Multitasking BBS products can run on single-tasking operating systems like CP/M and DOS by bringing along their own multitasking support. In effect, they are their own operating system. Figure 5.19 shows how multitasking support is done on a single and multitasking operating system. The advantage of using a multitasking operating system for a BBS is the ability to run other programs besides the BBS. It is even possible to run a DOS-based BBS on a multitasking operating system like OS/2 to gain the ability to run other applications along with the BBS. BBS products written specifically for multitasking operating systems do have a number of advantages, including better integration with other applications and higher efficiency.

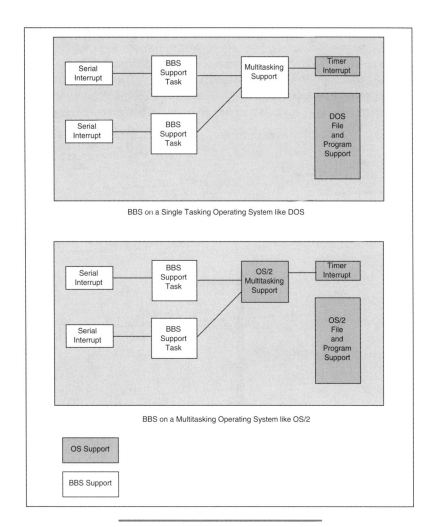

FIGURE 5.19 MULTITASKING BBS SUPPORT.

Regardless of the underlying multitasking support, the logical, internal BBS architecture is essentially the same for all BBS products. Figure 5.20 shows the basic BBS architecture. Each modem or LAN connection has its own support task, which interacts with the terminal-emulation program on the remote workstation. A support task is a portion of a program that handles a specific job and runs at the same time as other tasks. The support task uses the BBS menuing system to present a friendly interface to users. The support task will interact with other BBS support as the user traverses the menus. Mail, forums and file areas are accessed by the support task.

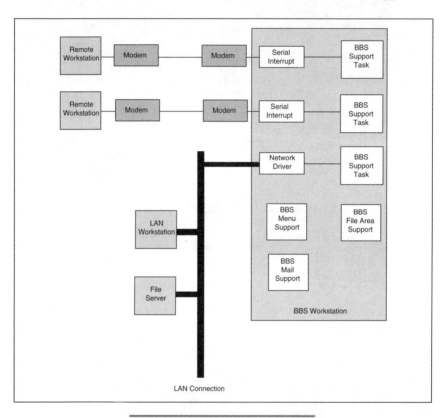

FIGURE 5.20 BASIC BBS ARCHITECTURE

The support task interacts with the terminal-emulation program on the remote workstation using a character-based protocol. There are four types of interaction, based upon the kind of terminal emulation employed, as shown in Figure 5.21. The first is simple line-oriented terminal-emulation. A line of text, ending with carriage return and line feed characters, is sent to the remote workstation. The remote workstation displays the line of text, scrolls the screen up one line, and displays the last line it received. The next step up uses *control* or *escape sequences* to perform special functions like cursor positioning and color changes. Like the carriage return and line feed characters, the control and escape sequences use special characters to tell the terminal emulator to perform a particular function. Graphic support, like RIP, uses the same type of escape sequences but the functions are graphically-oriented. Lines and bitmaps can be drawn in addition to text. The fourth type of interaction uses custom protocols. The function-encoding method is completely hidden by the workstation application and the BBS.

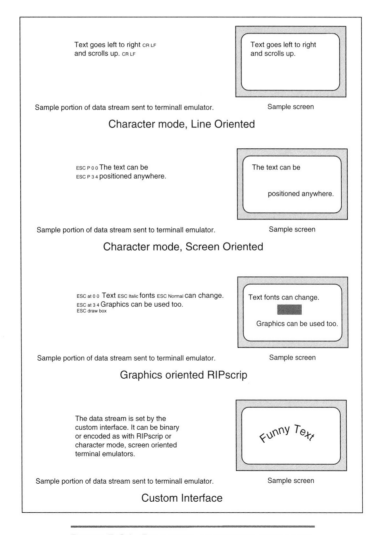

FIGURE 5.21 FOUR TYPES OF TERMINAL EMULATION.

Feedback from the remote workstation uses a matching kind of interaction. Function keys generate control or escape sequences. Mouse support, when available, encodes mouse positioning and button clicks using the same type of sequences. Luckily the details of this workstation and BBS interaction is hidden from users, other than the requirement for matching terminal-emulation selections on the remote workstation and the BBS.

Network-based BBS architecture builds on standard BBS support. The main areas of interaction with the LAN occur with BBS mail, file areas, and application-specific support. The latter often includes general database support, as well as custom applications such as order entry, fax on request, and even multiplayer games. Figure 5.22 shows how some of these areas interact.

Mail interaction can occur in two ways: a mail gateway and LAN workstation access. Mail gateways allow LAN users to use LAN-based mail systems to exchange mail with BBS users. LAN workstation access uses BBS mail directly. File area access can also occur in two ways: shared directories and LAN workstation access. *Shared directories* are file server directories that are accessible by the BBS and LAN users. Remote users leave and pick up files through the BBS and the file area, while LAN users access the directories directly. LAN workstations accessing the BBS exchange files with the file areas, just like remote users. In this case, the matching file areas can be located in directories that are not directly accessible to LAN users, including those on the BBS workstation's hard disk.

Application-specific support can be extremely flexible. Many BBS products include application developer's toolkits. These toolkits have been used by many third-party companies to develop add-ons for BBS products. Interaction with LAN users is application-specific. For example, a simple database access program could use a file-server-based data base to provide information to remote workstation users. The database could be accessed by LAN users using other applications or database front-end products.

Sophisticated BBS managers can develop custom applications using these same toolkits, but more often, the third-party add-on products are more suitable for most network-based BBS installations. These often have their own customization options. For example, order-entry systems and fax-on-demand products require a significant amount of customization before they can be used.

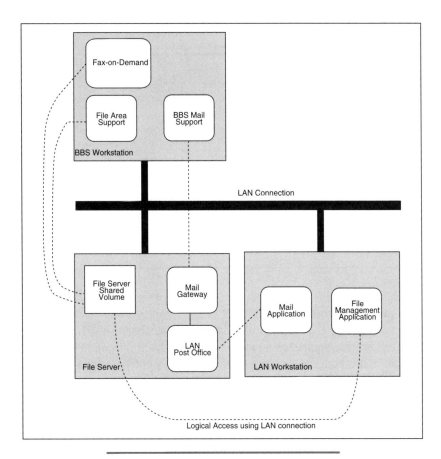

FIGURE 5.22 NETWORK-BASED BBS ARCHITECTURE

WHY USE A BBS FOR REMOTE LAN ACCESS?

Bulletin board systems have a number of advantages and disadvantages when used to remotely access a LAN. The following list summarizes these.

Advantages

Universal remote client availability
No charge for remote client software (typically)
Automatic new-user registration
Simple user interface
Security independent of network
Third-party add-ons often available

Disadvantages

Client configuration can be difficult or confusing
Telephone time not minimized
No direct access to LAN services or users

On the plus side, a BBS usually supports any kind of terminal-emulation program on the remote workstation. The interface presented may be text-only, but at least interaction is possible, and most services are available through the interface. Graphical interfaces require RIP support or custom client programs. Regular terminal-emulation programs are available for almost every computer and operating system, so BBS access is essentially universal. The generally good availability of terminal-emulation programs means a remote user can obtain the program based upon the hardware and software he/she has access to. Other remote LAN access methods normally require that specific programs be supplied to the user for a specific kind of remote workstation. Often the software is not compatible with the users machine, preventing remote access. Rarely does a BBS user have this problem.

Client software for other remote LAN access methods is typically licensed on a per-client basis; remote workstations simply require a terminal emulation program to access a network-based BBS. In fact this type of program is often already included with the software provided with the workstation, so no additional client software costs need be incurred. Shareware and freeware terminal-emulation programs are another low-cost alternative. Modems are also often bundled with terminal-emulation programs at no extra charge.

Shareware is a technique for selling software. You can freely distribute a shareware program but if you use it for more than a specified amount of time, usually 30 days, you are obligated to register the program. Registration normally includes a nominal fee, such as $10 or $25, which entitles you to unlimited use and often printed documentation and upgrades. Many of the programs found on BBS systems are shareware. *Freeware* is another term you may run into with BBS-archived software. Freeware is similar to shareware but there is no registration requirement. The author retains a copyright to the software but you are free to use and distribute it. In fact, many terminal-emulation programs and BBS products started out as shareware or freeware.

Automatic new-user registration can be a definite advantage if your family of remote users grows arbitrarily. For example, a network-based BBS supporting your customers has a potential new user each time a sale is made. All a new user needs is the BBS telephone number and the communication settings to access the BBS. Registration occurs when a new user first calls the BBS. The sysop is notified at this time. New users can be given unrestricted or restricted BBS access, which can then be upgraded by the sysop.

A BBS interface is fairly simple to use, even though BBS products allow rather sophisticated interfaces to be developed. Prompts, menus and forms are readily presented and easy to work with. Of course, proper wording and a clean menu and form-design helps.

A network-based BBS provides its own security for remote users. It is independent of the LAN security, so it is possible to have a secure network-based BBS while not using passwords for LAN workstation users. Network access is carefully controlled by the LAN manager or BBS sysop through fixed access points. BBS mail flows through a mail gateway, while file areas are placed on appropriate directories. BBS add-on products provide other means for remote users to interact with LAN users, and their security measures vary depending upon the product.

Third-party add-ons often available for commercial BBS products, and development toolkits are often available for those with programming expertise. The add-ons can provide a variety of services, from database searches to multiplayer games.

On the minus side, client configuration can be difficult or confusing for those unfamiliar with terminal-emulation programs, although regular BBS users will have no problem setting up their programs to access a network-based BBS.

Telephone time is not minimized when accessing a network-based BBS using a normal terminal-emulation program. The user must typically interact directly with the BBS menu system. Often, file transfers can be initiated with automatic hangup when the transfer completes. Some terminal-emulation programs have programmable macro support or full programming languages for customization. Macro support is a, limited programming language that can be used to recognize text being sent from the BBS and send text to the BBS. Programmable support is often used for making connections with commercial communications services or a BBS, and sophisticated programs can actually check for mail and files and download information automatically. Custom client programs often have this feature, which can significantly minimize telephone time.

A BBS typically provides no direct access to LAN services or users other than the mail and file areas already discussed, nor does a BBS normally provide remote control services or access to the LAN. Of course, some of these capabilities are possible if the appropriate add-on or custom BBS-support application is written. It is theoretically possible to have an add-on that provides selective file area access to file server directories based upon a remote user's request. Whether this add-on exists already, or if it can be written, depends upon the BBS product you choose.

Overall, a network-based BBS works very well if the remote users can be served using mail, file areas, forums and BBS add-on products. A network-based BBS does not work well as a remote LAN access method if direct LAN access is needed or direct access to users is necessary.

CONSIDERATIONS FOR USING A NETWORK-BASED BBS FOR REMOTE LAN ACCESS

There are a number of basic considerations which need to be examined before a network-based bulletin board system should be implemented. These considerations can help determine if bulletin board systems are suitable, practical and desirable. The following is a list of factors we will examine in more detail.

Considerations

- ✧ Access to LAN services (indirect)
- ✧ Ease of use by remote users (good)
- ✧ Network operating system (not important)
- ✧ Network protocol (not accessible)
- ✧ Telephone time (high)
- ✧ Number of simultaneous active lines (high)
- ✧ Performance (good)
- ✧ Scalability (good)
- ✧ Hardware requirements (low)
- ✧ Client licensing (low)

- ✧   Cost (low)

- ✧   Adding users (automatic or manual)

- ✧   General maintenance (minimal)

- ✧   Security (BBS security)

- ✧   Auditing (good to excellent)

- ✧   Automation (possible)

- ✧   Add-ons

BBS connections a network-based BBS provides indirect access to LAN users and services. BBS mail with gateways to LAN mail is one way for remote users to interact with LAN users. The same is true with BBS file areas. Files can be shared between LAN and remote users, but only through fixed directories on a file server. Access to LAN services is through BBS add-ons or custom applications.

A remote user accesses a network-based BBS using a terminal-emulation program. A network-based BBS is relatively easy to use remotely, although the initial configuration of the remote user's terminal-emulation program is often difficult for users who have not used one before.

The network operating system (NOS) is not usually an important item in choosing a network-based BBS; the limiting factor is whether the NOS supports the client that runs the operating system required by the BBS. Network protocols are not an issue either, since the remote user does not have direct access to them from the remote workstation.

Telephone usage tends to be high with a network-based BBS, since most interaction involves the user. Some terminal-emulation programs support macro- or script-language programming which can automate a connection, thereby minimizing telephone time, but creating these programs often requires time and programming talents; At the least it requires an understanding of the programming support and the time necessary to generate and test the program.

A network-based BBS has the potential for supporting the highest number of lines for the lowest cost of any remote LAN access methods. Often the only requirement for adding another line is a modem and a telephone line. Additional licensing may be required for the BBS software, and multiline serial adapters may have to be added, depending upon the number of lines supported. Most BBS products support at least a dozen lines from one workstation. Often a high-performance workstation can handle over a hundred lines. Some BBS products allow multiple BBS workstations to share a common database on a file server for even more lines with better performance.

A single line does not place much load on a network-based BBS, which is why even the average workstation can support many lines at one time. BBS performance is normally good even when many lines are transferring files, which places the heaviest load on the BBS.

A network-based BBS scales well. Multiple-line serial cards are inexpensive and relatively easy to install. Each typically adds eight or more serial lines. Most BBS products even support multiple cards. Today's PCs easily support these high-end configurations. In fact, the disk space available for files is often a more limiting factor, because many BBS installations are used as software distribution points.

Hardware requirements are comparatively low with respect to other remote LAN access methods. A single workstation is usually more than enough hardware for even a very large BBS. Multiple-line serial cards and modems are the primary costs for larger installations.

Client licensing fees tend to be low or non-existent. The terminal-emulation programs are usually the responsibility of the remote user. Terminal-emulation programs often come bundled with modems (a necessary piece of hardware), and with operating systems and environments like IBM's OS/2 and Microsoft's Windows. Shareware and freeware terminal-emulation programs are also plentiful if you have access to them. More sophisticated commercial applications often include macro support, plus a wider variety of terminal-emulation and file-transfer options.

Overall, the cost of using a network-based BBS is low. Hardware costs are low. Host software costs are reasonable and do not grow excessively as the number of lines is increased. Client software costs are also low-to-nonexistent. Maintenance can be minimal by allowing the BBS to perform much of the pruning automatically, often for users, mail, file areas and forums. Time is the usual parameter.

Users can be added manually by the LAN manager or BBS sysop, or users can be added automatically. Most BBS products support automatic addition of users. The first time a user calls in, the BBS lets the user select a user name (if they don't use their full name) and a password.

General BBS maintenance can be minimized, as mentioned earlier. It can also be distributed among a number of users as well. Most BBS products support remote management of mail, file areas, and forums. These sysops can be given limited management privileges, including the ability to give users access to features under the sysop's control.

Network-based BBS security is independent of the network the BBS workstation is attached to. User name and password support is the normal security method but modem callback support can also be used. Multiple passwords can control access to various features, especially those provided by add-on products.

A network-based BBS can be set up to provide very good auditing support. Early BBS products would generate a hard copy log on an attached printer, but most products now generate a disk file containing the specified audit information. Basic BBS audit trails track user login and logout times, while more complex audit trails may include files transferred and bulletins that have been read.

Automation is possible using two techniques. On the remote client end, the macro and programming languages found in more sophisticated terminal-emulation programs can be used to access the BBS automatically and do common operations with the press of a key. Programming support is also available for most commercial BBS products. These provide the tools needed to develop add-ons or to customize the BBS. Often the two techniques can be combined. At the extreme, custom applications can be developed for the client and the BBS.

BBS add-ons are available for a number of BBS programs. They can provide a wide variety of features, from Internet access to mail gateways for mixing LAN and BBS mail. If you can think of a BBS feature, you can probably find an add-on that provides it. Fax support, database support, order entry, sales, tech support, and multiplayer games are just a few add-ons you can find. Be careful though—most add ons work specifically with one vendor's BBS product.

Some BBS products can be set up so that one BBS can automatically connect to other BBS systems and exchange mail and files. FidoNet and PostLink are two protocols that provide this support. A BBS acts as a store-and-forward mail system when using these protocols. A mail message may move from BBS to BBS until it reaches the destination BBS, where a user can then pick it up.

A network-based BBS is an excellent remote LAN access method if the remote users can live with the requirements and limitations. Easy expansion and low cost are just two features you will encounter when considering a network-based BBS.

SOME EXAMPLES OF BBSES

Bulletin board systems come in a variety of implementations, most using the same technology, but some having unique features, such as the ability to use communications servers as gateways to host workstations on the LAN. Others allow different host and client operating systems and environments.

We will take a look at just two BBS products that are suitable for network-based BBS installation. They are Galacticomm's The Major BBS and Mustang Software's Wildcat BBS. Any BBS is a suitable remote LAN access port so long as it runs on a network workstation, and there are literally dozens of BBS products, both commercial and free. The two BBS products examined here are commercial BBS products. Both support a number of add-on products from the company as well as from third parties. Many other commercial BBS products exist with similar features and support.

Galacticomm Inc. sells BBS software as well as hardware. The Major BBS is a product line that handles BBS support from a single line to over a hundred. Galacticomm sells some add-on products and third parties sell even more.

Mustang Software Inc. sells both the BBS and client software. The Wildcat BBS product line is also tiered, so you can start a single-line BBS or plug in lots of multi-line serial boards. Qmodem is Mustang Software's terminal-emulation program that includes RIP support. It integrates well with the Wildcat BBS, but it is also a suitable system for accessing other BBS products.

The Major BBS and Wildcat BBS represent high-end, sophisticated BBS products. Many of the features in these products are unique, but most are common to all BBS implementations. Most of the sample screens shown for The Major BBS are character-mode, while the Wildcat BBS samples are graphical. Both support RIP, so they are both capable of presenting similar displays.

Galacticomm's The Major BBS

The Major BBS is for small, medium and large BBS installations. It runs on an Intel 386, 486 or Pentium processors with at least 4 megabytes of RAM. It supports two lines using standard serial ports and up to 256 lines using multi-port serial boards. Galacticomm Inc. sells hardware as well, so you can get a full-blown BBS directly from Galacticomm. The primary target for the hardware is medium to large installations requiring many lines.

The Major BBS supports Novell Netware connections as well through an add-on from Galacticomm. A custom LAN-based terminal emulator is provided, but it is character-based only. RIP support is provided only through serial line connections. The Major BBS supports a number of terminal-emulation modes, including ANSI color. For file transfers the following protocols are supported: Zmodem, Ymodem-G, Ymodem-Batch, Xmodem 1K, Xmodem, Kermit, and SuperKermit. Zmodem is the most popular and the most efficient. Most terminal-emulation programs support at least one of these file protocols.

The Major BBS is easy to install and configure. It includes support for add-on products and there is a programming interface option as well. Five standard BBS access models are provided. One can be selected, or a custom configuration can be set up during installation. The five standard models are:

1. Public   free access
2. Customer service   slightly restrictive
3. Sign up   initial auto-register only
4. Private   manual registration only
5. For Profit   6 different billing options

The Public model provides auto-registration and lets anyone access all services. Customer service also provides auto-registration, but some areas and services have restricted access. The Sign up modem lets new users register initially, but they are prevented from accessing any other services until a sysop raises their security level. The Private model provides manual registration of users by the sysop; new users calling in that have not been registered will not be allowed to log in. The For Profit model introduces billing to the Private model. Billing is based on access time. A user can pay ahead and be credited by the hour, day, week, or month, or he/she can be billed as needed. The models can be customized after installation as necessary. For example, a Public installation may be changed so that some forums and file areas are private, with the sysop selecting users who may access the private areas.

Figure 5.23 shows The Major BBS status screen that is shown on the workstation running the BBS. It provides a variety of views of the BBS status, configuration and active users. An operator can chat with active users, force disconnections and change some settings. Major reconfiguration and installation of add ons is typically done when the BBS is not running.

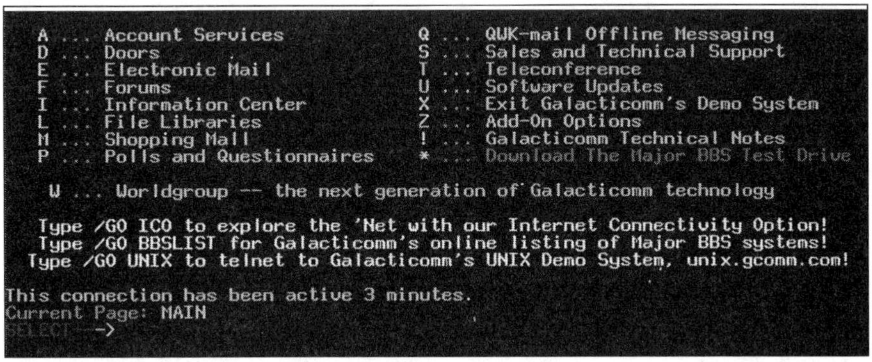

```
A ... Account Services          Q ... QWK-mail Offline Messaging
D ... Doors            .         S ... Sales and Technical Support
E ... Electronic Mail           T ... Teleconference
F ... Forums                    U ... Software Updates
I ... Information Center        X ... Exit Galacticomm's Demo System
L ... File Libraries            Z ... Add-On Options
M ... Shopping Mall             ! ... Galacticomm Technical Notes
P ... Polls and Questionnaires  * ... Download The Major BBS Test Drive

    W ... Worldgroup -- the next generation of Galacticomm technology

   Type /GO ICO to explore the 'Net with our Internet Connectivity Option!
   Type /GO BBSLIST for Galacticomm's online listing of Major BBS systems!
   Type /GO UNIX to telnet to Galacticomm's UNIX Demo System, unix.gcomm.com!

This connection has been active 3 minutes.
Current Page: MAIN
SELECT  ->
```

FIGURE 5.23 THE MAJOR BBS MAIN STATUS SCREEN.

Figure 5.24 shows a sample main menu screen viewed from a Windows based terminal-emulation program. It is a character-mode display, but The Major BBS also supports RIP terminal emulation for graphic presentations. Figure 5.25 shows the menu tree design screen for a main menu. The menu design program runs independently, and modifies a menu database used by the BBS. A separate RIP design program is available as an add-on. RIPterm is included with The Major BBS. RIPterm is a basic terminal-emulation program that supports RIP. It can be freely distributed for use with The Major BBS.

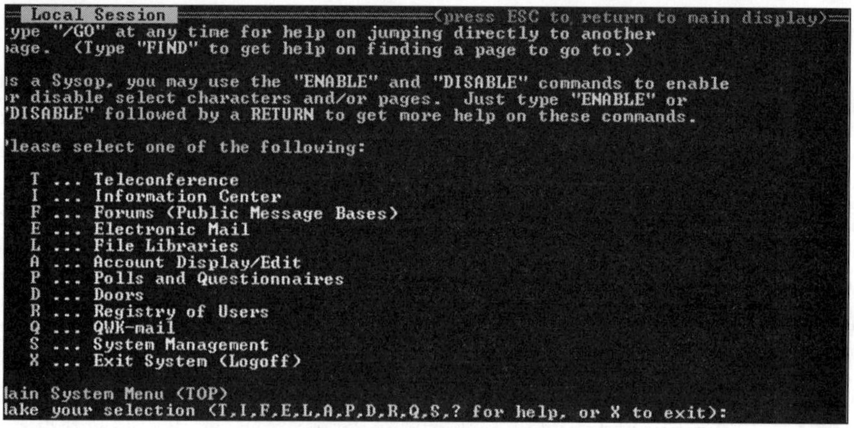

```
 Local Session                       (press ESC to return to main display)
ype "/GO" at any time for help on jumping directly to another
age.  (Type "FIND" to get help on finding a page to go to.)

s a Sysop, you may use the "ENABLE" and "DISABLE" commands to enable
r disable select characters and/or pages.  Just type "ENABLE" or
DISABLE" followed by a RETURN to get more help on these commands.

lease select one of the following:

   T ... Teleconference
   I ... Information Center
   F ... Forums (Public Message Bases)
   E ... Electronic Mail
   L ... File Libraries
   A ... Account Display/Edit
   P ... Polls and Questionnaires
   D ... Doors
   R ... Registry of Users
   Q ... QWK-mail
   S ... System Management
   X ... Exit System (Logoff)

ain System Menu (TOP)
ake your selection (T,I,F,E,L,A,P,D,R,Q,S,? for help, or X to exit):
```

FIGURE 5.24 A SAMPLE MAIN MENU SCREEN.

```
 Menu Tree
 TOP
    ┬TELE
    ┼INFO┬
    │     ├ABOUTUS
    │     ├SYSCONFIG
    │     ├YOURBBS
    │     ├GLOBALS
    │     └HELP
    ├FORUMS
    ├EMAIL
    ├LIBRARY
    ├ACCOUNT
    ├POLLS
    ├DOORS
    ├REGISTRY
    ├QWK
    ├REMOTE
    └EXIT


 help   edit          goto   add    delete        search        exit
 F1     F2     F3     F4     F5     F6      F7     F8     F9     F10
```

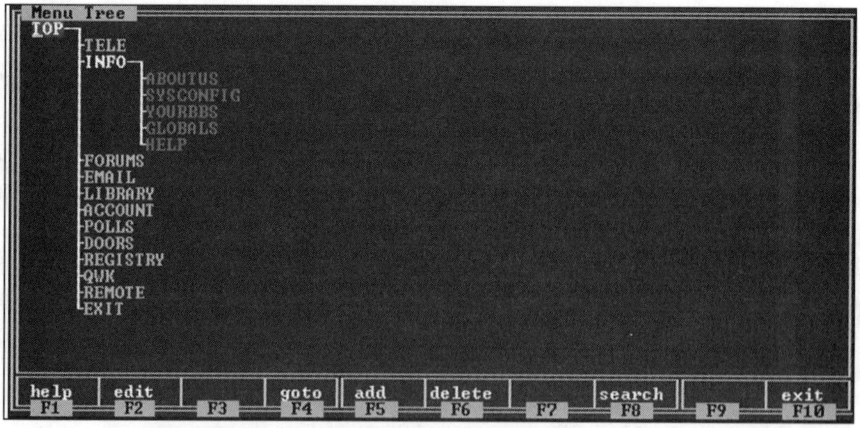

FIGURE 5.25 A MENU TREE DESIGN SCREEN.

The Major BBS menuing system supports polling and questionnaires, as well as basic menu- and bulletin-presentation support. It also supports the QWK protocol used by many offline mail-reader programs; these programs are specialized communications programs that can call into a BBS like The Major BBS and automatically log in, download messages, files, and forum information, and upload response messages and files. The protocol uses a compressed ZIP file for greater efficiency. (ZIP is a common file-compression format used on BBS systems). It is from PKWare of Wisconsin and is available as shareware.

The Major BBS supports a variety of security options based upon user names and passwords. Figure 5.26 shows the security screen on the BBS workstation. The Major BBS uses a technique called Locks and Keys, which is similar to the permission names and passwords used on a local area network. A user has a user name and password for gaining initial access to the BBS. Additional passwords can be given as other services or data is accessed. Something locked is inaccessible without the matching key/password. Mail, teleconferencing, forums and file areas can be protected in this fashion. Even portions of the menu system can have limited access. For example, a user may have access to the mail menu, but not the mail management menu.

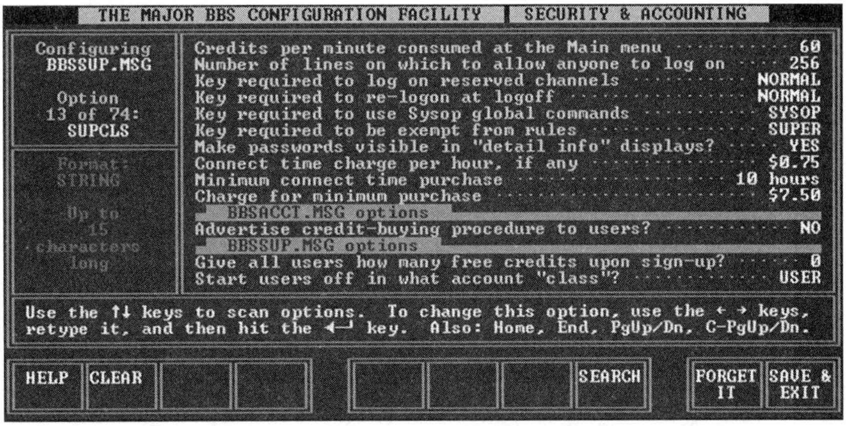

```
┌─────────────────────────────────────────────────────────────────────┐
│      THE MAJOR BBS CONFIGURATION FACILITY  │  SECURITY & ACCOUNTING   │
├─────────────────────────────────────────────────────────────────────┤
│  Configuring   │ Credits per minute consumed at the Main menu .... 60 │
│  BBSSUP.MSG    │ Number of lines on which to allow anyone to log on  256│
│                │ Key required to log on reserved channels ...... NORMAL│
│    Option      │ Key required to re-logon at logoff ............ NORMAL│
│   13 of 74:    │ Key required to use Sysop global commands ...... SYSOP│
│    SUPCLS      │ Key required to be exempt from rules ........... SUPER│
│                │ Make passwords visible in "detail info" displays?  YES│
│    Format:     │ Connect time charge per hour, if any .......... $0.75 │
│    STRING      │ Minimum connect time purchase .............. 10 hours │
│                │ Charge for minimum purchase ................... $7.50 │
│    Up to       │ ── BBSACCT.MSG options ──                             │
│     15         │ Advertise credit-buying procedure to users? ...... NO │
│  characters    │ ── BBSSUP.MSG options ──                              │
│    long        │ Give all users how many free credits upon sign-up? 0 │
│                │ Start users off in what account "class"? ...... USER │
├─────────────────────────────────────────────────────────────────────┤
│ Use the ↑↓ keys to scan options.  To change this option, use the ← → keys,│
│ retype it, and then hit the ↵ key.  Also: Home, End, PgUp/Dn, C-PgUp/Dn.│
├──────┬───────┬─────────┬─────────┬─────────┬────────┬───────┬────────┤
│ HELP │ CLEAR │         │         │         │ SEARCH │FORGET │SAVE &  │
│      │       │         │         │         │        │  IT   │ EXIT   │
└──────┴───────┴─────────┴─────────┴─────────┴────────┴───────┴────────┘
```

FIGURE 5.26 THE MAJOR BBS SECURITY SCREEN.

Remote management (see Figure 5.27) is possible with The Major BBS. This allows remote sysops to manage and prune forums and file areas without needing access to the BBS workstation. Many but not all management operations can be performed remotely. Like other aspects of The Major BBS, management support can also be controlled by the security system. This means that the master sysop can delegate work to other sysops, but still retain overall control. General BBS activity can be viewed at the BBS workstation as shown in figure 5.28.

```
┌─ Local Session ─────────────────────<press ESC to return to main display>═══
│                   R E M O T E   O P E R A T O R   M E N U
│
│ SENDALL => Send Message to All        SYSTATS  => View Overall Statistics
│    SEND => Send Message to User-ID    MODSTATS => View Module Usage
│   LOGON => Edit BBS Log-on Message    DEMSTATS => View System Demographics
│                                       CLSSTATS => View Class Statistics
│ ACCOUNT => Accounting functions
│  DETAIL => Detail Info on User-ID      EMULATE => Emulate a channel
│   AUDIT => Display the Audit Trail     MONITOR => Monitor All mode
│   USERS => Stats of Users Online         INPUT => Monitor Input mode
│  SEARCH => Account Database Search      CHANGE => Change Channel Status
│
│  HANGUP => Disconnect a User-ID           TYPE => DOS TYPE command
│ SUSPEND => Suspend/Unsuspend a User-ID    COPY => DOS COPY command
│ PROTECT => Protect/Unprotect a User-ID  RENAME => DOS RENAME command
│  DELETE => Delete a User-ID                DIR => DOS DIR command
│SHUTDOWN => Shutdown the System              MD => DOS MD command
│ CLEANUP => Force Cleanup or Event           RD => DOS RD command
│TRANSFER => Transfer files                  DEL => DOS DELETE command
│   SYSOP => Edit a User-ID's Access
│
│REMOTE SYSOP
│Select an option (or ? for menu): _
```

FIGURE 5.27 THE MAJOR BBS REMOTE MANAGEMENT SCREEN.

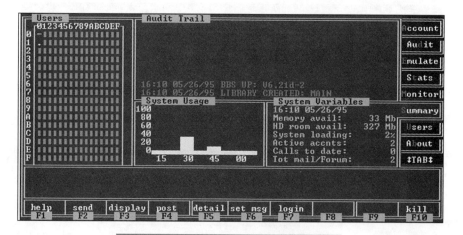

FIGURE 5.28 THE MAJOR BBS ACTIVITY SCREEN.

The Major BBS supports multiuser teleconferences or *chat* sessions. A two-user *chat* session allows two users calling in on different lines to converse by typing messages to each other. The multiuser version works the same way. Messages typed in by a person are sent to each user in the conference, prefixed with the name of the originator.

The Major BBS mail is rather sophisticated. It supports file attachments, carbon copies, distribution lists, and even *return receipts*. The latter are messages returned to the sender when a recipient reads a message. Figure 5.29 shows the mail's full-screen editor. The Major BBS also supports a line-oriented editor for terminal-emulation programs that cannot support the screen-oriented editor. File attachments are uploaded using standard file protocols. The Major BBS mail system can be linked to LAN mail systems using the MHS mail gateway. This can also hook BBS mail into other mail support that may be installed with the LAN mail system, such as Fax support or links to other mail systems.

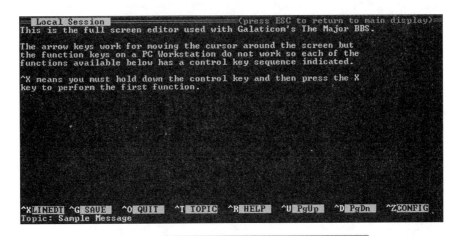

FIGURE 5.29 THE MAJOR BBS MAIL FULL-SCREEN EDITOR.

The Major BBS supports up to 3,500 public forum areas. Forums are a collection of messages. Anyone with access to a forum can read the messages left in the forum. Message-threading is supported. A *message thread* is a sequence of messages left in response to each other. A thread starts with a single message, but a message thread can include hundreds of messages. Message threads usually have themes and most BBS products simply show the subject of the initial message and the number of messages in the thread when you scan a forum. The Major BBS uses the same kind of editors for both mail and forum messages, so you can attach files, use the line- or screen-oriented editor, and view the messages in the same fashion. You can even search for messages with a particular keyword.

The Major BBS supports up to 10,000 file areas, which can be placed ion any directory available to the BBS workstation. This includes network directories if the workstation has access to a network file server. You can scan file areas and tag or mark a file for later upload. This is handy when looking for many files. Figure 5.30 shows a sample file-transfer screen on the remote workstation. The terminal-emulation program shows the file-transfer status, while the text in the window shows the interaction with the BBS prior to the start of the file transfer. The file-transfer status box will be removed when the transfer is complete, and the terminal-emulation screen will show the subsequent status report from the BBS workstation.

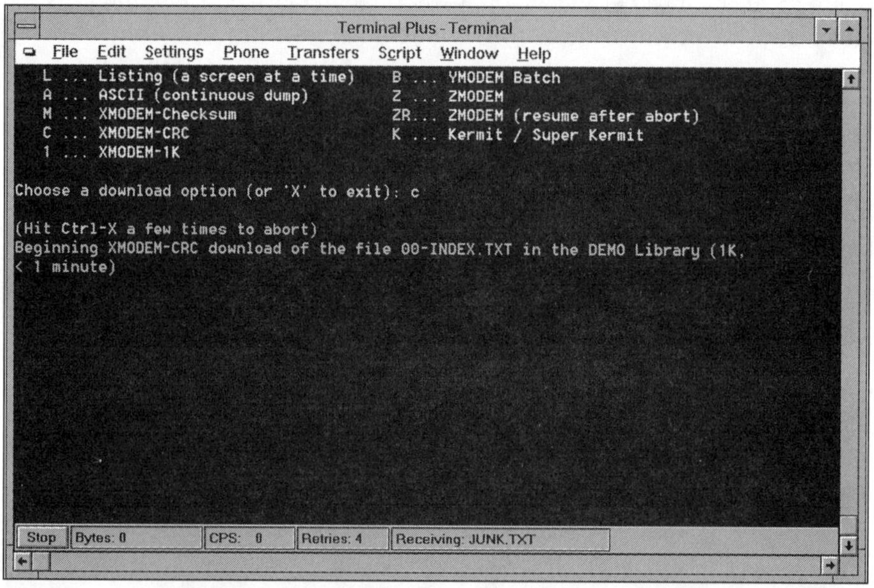

FIGURE 5.30 THE MAJOR BBS FILE-TRANSFER SCREEN.

Figure 5.31 shows a sample audit trail and report. The Major BBS supports a number of different report formats. It is even possible to use the user database to generate mailing labels. This is handy when hardcopy information must be sent to users. Of course, the accuracy of the user list can vary especially when auto-registration is used.

The Major BBS supports a wide variety of add-ons. Galaticomm sells a number of these add-ons, but third-party vendors sell many as well. Some of Galacticomm's offerings include the Entertainment collection, the Advanced LAN options, the Shopping Mall and Fax support. The Entertainment collection includes a number of single and multiplayer games. You only need to install the ones you like. The Advanced LAN option is needed for NetWare workstation access using Novell NetWare's SPX communications protocol. An active LAN connection is considered a line for the BBS license. Even LANs with a large number of users can be supported with a BBS that has only a few lines, since even LAN users will not remain connected to the BBS for an extended period of time. In fact, LAN users tend to place less of a load on the BBS because their connection speed is so much higher. The Shopping Mall lets you sell goods and services through the BBS. It handles order entry and invoicing through a BBS connection. Users can search for goods and services listed in the Shopping Mall's database. Orders can be placed, with the Shopping Mall software handling discounts, shipping charges, and sales tax. The Fax support lets you attach a Fax-modem to a serial port on the BBS workstation for sending FAXes. You can send a fax using the mail system or by requesting a file from a file area be sent using the fax modem. Text and graphics files can be sent using this procedure, and billing feature can be used to pay for the cost of sending a fax.

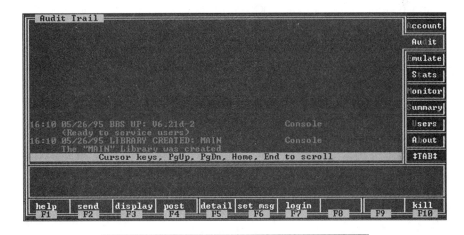

FIGURE 5.31 THE MAJOR BBS AUDIT TRAIL AND REPORT.

The Major BBS provides a number of features that make it ideal for a remote LAN access system. Its ties to LAN-based mail through the MHS gateway provides indirect access to LAN users. The LAN-based access to the BBS lets LAN users utilize BBS features directly.

Mustang Software's Wildcat BBS

Mustang Software sells both the Wildcat BBS and Qmodem Pro, a highend terminal emulator. Qmodem Pro supports RIP, along with a number of other features which make it a good companion to the Wildcat BBS, but it is suitable for accessing other BBSes and commercial systems like MCI Mail and CompuServe. Likewise, the Wildcat BBS can be accessed using any terminal-emulation program, including Qmodem Pro.

The Wildcat BBS comes in a number of versions for small, medium and large systems. It is also ideal for LAN use. The Wildcat BBS program can be used to access BBS facilities as if you called in through a modem connection. Two or more BBS programs can be run on different workstations in a LAN from a common directory on a file server. All copies will use the same BBS database. Add a mail message from one workstation, and the message can be picked up from another workstation running the Wildcat BBS software. This approach allows LAN users to access the BBS, and it also allows multiple BBS workstations to support multiple serial lines. A total of 250 connections can be handled by a single database.

A Wildcat BBS workstation needs at least an Intel 386 running DOS with 4 megabytes of RAM. A network interface is optional. The Wildcat BBS network support should work with almost any DOS-compatible network. The Wildcat BBS can also be run on multitasking operating systems such as IBM's OS/2, Microsoft Windows, and DESQview.

The Wildcat Status screen, shown in Figure 5.32, is viewable from any workstation running the Wildcat BBS software. The menu selections on the left let a system operator access other features, including logging in as a BBS user.

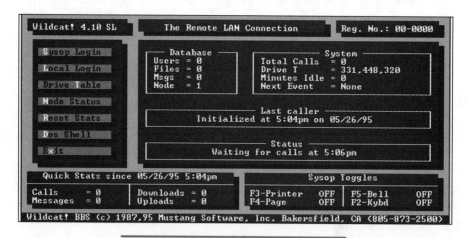

FIGURE 5.32 The Wildcat BBS status screen

Figure 5.33 shows a sample Main menu screen displayed on Qmodem Pro using RIP. Pretty snazzy. RIP presentations can be created using a text editor, but you must know the character sequences needed to draw items like lines and circles. Programs like RIPaint are available from Mustang Software. Figure 5.34 shows the menu design program for creating character-based menus and the overall menu structure.

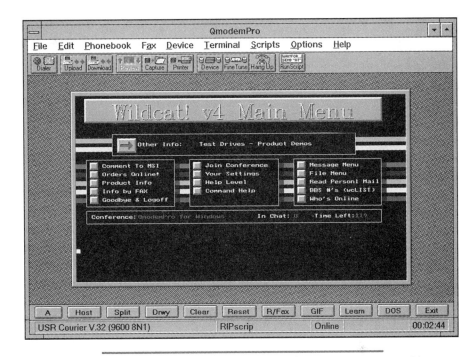

FIGURE 5.33 A SAMPLE WILDCAT BBS MAIN MENU SCREEN.

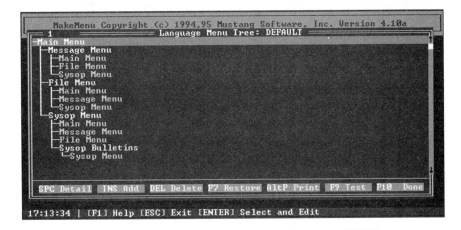

FIGURE 5.34 THE WILDCAT BBS MENU TREE DESIGN SCREEN.

Wildcat BBS supports up to 1000 unique security profiles. Figure 5.35 shows one of the security-setting screens available to a sysop. Local and remote management is possible. Figure 5.36 shows what a Wildcat BBS remote-management screen looks like. The Wildcat BBS supports the typical user name and password security, which also controls access to BBS features. It also supports Caller ID if you have a modem that supports the feature.

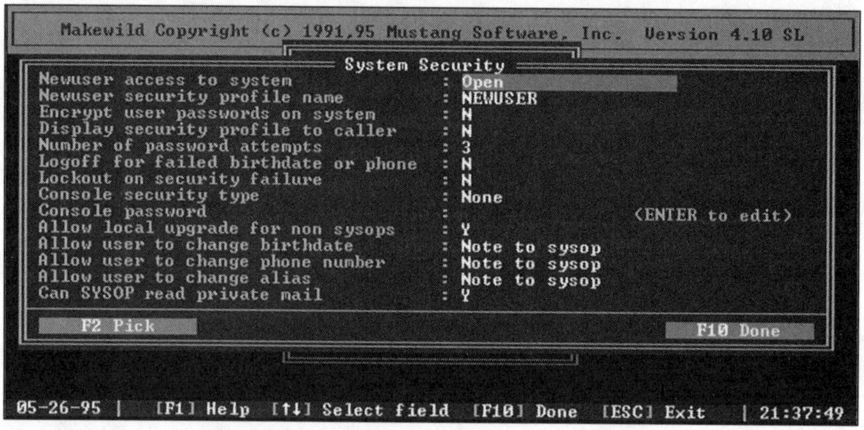

FIGURE 5.35 THE WILDCAT BBS SECURITY SCREEN.

FIGURE 5.36 THE WILDCAT BBS MANAGEMENT SCREEN.

The Wildcat BBS supports the standard BBS features such as mail, forums and file areas. The mail system supports line-oriented and screen-oriented editors. It even has a spell checker. The mail system supports group lists, carbon copies, return receipt mail, and file attachments. Links to other mail systems are extensive. The wcGATE add-on supports links to the Internet, MHS, FidoNet, and PostLink. PostLink was developed for RelayNet International Message Exchange (RIME). It is also used with some Echomail networks. RIME uses the Universal Text Interface (UTI) for message exchange, which allows messages to be converted to the native mail format (which may be different for sender and receiver). Wildcat also supports QWK mail access for automatic pickup and delivery of mail by a remote user.

The Wildcat BBS supports up to 32,000 file areas. It even supports CD-ROM drives with multi-disk changers, providing potentially vast amounts of information. The following file-transfer protocols are supported: Zmodem, Ymodem-G, Ymodem-Batch, Xmodem 1K, Xmodem-CRC, Xmodem, and Kermit. Figure 5.37 shows Qmodem Pro performing a file transfer with a Wildcat BBS. A GIF (Graphics Interchange Format) thumbnail previewer is available with appropriate RIP support.

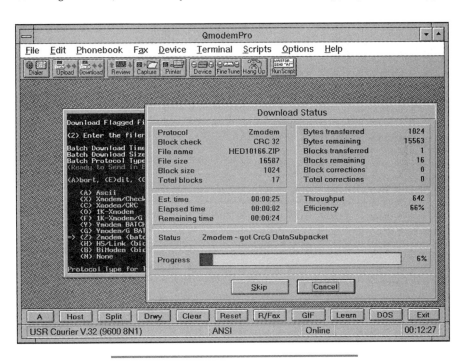

FIGURE 5.37 QMODEM PRO FILE-TRANSFER SCREEN.

Mustang Software also sells other add-ons such as wcCODE, a programming interface, and wcPRO, a statistics and fax-support package. The fax support allows faxes to be sent via mail, and files in the file areas can be sent via a fax-modem.

Qmodem Pro for DOS and for Windows (separate packages) are ideal products to access a Wildcat BBS. They support RIP as well as a number of character-mode terminal-emulation types. They also include support for accessing other systems, such as MCI Mail and CompuServe, and can also be used to create mail offline (see Figure 5.38) and upload it automatically.

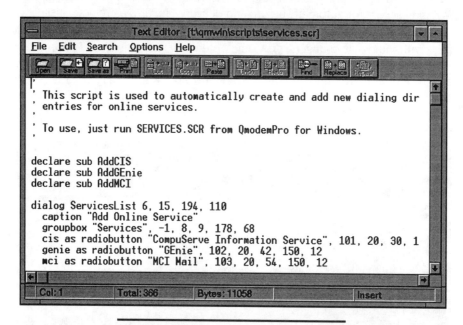

FIGURE 5.38 QMODEM OFFLINE MAIL CREATION.

Mustang Software's products represent a good remote LAN access method. They are especially flexible when used to provide access to LAN users; not all BBS products are capable of using a common BBS database from multiple LAN workstations. Like other high-end BBS products, they support add-on products from both the BBS vendor and third parties.

REMOTE FAXING

Remote fax support is a limited form of remote LAN access. Fax exchange is appropriate for text and graphics, but not for data files. Fax exchange is an interesting form of remote LAN access because it can often be accomplished without the use of a remote PC. In this case a fax machine replaces the PC.

REMOTE FAXING

Remote fax support can take many forms, but it basically comes down to three modes of operation: receiving a fax sent by someone else (*incoming*), receiving a fax you request (also called *fax-on-demand*), and sending a fax to a LAN user (*outgoing*, see Figure 6.1). Only one operation, receiving a fax you request, is of note. Sending a fax from a LAN workstation is a relatively simple and common operation these days, sending a fax to a user on the LAN is not quite so simple or as common. Receiving a fax you request is notable because it involves no additional user intervention. While this chapter concentrates on this aspect of remote fax support, we will look at all aspects of LAN-based fax support to see how they are integrated— most fax products that support remote fax requests also support general sending and receiving of faxes.

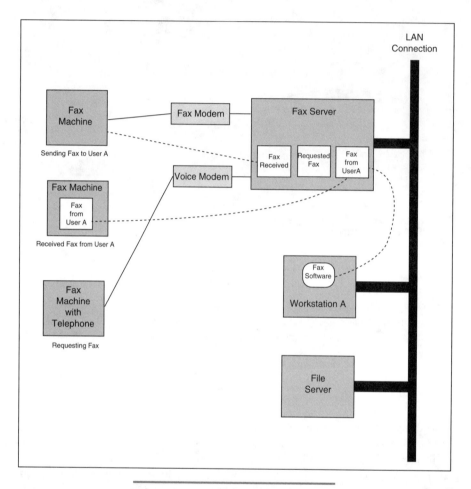

FIGURE 6.1 THREE FAX MODES FOR LANs.

Outgoing and fax-on-demand support are a relatively easy to implement. Incoming fax support is more problematic when there are a number of possible recipients, which is normally the case with a LAN-based system. The idea is to be able to send a fax and have it delivered to a user on the LAN. There are three basic techniques used to solve this problem (see Figure 6.2) in addition to manual distribution: automatic delivery using direct inward dialing (DID); automatic delivery using a touch-tone phone (dual-tone multiple-frequency or DTMF); and automatic delivery using optical character recognition (OCR). Manual distribution places all incoming faxes into a single folder. Someone must then view the faxes individually and forward them, usually via electronic mail, to the proper recipient.

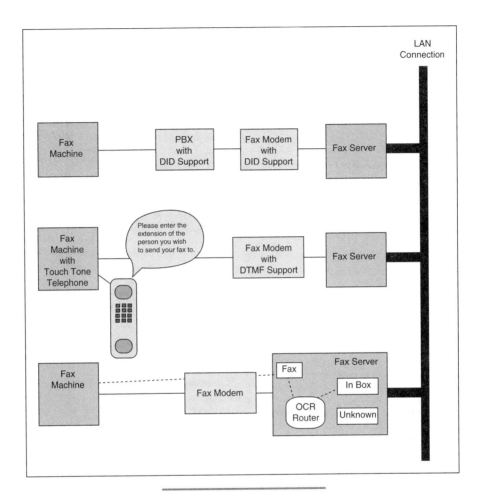

FIGURE 6.2 INWARD FAX SUPPORT.

Automatic delivery using DID requires a fax board that supports DID. The phone company provides a single line with multiple phone numbers associated with it. The fax board can determine which phone number was called when it receives a fax. Individual recipients are assigned a particular phone number. DTMF support also requires a special fax board, although these tend to be less complex and less costly than DID-compatible fax boards. The caller must be using a Touch-Tone telephone and two numbers must be dialed, the first being the telephone number and the second being the routing number. The latter is entered after the fax modem answers the initial call. A recipient is assigned a routing number. OCR support is used in a limited number of cases. It uses the manual distribution technique, except that an OCR program replaces the person who views the faxes. OCR support tends to require a fixed cover-letter format and font.

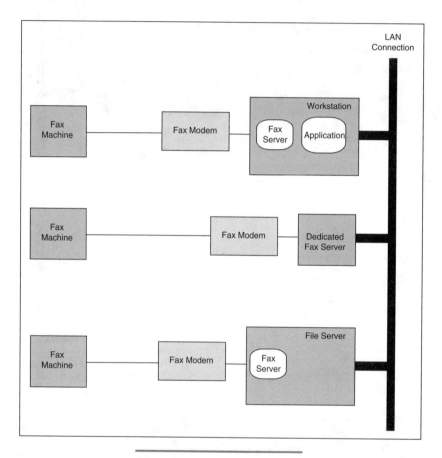

Figure 6.3 Three fax platforms.

Fax-on-demand involves sending faxes from the LAN to your fax machine, which is easy. The hard part is figuring out what faxes to send and where to send them. A variety of techniques are available to do this. For example, one common technique uses a voice-based prompting system. A caller hears a computer-generated voice that presents a list of options, just like a voice-mail system. The caller responds using the keys on a Touch-Tone (DTMF) telephone. Some systems combine the features of voice mail and fax-on-demand. The difference between a voice-mail system and a latter system is that the fax-on-demand prompts eventually ask for a phone number and a number that indicates which fax documents to send. Often the initial fax option is to send a fax, and it contains a list of fax documents and their associated numbers.

Fax-on-demand requests can also come through a number of computer-generated requests. Many mail systems support fax mail gateways as well as remote workstation gateways. Combine the two with a work-flow system and you can send a message from a remote workstation to the work-flow system through the mail gateway. The message is the request for the fax to be sent, along with the phone number to send it to. The work-flow system generates a message that is sent through the fax mail gateway to the fax machine.

A bulletin-board system (BBS) equipped with a fax gateway may be used in a similar fashion, although many BBS products have the fax support already integrated with the mail or file-area system. You select a message or file to send and enter the fax number. Often the same modem is used for BBS access and fax support, so faxes are sent after you hang up. Dedicated fax-on-demand systems with computer access work like a BBS with a fax gateway; the main difference is a lack of other BBS functions by the dedicated fax-on-demand system.

Just to show how far this access method can go, you need to take a look at the Internet. Some World Wide Web (WWW) servers allow faxes to be requested through them. A WWW page is displayed using a WWW viewer program. There is a connection across the Internet between the viewer and the server. The page of interest would be a form that includes a field for the phone number and a selection of documents to be sent. The form can contain buttons, so there is probably one that sends the documents. Clicking on the buttons sends the request to a program on the WWW server. The program may send a message to a fax server, or the WWW server may also be a fax server. Eventually the fax gets sent.

Another interesting fax-on-demand request mechanism uses a specific set of forms and OCR. You must have access to a request form. For example, a form could be included as part of a magazine or catalog. You fill out the form, placing the phone number in the appropriate blocks and check off the items you want. You fax the completed form to the system that receives the fax, which processes the form through the OCR software and determines the phone number and the document request from the results. The requested documents are then faxed back.

LAN fax support can be divided into three support platforms, based on where the server software runs. The platforms include file-server-based, dedicated-fax-server-based, and workstation-based, as shown in Figure 6.3. All can be part of a LAN. The workstation-based systems can also be used as standalone systems. All platforms essentially operate in an identical fashion with respect to the remote users and the LAN users; only the internal flow of information changes.

A file-server-based platform has fax-server software running on the file server; the software uses fax modems attached to the file server. Outgoing faxes sent by LAN users are delivered to the file-server-based software, where they are queued to be sent. The faxes are then sent using the modems, depending on various options that may be available including delivery time and fax priority. Delivery of files to the server can be done using dedicated fax software or via electronic mail gateways. In the latter case, a user sends a mail message where one or more recipients have fax destinations that include a phone number and optional information such as the preferred delivery time.

Dedicated fax servers attach to a network. A fax is sent from a workstation to the fax server, either directly or indirectly. Some fax servers maintain their own queues, while others use a queue on a file server. A fax is sent to the queue and is removed by the fax server when the fax can be sent. Incoming faxes are handled in a similar fashion. They can be held in the fax server, moved to a file server, or even printed on a network printer. Dedicated fax servers come in all shapes and sizes, from single fax modems through rack-mounted systems with multiple fax modems on a single card.

A workstation-based fax server can be dedicated to the task or it can be used to run applications while also being a fax server. Some dedicated fax servers are workstations that have been customized. The advantage of a workstation-based fax server is the ability to make use of existing equipment, including the LAN. Often the fax server software can operate with different network operating systems, and some server systems do not even care which network operating system is used. Dedicated fax servers often work with only one kind of network operating system, typically Novell NetWare, or a limited number of network operating systems.

Another workstation-based fax system uses BBSes, which were discussed in Chapter 5. The fax server software is incorporated with the BBS software. Faxes can be sent from the BBS using a number of different techniques. BBS mail can be set up so that a mail recipient can be designated as a fax phone number. A BBS user can also request that files be sent to a fax number. A BBS can often use the same modem for receiving an incoming call and sending a fax—at different times, of course.

Remote fax support is suitable for single or multiple telephone lines. Some single-line systems for standalone workstations can also be used for remote LAN access by placing the fax workstation on the network and letting it use files on the network file server. Multiple-line systems are usually expandable to dozens of lines. A number of vendors sell fax-modem adapter cards with more than one modem per card. Cards with a single modem are standard fare for workstations. Putting multiple modems on one card lets a workstation handle dozens of lines simultaneously. Often four modems are placed on a single card.

Software support is often the deciding factor in purchasing fax-modem cards. Fax software often supports a wide variety of single-line modems, but more limited support is found for the multiple-line modems needed in larger installations.

Remote fax support is a suitable remote LAN access method for a variety of applications. It will not provide direct access to the LAN, but it will provide indirect access to LAN users if incoming faxes can be moved into the LAN mail system. Fax-on-demand installations provide remote users access to LAN data, but only data that can be sent as text or graphics. Fax support does have one advantage: you only need a telephone and a fax machine. Fax machines are still more common and easier for many people to use than computers.

REMOTE FAXING: A USER'S VIEW

A remote user has a relatively simple view of a remote fax system. A remote user can perform three basic operations (Figure 6.4): sending a fax to the LAN, receiving a fax from a LAN and requesting a fax (fax-on-demand). It is also worth remembering a LAN user's fax capability—a LAN user can both send and receive a fax.

The LAN user's ability to send a FAX is common to every fax server or fax application because of the ease of implementation. The send operation may be initiated using a variety of different techniques, depending on the software involved. For example, a standalone fax program may provide its own editor to write a note to be faxed, or you may be able to select a file to send. Fax support may also be integrated with the mail system, providing a way to designate recipients as fax users so that the mail message is sent as a fax.

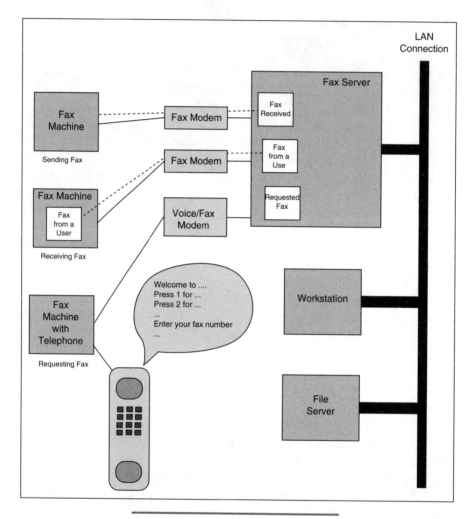

FIGURE 6.4 REMOTE USER FAX CAPABILITIES.

It is on the receiving side that things become more difficult. Figure 6.5 shows the typical flow for incoming faxes. The best case is where a fax is sent directly to the LAN user's workstation, but since this is a LAN book we want to see what happens in a shared environment. The most limited case has a fax being received by a fax server and placed into a queue. Someone must view the fax and then forward it, usually through the LAN mail system, to the recipient. This is the same type of manual distribution that occurs with a common fax machine, where all incoming faxes wind up in the same bin.

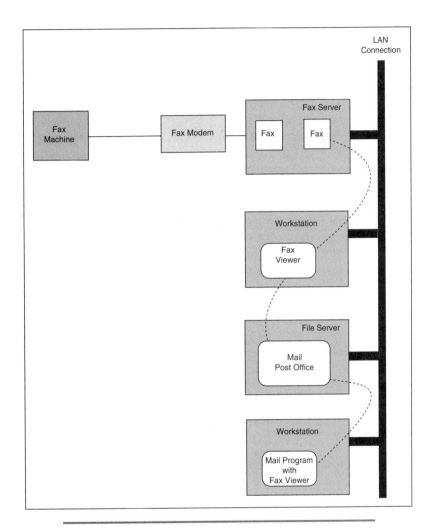

FIGURE 6.5 INCOMING FAX SUPPORT INCLUDING MANUAL DISPATCH.

There are one transparent and two nontransparent automatic routing methods for our remote user. The transparent routing method uses direct inward dialing (DID). DID is done in conjunction with your telephone company. Each LAN user who will receive faxes is given a telephone number. The fax modem is attached to a single line, which will indicate what phone number was used to place the call. The fax modem forwards this information to the fax server software for routing purposes. Multiple incoming lines can handle multiple DID phone numbers so that a single fax modem is not overwhelmed by a large number of incoming faxes. DID is the most transparent routing mechanism because the sender and receiver need to do nothing special to have the fax routed automatically.

The first nontransparent routing method uses a Touch-Tone phone (DTMF). The sender must dial a phone number and wait for the fax modem to answer. The sender must then dial one or more digits (essentially the receiver's fax extension), to indicate who should receive the fax. Each person is assigned their own fax extension number so a fax can be routed to them. What happens when the phone is initially answered depends on the fax modem and software installed. The minimum configuration uses a conventional fax modem; in this case, the caller hears nothing and must know when and how to enter the extension. Some fax modems are also equipped with voice output, or they may be connected to a computer-controlled voice output adapter. With the appropriate software, the caller can be presented with a voice prompt indicating what he or she can do. The basic case, presented now, is to enter the extension of the recipient. Fax-on-demand support lets the user choose more options using a Touch-Tone phone. The caller must initiate sending the fax after the extension is entered. DTMF routing works best with voice prompts and manual dialing. Problems can often occur when the caller uses a fax machine or fax modem that is set up to dial a number and then send the fax. Adding the extension to the end of the phone number does not work, because it must be entered after the call is initially picked up. Some fax machines and most fax software let the caller include delays between numbers to be dialed; in this case the delay needs to be added between the phone number and the extension. Experimentation is sometimes required here because the amount of time needed to make the initial connection can vary by a second or two. Another minor problem that occasionally crops up is the speed of dialing the extension. Fax modems can dial very quickly, but sometimes the DTMF support at the receiver's end cannot keep up, so the extension is not recognized. Fax modems can often be configured to dial at slower rates, which fixes the problem. Unfortunately, the instructions on how to do this are often hidden in the fax modem's manual.

The second nontransparent routing method uses optical character recognition (OCR) on the cover page, which is normally the first page sent. A typical cover page includes the name of the sender and the name of the recipient. OCR routing typically requires a fixed-format cover page and typed names; a cover page with handwriting goes into the manual routing bin. The entire fax is received and then passed on for processing by the OCR support. The first page is converted to text and the text is then searched for appropriate keywords like TO and FROM. The text following these keywords is assumed to be the name of the recipient and sender. This information is used to route the fax to the recipient. The fax goes into the manual routing bin if the recipient is not on the list of LAN users.

OCR routing is very accurate and relatively easy when a fax is sent from a fax modem. The information in the fax, especially the cover page, is generated by the computer. The only trick is to use a font that faxes well, such as Helvetica, and to make the font size large enough for the OCR software to accurately convert the graphical fax image to text. A size of 10 to 14 points works quite well. Even hand-printed text can be converted if the printing is clear and consistent.

A variation on text-based fax routing is the check-box-oriented fixed-format cover page. The cover page is given to anyone intending to send faxes to the recipient. Check boxes on the page indicate who or what group should receive the fax. The software at the fax server simply compares the graphical image of the first page to its internal version of the cover page for orientation. The software then examines the check box positions for a light or dark area and processes the fax accordingly.

Fax-on-demand is a realm that some users may be familiar with, while other users may have never encountered this type of service. The remote user calls a workstation on the LAN to select one or more documents to retrieve and then supplies a phone number to send them to. Additional information may be required if the caller must pay for the return phone call or the information in the documents. Typically this service is provided free of charge as a customer service benefit.

The initial call can be made to a computer interface, such as a BBS system (Figure 6.6) or a mail gateway (Figure 6.7). It can also be a call to a voice-prompting system (Figure 6.8), possibly integrated with a voice-mail system. Finally, there is the OCR request method (Figure 6.9) that is similar to OCR-based routing of incoming faxes.

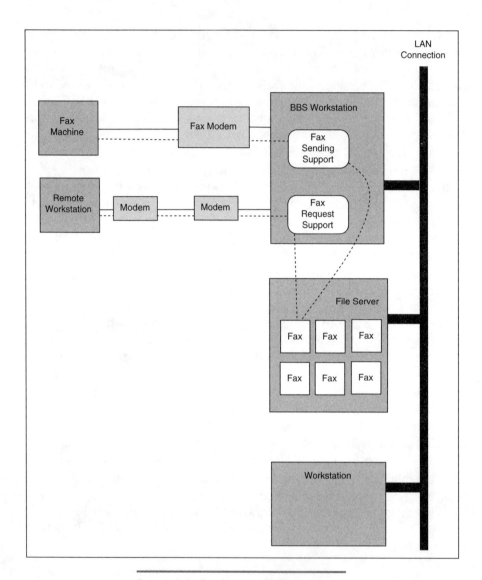

FIGURE 6.6 FAX-ON-DEMAND BBS REQUEST.

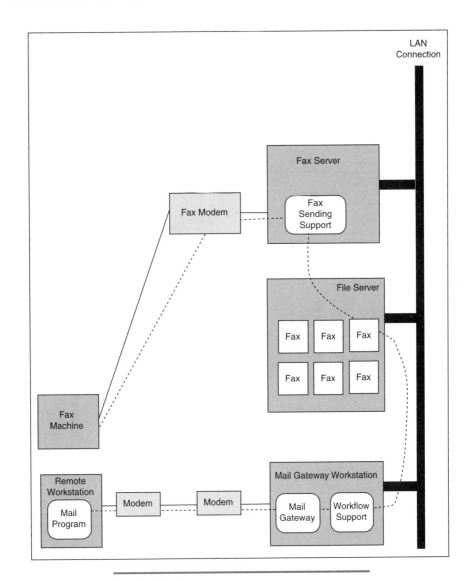

FIGURE 6.7 FAX ON DEMAND MAIL GATEWAY REQUEST.

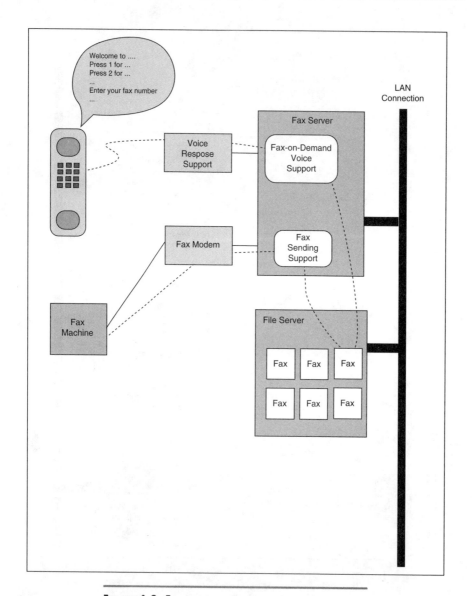

FIGURE 6.8 FAX-ON-DEMAND VOICE PROMPTED REQUEST.

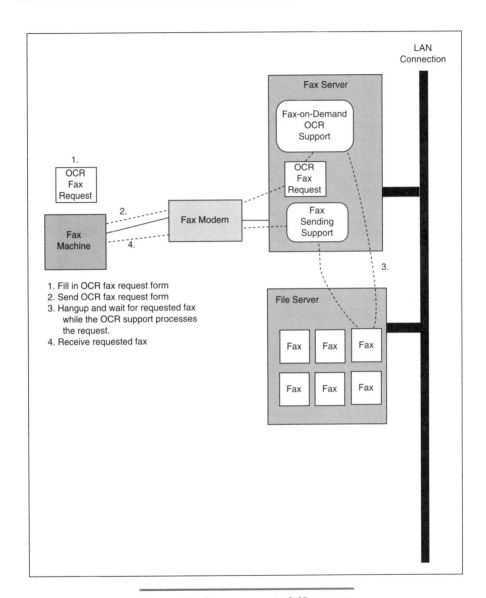

1. Fill in OCR fax request form
2. Send OCR fax request form
3. Hangup and wait for requested fax
   while the OCR support processes
   the request.
4. Receive requested fax

FIGURE 6.9 FAX-ON-DEMAND OCR REQUEST.

The computer-oriented interface may be a part of another remote LAN access method, such as a BBS, that provides other services in addition to fax-on-demand. Each interface is different, but the procedure and results are the same. The remote user calls in, select the documents to download, hangs up (or sometimes the same connection is used for the fax), and the fax is sent from the fax server. The fax transmission support may be part of the request support or it may be independent (see Figure 6.10).

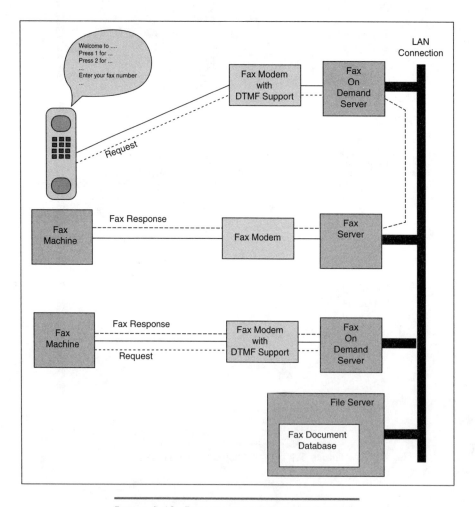

FIGURE 6.10 FAX-ON-DEMAND RESPONSE METHODS.

Using a BBS fax-on-demand system starts with the remote user calling the BBS using a terminal emulation program. The user then logs in and navigates the BBS menu system until he or she gets to the section supporting fax requests. This area and the type of support varies with each BBS and each BBS product, but in general users are presented with a list of documents or files that can be faxed. The user selects the documents he or she wants and then supplies a fax phone number as an address. After the user disconnects from the BBS, the documents are sent to his or her fax machine.

A mail gateway fax-on-demand system is often built using a work-flow system. The remote user creates a mail message with a list of documents to be faxed. The message also includes the fax machine phone number. The message is then delivered through the mail gateway. Once the message is in the post office, the work-flow system takes over and picks up and processes the message. The requested documents are then sent to the fax transmission program for delivery to the remote user. The fax transmission program is often part of the mail system, so the workflow software simply sends the documents as mail messages, using the message-supplied phone number as the address of the recipient.

Voice prompting is found in voice-mail systems' and fax-on-demand systems using voice prompting operate in the same fashion: you place a call, and when the call is answered you hear a voice telling you about the options you can choose by pressing a button on your touch-tone phone. Eventually you select one or more documents and the system asks you for the fax machine's phone number. You dial the phone number, hang up, and wait for the documents on your fax machine.

Fax-on-demand OCR requests use a fax machine to send the request, and the same machine can be used to receive the requested documents. Typically a preprinted form is supplied to the requester, either in a magazine or the back of a manual. You fill in the check boxes to indicate the documents to send. Boxes for the phone number are supplied. You need to write the numbers clearly, but OCR of a limited character set, such as digits only, is much more accurate than scanning text. The request form is faxed to the fax-on-demand system, which receives the form, processes the information supplied, and sends back the requested documents.

Faxing the requested documents can be done using a variety of methods. Low-volume systems can use the same phone line and hardware used to handle the initial request to send the requested fax. Turnaround can be quick, but subsequent requests cannot be processed until the documents have been sent. Medium- (4-14 telephone lines) to high-volume systems separate the fax transmission from the caller support side. Fax modem telephone lines are dedicated to sending faxes.

Caller support voice prompting lines are dedicated to receiving calls and allowing callers to select documents to fax. The number of fax-modem telephone lines used on this side is often less than on the request side, because it often takes more time to request a document than to send it. Outgoing faxes can also be queued, so you only need enough modems to empty the queue fast enough for the delay between a request and receiving the document to be moderate.

Fax-on-demand systems can only send printed documents, not just any data files, such as a spreadsheet file. You can include a printed version of a spreadsheet in the list of documents but when you receive it you see only the values, not the underlying equations. Users still like these systems because they are simple to use and they work with any fax machine.

REMOTE FAXING: A LAN MANAGER'S VIEW

Setting up and maintaining LAN fax support and fax-on-demand systems can be a simple process for a single-line system, but multiline systems require more work and expertise. The three types of fax support already discussed include sending faxes, receiving faxes and fax-on-demand support. Integration with the LAN can vary, but in general LAN fax support can be a very powerful tool. Issues such as security are less important with fax support compared to other remote LAN access methods because of the limited type of information, printed documentation, that is being exchanged. Printed documentation is anything you can put on paper. Printed documentation can be sent via fax, and even fax-on-demand systems typically control the documents that can be requested.

A LAN user can send and receive faxes to and from a remote user by a number of straightforward methods: using fax modems attached to workstations, to communications servers, and to fax servers. Fax modems attached to workstations are typically dedicated to the workstation's user; single-user fax software can be used here to send and receive faxes. Installation is straightforward and the LAN manager does not have to be involved in day-to-day operation. Fax modems on a communications server are used in a similar fashion to fax modems on a workstation; the difference is that a fax modem on the communications server can be used by any LAN user, but only by one user at a time. Installation and maintenance of the communications server is straightforward, but users must be trained to use the server-based modems.

Receiving a fax on a standalone fax modem attached to a LAN workstation is straightforward for the workstation's user, since the phone line is dedicated to the fax modem. Fax modems on communications servers can be set up to receive a fax, but it is more difficult to determine which phone number is to be called to send the fax. One way to do this is to include the phone number in the modem name used with the communications server software. A LAN user uses a fax modem on the communications server and tells a remote user what number to call. Training users how to do this can be difficult. It is useful for receiving occasional faxes, but not for daily use because it is often difficult to reserve a particular modem every day. Fax servers tend to be more useful for receiving faxes.

Fax servers can be divided into two types: dedicated and integrated. *Dedicated* fax servers come with their own software for accessing the server. Access includes the ability to send and receive faxes. Installing dedicated fax server software is usually an easy process. Fax server software can run on network file servers, dedicated fax server workstations, and even on nondedicated workstations. The actual location of the fax server normally has no effect on the operation of the fax client software. Yes, this is a client/server application. The server usually requires little maintenance once it is installed. Server operation is normally automatic and a LAN manager need only check it when something is not working properly.

An *integrated* fax server is one that works with other software, such as mail or a BBS. Internally, the integrated fax server operates in the same fashion as a dedicated fax server. On the remote user side, the operation is also the same. The difference is that the LAN user works with the fax server software integrated with other other software, such as the LAN mail system. In this case, sending a mail message can result in the message being sent through the fax server. Likewise, received faxes are delivered through the mail system.

A fax server system can route incoming faxes using the four techniques already discussed, including manual routing and the three types of automatic routing using DID, a Touch-Tone phone (DTMF), and OCR. The technique selected by the LAN manager will affect the amount of work at installation time and the amount of daily maintenance involved. The estimated number of incoming faxes often dictates the choice of routing techniques.

Manual routing is usually the best choice when the number of incoming faxes is expected to be low. All incoming faxes are placed into a common folder. The folder may often be accessed by the entire LAN population, or it may be restricted to a few users. If you as a user are expecting a fax, you can periodically check the folder, or someone can be assigned to periodically check the folder and forward faxes to the appropriate parties. Letting everyone access the folder can cause problems if confidential faxes are received. Assigning one or more users to perform this job is one way to limit access to incoming faxes, but timely delivery is not guaranteed unless one happens to be one of the select few with access to the folder.

Automatic routing of incoming faxes is better for the caller and for the LAN user, when it works. DID is the most transparent, but also the most complex to implement. LAN managers must deal with the local telephone company or with a PBX vendor if a local PBX provides the DID support. Special modems are required to handle DID support, and the fax server software must also accommodate these modems. Initial setup can be very complex, but the payoff is transparent operation for both sender and receiver.

DTMF routing is easier to implement because it does not involve the telephone company or a PBX vendor. It does require special modems and matching fax server software. DTMF and DID routing require about the same amount of work by the LAN manager at the fax server end. A phone number and matching user name is kept in a table used by the fax server software to route incoming faxes. The LAN manager must set up the table and change it when users are added or removed from the LAN. Some systems provide voice prompting when a call comes in, but this normally requires recording a short message. Matching voice support is required by the modem, or the voice support may be provided by another workstation adapter connected to the same telephone line as the fax modem.

OCR routing support varies, depending on the fax server product and the complexity of the form being scanned by the OCR software. Unlike the other two automatic routing methods, OCR routing includes manual routing support, because OCR routing is not foolproof; DID and DTMF routing can always recognize who should receive an incoming fax. OCR routing works by scanning the first page. If no information can be garnered from the cover page, the entire fax gets dumped into the manual routing folder. OCR routing requires the same kind of setup as DID and DTMF routing. A table of names and routing information is set up by the LAN manager for use by the routing software after the cover page is converted to text by the OCR software. Training is often an issue for accurate operation; otherwise OCR routing winds up being manual routing because unrecognized cover pages cause the faxes to be placed into the manual routing folder.

The amount of work involved in setting up and managing a fax-on-demand system depends a great deal on the number of lines, the intended audience, and the choice of software. Single-line systems like Creative Labs PhoneBlaster are relatively easy to install and configure. Unfortunately, increasing the number of lines using this type of product is difficult because each workstation must be managed individually, and a workstation is required for each telephone line.

Small (more than 2 lines), medium (4–10 lines), and large fax-on-demand system setup is complex simply because of the amount of hardware and number of telephone lines involved. These multiline systems normally split the request operation from the actual sending of a fax. Fax transmission is often done using conventional dedicated and integrated fax servers.

The fax-on-demand request methods require different setup procedures. BBS and mail-based requests are often available as an option to the standard BBS and mail products. It is even possible to link Internet access to a LAN mail system, and in turn to the fax support in a mail gateway. A user can request a document through an Internet-based application, and the subsequent mail message is routed to the fax server, or possibly to a work-flow application, which then directs that another message, containing the requested documents, be sent through the fax server.

Document management can become a major issue for a LAN manager if the available documents change regularly or if the number of documents is large. The way documents are made accessible and how the documents are described can make the LAN manager's job either easier or more tedious. For example, a fax-on-demand system that has users enter a multidigit code to select a document may be able to automate the document management solution by placing all document files into a single directory and using the file names as code to select them. Alternatively, a database, or a less-than-conventional database like Lotus Notes, can be used to maintain the document list. The one thing to remember about the documents is that each document needs a description or number in addition to the contents of the document.

Fax-on-demand documents are often accessed by LAN users as well, although access is through the LAN instead of the fax machine. Fax software often prefers the document to be readily converted to a fax format for fast transmission. Some products can convert different file types to their internal fax format just before the fax is sent. Keeping the documents in a form that both the LAN user and fax software can use makes the LAN manager's job easier. Adobe Acrobat's PDF files are one way to do this. PDF files can be viewed using a PDF viewer such as Adobe Acrobat's Reader program; the same PDF files can be sent by some fax servers.

Finally, there is the issue of usage audits. Tracking how many fax requests are made and what files are requested most often can be useful in planning future upgrades. Most fax-on-demand systems record what occurred during the day, but often this information is raw data that must be analyzed.

Setting up support for allowing LAN users to send a fax to a remote address is the easiest job. Setting up a system for receiving a fax is more complex, but there are alternatives. Setting up a fax-on-demand system can be very complicated for medium-to-large installations because of the logistics and the complexity of the hardware and software involved. Still, for many companies the cost and complexity are acceptable, considering the kind of service such a system provides.

WHAT ARE REMOTE FAXING SYSTEMS AND HOW DO THEY WORK?

While the actual process of fax transmission and data storage is complex and interesting to some, we will not be covering it in this book. What we *will* be covering in this section is how received faxes can be routed and how fax-on-demand systems work. We will not be looking at how a fax is sent, because it is a relatively straightforward process done by the fax software; essentially, a document and a phone number are required and the fax modem is used to send the document. But first a quick note about fax file formats.

The actual sending and receiving of a fax is handled by the fax modem and the fax software. The fax software typically uses its own graphics file format for storing the data sent or received. Sending a fax from a workstation is typically done using a document not in this format. Where and when the user's document is converted from its native file format (for example, text file or word processing file, depending on the application) to the fax format depends on the fax software, and the conversion is usually transparent to the user. Received faxes are typically saved in the fax software's graphics file format and users can view a fax using the fax software's own viewing program. The fax software often has the ability to save a fax using standard graphics file formats such as .BMP, .PCX, and .GIF.

The automatic routing of incoming faxes and faxes on demand often use identical hardware that requires similar software support. Thus, we will look at the rating techniques themselves, instead of how they work individually for routing incoming faxes and faxes on demand. The techniques include DID, DTMF (Touch-Tone phones), and OCR. We will address voice prompting, along with voice recording. Voice recording is how voice-mail systems operate, and we mention it here simply to show how the hardware and software are integrated to provide this support, as well as to show how it integrates with the fax support, because the two are often found in the same product.

Figure 6.11 shows how the hardware may be configured. Some products integrate all types of support onto a single card, while others spread the support across multiple cards. The integrated products are typically found in single-line products, while multiline products have only one or two types of support on a single card. Support from one card is combined with support on another card, using external cabling. These cards are often configured to support multiple lines and are found in larger installations. You may notice that OCR support is not listed as a hardware-support option; OCR typically uses software support and is applied after a fax has been received and saved as a graphics fax file.

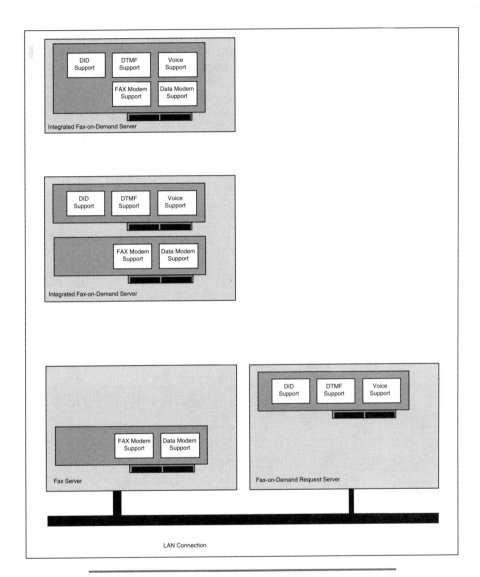

FIGURE 6.11 FAX BOARDS AND DID, DTMF, AND VOICE-SUPPORT
(INTEGRATED AND SEPARATE).

DID support (Figure 6.12) is normally used only for incoming fax routing. DID support is provided by standard hardware and protocols used by your local telephone company and PBX vendors. Modems that support DID hide the hardware details and provide the software with access to the DID information, which is supplied each time a call is answered. The information is simple—the phone number—and the hardware connection procedure is automatic, so that is about it.

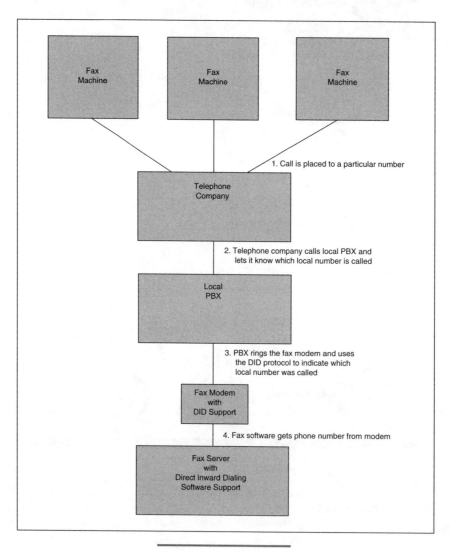

FIGURE 6.12 DID SUPPORT.

DTMF support (Figure 6.13) is typically integrated with the fax modem. The modem already detects tones to communicate with the modem at the other end of a connection, so just a minor change is needed for most hardware to detect the DTMF tones generated by a Touch-Tone telephone. The modem must normally be set up to detect tones, and this is normally done after it answers a call. The modem lets the PC know when and which tone is detected when the caller presses a key.

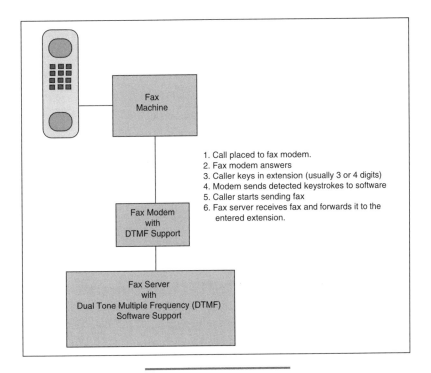

1. Call placed to fax modem.
2. Fax modem answers
3. Caller keys in extension (usually 3 or 4 digits)
4. Modem sends detected keystrokes to software
5. Caller starts sending fax
6. Fax server receives fax and forwards it to the entered extension.

FIGURE 6.13 DTMF SUPPORT.

Voice support is divided into input and output support. *Input support* is used to record voice messages in a voice-mail system; it converts analog signals to digital data that can be stored as a file. The file can be played back using a digital-to-analog conversion unit, otherwise known as a PC *sound board*. It is the same type of support used for voice *output support*, except the output is sent to a speaker in one instance and to the telephone line on the other. When you call a voice mail system voice prompts are presented as voice output .

WHY USE REMOTE FAXING FOR REMOTE LAN ACCESS?

Remote fax systems have a number of advantages and disadvantages when used to remotely access a LAN. The following list summarizes these.

Advantages

Requires only a fax machine at the remote site

Remote access tools often minimal

No charge for remote client software (typically)

Simple user interface

Telephone time minimized

Fax-on-demand may integrate with other systems

Disadvantages

Requires a fax machine at the remote site

Limited information exchange (fax data)

Manual routing of faxes received on a LAN

Host configuration can be difficult

No direct access to LAN services or users

On the plus side, remote fax support requires a fax machine at the remote site. This is both an advantage and a disadvantage: fax machines and fax modems, which can cost as little as $50, are generally available in most offices, but if you do not have access to a fax machine or fax modem, you are out of luck.

Remote fax access tools are minimal. The minimum is a fax machine or a PC with a fax modem. This is sufficient for sending or receiving faxes. Fax-on-demand requires an access mechanism; systems that use voice prompting only require a Touch-Tone telephone. Computer access through a BBS, a mail gateway, or even the Internet requires a communications program. The type of communications program depends on the type of system to be called. Minimally, a terminal-emulation program will be needed. The minimal requirements at the remote site either obviate the need for remote client software or minimize it. A terminal emulation program, if required, can be obtained for a *minimal* cost, under $80. Terminal emulator programs are also bundled with operating systems like Windows and OS/2.

Faxing is successful because the interface is very simple. Receiving a fax is automatic, and sending a fax normally requires just a few keystrokes and entering the phone number. Routing of faxes received on a LAN are the responsibility of the

LAN fax support, not of the sender. Fax-on-demand requires a fax machine that can receive the requested documents. The request procedure is usually very simple. Voice prompting with Touch-Tone responses will be familiar to anyone who has called into a voice-mail system, most telephone and electric companies use one as a front end for customer support. All you need to do is follow the directions and make the appropriate selections by pressing a key on the telephone.

Telephone time tends to be low for remote fax access. Sending and receiving a fax goes relatively quickly, and most documents are only a few pages long. A phone call only lasts long enough to transfer the document. Fax-on-demand requests can often take longer to make than faxing the requested document, but this time is normally minimized because no one wants to listen to the voice prompts any longer than he or she has to.

Integration with voice-mail systems can be an advantage for fax-on-demand systems. The first voice prompt can include an option to enter the fax-on-demand system. Subsequent prompts walk you through the fax-request procedure. BBS-based systems combine a standard BBS with fax-request support. Even the Internet can act as a gateway for fax requests using World Wide Web (WWW or Web) servers and a WWW viewer at the remote workstation.

On the minus side, as we have already seen, is the requirement for a fax machine or a fax modem to be installed at the site to receive or send a fax. Luckily, these tend to be quite common and keep getting cheaper.

Remote fax access works well if the information you want to transfer can be sent using a fax machine. Text and drawings fax well, but binary data does not. Unfortunately, even faxing text and data may give you only a document you can view. A computer with OCR and fax software is necessary to convert a fax document in to machine-readable form. The fax software receives a fax and saves it as a graphics file. The OCR software processes the graphics file and converts it to a text file.

Routing of incoming faxes is an issue when receiving faxes on a LAN. Manual routing is workable, but not necessarily timely. Automatic routing may be available, but the cost may not be in line with what you want to pay. Direct inward dialing (DID) is the most transparent option for the remote user. Each LAN user is assigned a phone number, and the fax server can determine which phone number was dialed when it answers an incoming call. A low-cost but less-transparent option uses fax modems that can recognize Touch-Tone telephone tones (DTMF). A fax is sent by first calling the fax modem and then dialing an additional number to select the recipient. The fax is sent after the additional number is entered.

Host configuration can be difficult, depending on the support provided. Sending a fax from a LAN is the easiest option to install and configure. Most LAN-based fax servers provide this option. Manual distribution of incoming faxes is typically included with this sending support. Automatic distribution is more complex and depends on whether DTMF or DID is supported. Both require an initial matching of users to phone numbers. Luckily, this job only needs to be done once.

The major limitation of remote fax support is that it provides no direct access to LAN services or users. The closest you can get is to send a fax to a LAN-based fax server.

Remote LAN access using a fax machine provides many advantages, but there are significant limitations. Keep these in mind when choosing a remote fax access system.

SHOULD YOU USE REMOTE FAXING FOR REMOTE LAN ACCESS?

There are a number of basic considerations that need to be examined before a remote faxing system should be implemented. These considerations can help determine if remote faxing is suitable, practical, and desirable. The following is a list of the considerations we will examine in more detail.

Considerations:

- ✦ Access to LAN users (none)
- ✦ Access to LAN services (none)
- ✦ Ease of use by remote users (good)
- ✦ Network operating system (not important)
- ✦ Network protocol (not accessible)
- ✦ Telephone time (minimal)
- ✦ Number of simultaneous active lines (high)
- ✦ Scalability (good)
- ✦ Performance (good)
- ✦ Hardware requirements (varies)
- ✦ Client licensing (none)
- ✦ Cost (low)
- ✦ General maintenance (minimal)

❖ Security (good)

❖ Auditing (good)

❖ Automation (not possible)

❖ Integration with voice mail system (possible)

Remote faxing is not the remote LAN access solution to choose for directly reaching LAN users or services. *Documents* are the thing with remote fax support. Indirect access to users through the mail system is possible with some remote fax systems, especially when they are used with LAN mail gateways.

Ease of use by remote users is good for all aspects of remote faxing. Sending a fax to a LAN system is the same as sending a fax between fax machines; receiving a fax is also the same. Fax-on-demand systems vary on how a fax document is selected and how the destination phone number is supplied. Voice prompting is easy for anyone to use, and Touch-Tone telephone data entry is slow but accurate and easy to do. It is also a familiar technique used for a variety of voice-mail systems. BBS access to fax documents requires a remote workstation with terminal-emulation but this is not much more difficult to use than a voice-based system.

The network operating system and network protocol are not usually issues when dealing with remote fax support. The remote user has no access to either, and the remote fax server software only needs to deal with a network operating system if it uses communication protocols for interaction with workstations on the LAN.

Telephone time is normally minimal with remote fax systems, including fax-on-demand products. Most fax documents wind up being a few pages that transfer in a few minutes, depending on the complexity of the documents. Selection of the document often takes more time than sending the document itself. In fact, installations that use different lines for accepting requests and sending a fax will have fewer lines for sending, because responses can often be delayed without causing a problem and because the documents can be sent quickly.

The number of simultaneous active lines can be high, although the actual number will depend on the software used to implement a remote fax system. Some single-line software will not be readily expandable, but multiline fax software typically expands well to dozens of lines. Multiple-port serial or modem boards can help in this case.

Performance of a remote fax system is good, although it is limited to the speed at which a fax can be sent. The current crop of fax machines uses 9,600-baud transfer rates, although they can usually slow down to accommodate slower fax machines or poor-quality telephone lines. Faster fax support is available, but it is less standard than the 9,600-baud variety. The advantage of fax support is that it is relatively standardized, and fax machines and fax modems from different manufacturers work well together.

Hardware requirements vary depending on the software chosen and the kind of solution needed. Fax-on-demand voice systems for single-line installations often use a single adapter board for both the voice support and the fax modem. Multiple-line installations typically use separate voice boards and fax-modem boards. In this case the incoming requests and outgoing responses are often segregated.

Client licensing is usually not an issue because client software is usually unnecessary. Receiving or sending a fax requires a fax machine or a fax modem, but these are often already available. Voice-response systems often require a Touch-Tone telephone at the caller's end, but these are also relatively common. Terminal-emulation programs, needed to access a BBS that supports fax-on-demand installations, are relatively inexpensive or are included with some operating systems. Remote fax support that uses mail gateways may have additional costs at the client end.

The cost of installing and operating a remote fax system is relatively low compared to the number of users that can be supported. Large multiple-line systems can cost a great deal, but they will support a very large user base. Single-line approaches can be relatively inexpensive, but they tend to be limited in the area of expansion.

General maintenance of remote fax support tends to be minimal. Outgoing faxes from LAN mail systems are relatively transparent to users and involve minimal maintenance after installation. Checking logs is often the extent of general maintenance; incoming fax support requires more maintenance, depending on the routing method used. Dropping all incoming faxes into a single folder requires a good deal of human support if many faxes for different recipients are received on a regular basis. Automatic distribution requires additional support only when it doesn't work. Automatic distribution can be done using a variety of techniques, including direct inward dialing (DID), Touch-Tone telephone (DTMF), and optical character recognition (OCR). Fax-on-demand maintenance is on the same order as incoming fax support, and it depends on the technique used to request a fax.

Security is good with respect to remote users because only documents can be sent or retrieved. Document security on the LAN may be an issue, but this is readily managed using the network's security measures, which may be augmented by the fax software.

Most fax systems support auditing of some sort. The minimal audit trail includes time, phone number, and call duration. More detailed audit trails include file names, mail information, and related information.

Automation is not possible with fax systems. Because information cannot be exchanged, only sent or received and only as copies of printed documents. Fax-on-demand and routing of incoming faxes can be done automatically, but this is not the same thing. Automation involves a remote user automatically invoking operations on the LAN, which cannot be done using a fax connection.

Integration with voice-mail systems is possible with some fax systems, especially fax-on-demand systems. Of course, voice-mail systems can also route calls to a standalone fax system.

REMOTE FAXING: SOME EXAMPLES

Remote FAXing support comes in a variety of implementations. We will ignore the typical stand-alone fax server that provides outgoing fax support and limited incoming fax support and concentrate on the more unique fax server support, such as OCR routing of incoming faxes and fax-on-demand systems.

Some fax systems are implemented in software and run on the network file server. This is fine for low-volume applications; however, placing the fax server on its own workstation often provides better performance and increases the overall reliability of the network. It also allows different people to manage the network file server and network fax server. Splitting the two lets you place the file and fax servers in a place this is convenient for use and wiring. For example, placing the fax server near the telephone wiring closet can minimize wiring chores.

The first product we will look at is Mitek's NIF. It is a typical LAN-based fax server, with the ability to send and receive faxes. The outgoing fax support is not surprising, but its routing of incoming faxes is. NIF uses OCR routing. It scans the first page after the fax is received to determine who should receive the fax. Typewritten faxes work best with the router, but even hand-printed faxes can be routed.

The U.S. Robotics dedicated fax server is presented as an example of the typical network fax server. It supports multiple lines and plugs directly into the LAN. A typical network fax server can also be a standard workstation running fax server software.

Next we move into the realm of fax-on-demand support. Starting at the low end, we take a look at Creative Labs' PhoneBlaster. It is a single-line fax system with limited fax-on-demand support. I include it because the PhoneBlaster is ideal for many small offices and home offices with a peer-to-peer LAN.

Mustang's Wildcat BBS has a fax-on-demand option. It is one way to combine remote LAN access methods. Mustang's BBS support was addressed in Chapter 5, so we will concentrate only on the fax support here.

Moving up a notch, we have Ibex's RoboFax. It supports one to four telephone lines and represents an inexpensive system that is suitable for small to medium-size companies. Ibex also sells a high-end system called FactsLine. It can be hooked up with a Lotus Notes database for sophisticated document distribution.

While OCR routing and fax-on-demand support are often provided in a stand-alone product, some fax server products include options for this type of support.

Mitek NIF: OCR Routing

Mitek Systems Inc. (San Diego, CA) sells a network fax server product called NIF. NIF lets you send and receive faxes just like a typical network fax server, but it routes incoming faxes using OCR.

NIF comes with front-end applications for creation and viewing of faxes on LAN workstations. It is designed to work with any network, although the fax server and LAN workstations are expected to run Microsoft Windows. Sending a fax can be done using the NIF front-end application or the NIF-supplied fax printer driver. The printer driver works just like drivers found in other fax products. You select the printer driver as the default printer and then print a document from any Windows application. The printer driver will prompt you for the name or names of the people who are to receive the fax. The driver then takes the information sent by the application and creates fax files to be sent later. These files will be used by the fax server when sending the fax.

Incoming faxes are received by the NIF fax server like any other fax server. It answers the incoming call, receives the fax, and saves it as a fax file on the server. It then hangs up the phone. At this point NIF's incoming routing procedure comes into play, as shown in Figure 6.14. The fax file is in a format that NIF's OCR support can read. The first page is converted to text by the OCR support. The text is then scanned for keywords like To and Dear. The text following these keywords is used to route the fax to the appropriate person's in box. You can add keywords to the default list, which is handy if you are expecting faxes from overseas.

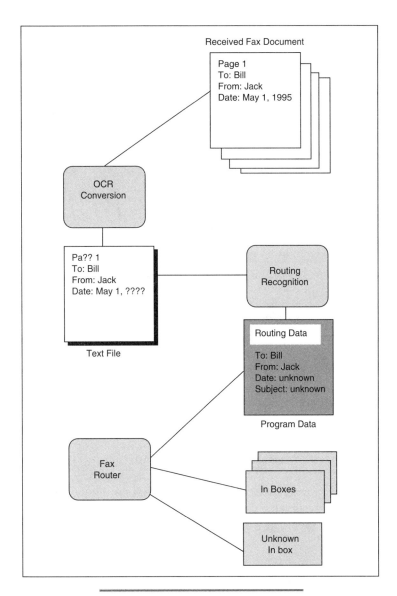

FIGURE 6.14 NIF OCR ROUTING DIAGRAM.

Once NIF has found potential routing text located near the keywords it uses this text to scan the address book for possible destinations. It compares the text using a variety of techniques, including checks for first names only. Address book entries also include a field where you can include intentional mispellings.

NIF's OCR support works well with printed faxes and with legible hand-printed text. Figure 6.15 shows a few samples of text that could and could not be used to route a fax automatically.

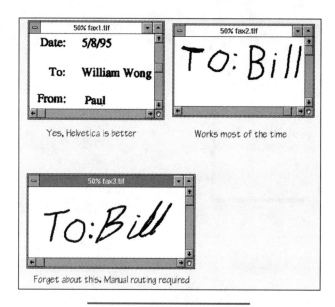

FIGURE 6.15 FIRST PAGE SAMPLES.

If the OCR support cannot figure out to whom to deliver the fax, then the fax is placed in the general in box, where it must be routed manually. This in box can have restricted access, or everyone can have access to it. In either case, someone must view the fax to see who should receive it and then forward it to the appropriate person.

NIF's OCR routing support is not unique, but not all fax servers provide this option. Since more faxes are being sent from computers, however, OCR routing makes sense.

U.S.Robotics Fax Server: Dedicated Network Fax Server

U.S. Robotics (Skokie, IL) is a well-known manufacturer of data and data/fax modems. It also sells communications and fax servers.

The SA FAX Server, shown in Figure 6.16, is the product we want to look at. It is designed to plug into an Ethernet or Token Ring Novell NetWare network and to support multiple fax lines. The fax lines can be set up to handle incoming or outgoing fax operations. It supports routing of incoming faxes using DTMF, caller ID, and OCR support; manual routing is the default. The fax software is based on FACSys for Windows and DOS from Optus Software, Inc.

Figure 6.16 SA FAX Server.

The SA FAX Server includes two serial ports, which are attached to external modems like the Sportster V.34 modem shown in Figure 6.17. This allows a single-line or dual-link configuration to be supported by each fax server. Multiple fax servers can be placed on one network.

Figure 6.17 U.S. Robotics Sportster V.34 modem.

Outgoing faxes are handled in the normal fashion. Front-end applications are provided for DOS and Windows from which incoming faxes can be viewed and files sent. Printer drivers are also included, so that applications can print directly to a fax printer driver, which prompts the user for the destination. The fax document is then handed over to the fax server, which sends it out at the appropriate time.

Incoming faxes are received by the fax server and kept on the Novell NetWare file server. The faxes can be routed automatically if the appropriate routing options are available. Users can pick up a fax at any workstation.

While a workstation can provide the same kind of support as the SA FAX Server, the SA FAX Server is more economical, compact, and secure than a workstation. There is no keyboard or monitor to contend with, and access to the server is restricted by passwords. A LAN manager can configure and control the server from any workstation on the network.

Creative Labs PhoneBlaster: Voice-Based Fax-On-Demand

Creative Labs PhoneBlaster is a multifunction ISA adapter that has a variety of features, as shown in Figure 6.18. I will also discuss the PhoneBlaster in Chapter 8, where its multimedia features are highlighted. The PhoneBlaster includes a Sound Blaster 16 audio board and an IDE CD-ROM interface, making it an ideal multimedia add-on to a workstation. It also contains a data/fax modem and DTMF and voice support on the telephone line. The data modem can be used with standard modem applications like terminal emulators. The fax modem can be used to send and receive faxes. The DTMF and voice support lets it provide a voice-mail system with optional fax-on-demand support. It is the fax-on-demand support that we want to examine in detail here.

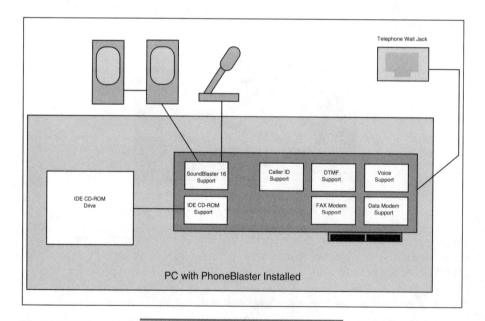

FIGURE 6.18 PHONEBLASTER ARCHITECTURE.

The PhoneBlaster comes bundled with a product called Ancilla from Kalman. It provides an integrated voice-mail system that also lets you send and receive faxes and allows callers to request faxes. The voice-mail system uses a fixed menuing system. You can record new voice prompts and add voice-mail boxes, but you cannot change the procedure used by the voice-mail system to prompt users or select what keys are to be pressed to perform particular functions. The advantage is instant availability once the hardware and software are installed; the disadvantage is limited customization.

The fax-on-demand support is linked to mail boxes. Up to 10 fax documents can be associated with a particular mail box. Figure 6.19 shows the fax-on-demand setup screen. The documents can be audibly annotated. A caller navigates through the voice prompts to pick up a fax document. Once they are at the mail box prompt, the caller can select the document and have the fax sent using the same telephone connection, or a phone number can be provided by the caller so the fax can be sent to another telephone line. The latter can be disabled to prevent callers from sending long-distance faxes without paying for them.

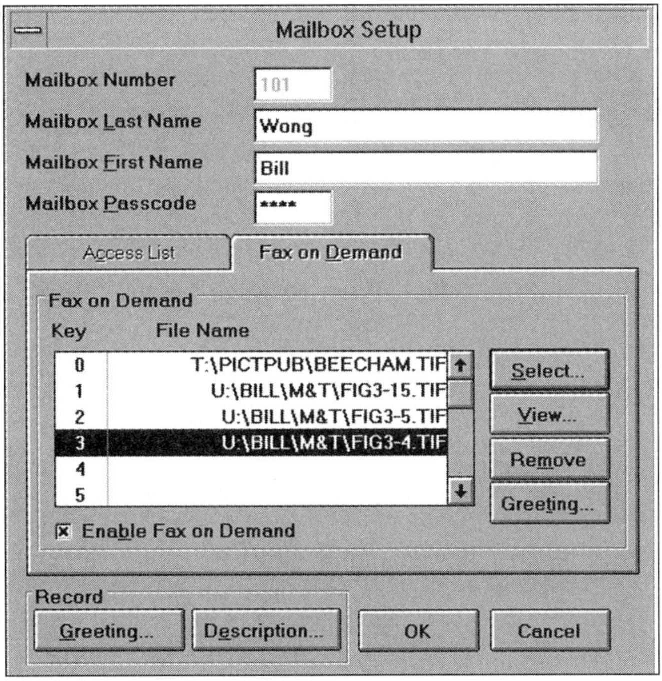

FIGURE 6.19 FAX-ON-DEMAND SETUP SCREEN.

While the voice-mail configuration is limited, it is more than adequate for a small office or home. The system is designed to operate on a stand-alone workstation, but you can easily incorporate it into a LAN environment and place the fax documents on a file server. The voice prompts can also be placed on the file server. Putting the files on a commonly accessible file server lets you change the prompts and documents from any workstation.

The PhoneBlaster hardware is more capable than the Ancilla software, and you may be able to find a third-party product that takes advantage of the hardware or is more flexible in the customization. The price is hard to beat, however; for less than $250 you get the hardware and bundled software. The price is about what you would pay for a modem or a multimedia audio board, so whatever way you look at it you get something for free.

Mustang's Wildcat BBS: BBS-Based Fax-On-Demand

Mustang's Wildcat BBS was highlighted in Chapter 5. As a remote LAN access method, a network BBS can provide a number of services, many of which are add-ons from the vendor or a third party. The fax-on-demand support is part of the wcPRO add-on that is available from Mustang. Figure 6.20 shows how the pieces fit together. The wcPRO module is software that works with a fax modem. The modem must be a data/fax modem if the BBS uses a single line. A Wildcat BBS can support multiple modems so that it is possible to use one fax modem for sending and the other data modems to allow users to access the BBS. Each modem requires its own telephone line.

The Wildcat fax-on-demand support allows a caller to request a fax document while interacting with the BBS. The user must be using a terminal-emulation program to access the BBS. The fax support is incorporated as part of the BBS menu structure by the system operator (sysop). Documents can be chosen from menu items or a file area. The caller chooses the documents and then supplies the telephone number of the fax machine to receive the documents. The BBS can support multiple users simultaneously using multiple modems. Fax requests are queued so that a single fax modem can be used to send faxes to multiple users, even though they may have requested the documents at the same time. Multiple fax modems can be used in high-demand situations.

A BBS has the advantage of being able to provide the caller with a fax or the file used to generate the fax. For example, a price list may be useful in printed form via a fax because it includes drawings. The file format may be one that the caller cannot print, so the fax is an ideal way of getting the price list. In other cases, the caller may be able to use the file and will download it using the terminal-emulation program instead. Another alternative is where a caller sends the fax to a different location. For example, a salesperson may want to fax the latest price list to a customer. The salesperson calls the BBS and selects the document, providing the customer's fax phone number as the destination.

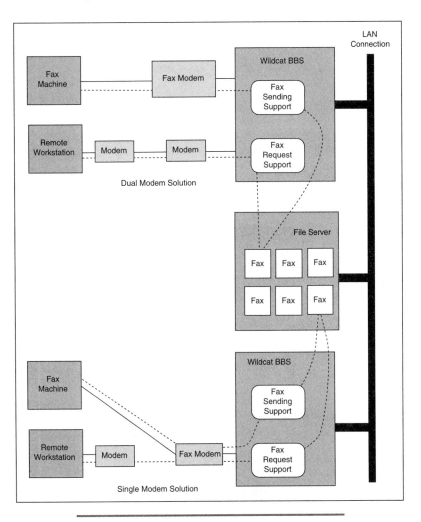

FIGURE 6.20 MUSTANG WILDCAT BBS FAX ARCHITECTURE.

The BBS has the advantage of being able to provide more details about the files than a voice-prompting system. It is also possible to create a file describing some or all of the documents that are available so the file can be downloaded and reviewed off-line. Voice-mail systems cannot provide this type of information in a timely fashion. The closest approximation is to have a fax document that contains a list of documents and their descriptions so that a caller can download that document first.

Adding fax-on-demand to a BBS is relatively easy. For a company with a single-line BBS and a data/fax modem, it is an ideal low-cost solution.

Ibex RoboFax and FactsLine: Fax-On-Demand

Ibex Technology Inc. (Placerville, CA) sells two fax-on-demand products: RoboFax and FactsLine.

RoboFax uses a voice/fax board from National Semiconductor, shown in Figure 6.21. A fax-on-demand server can use up to four boards. Large installations will want to check out Ibex's FactsLine product. The single-line version of RoboFax is called RoboFax-Pro Lite, while the more expensive multiline version is named RoboFax-Pro. A single-line system costs less than $800.

FIGURE 6.21 ROBOFAX ADAPTER.

Figure 6.23 shows RoboFax's architecture. One to four voice/fax boards are plugged into a standard IBM-compatible PC. The PC may be a workstation on a LAN or a stand-alone workstation. Fax documents can be located on the workstation's hard disk or on the LAN. Placing the files on a LAN's file server allows the documents to be updated from any workstation on the LAN. The menu system is kept in a database, which can be modified only when the fax-on-demand server is not running the RoboFax software, so it is usually a good idea to keep the database on a workstation where it cannot be accidentally updated.

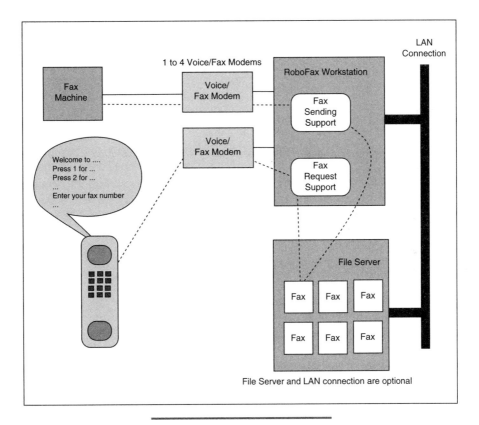

Figure 6.22 RoboFax architecture.

RoboFax uses the standard voice-prompt system with DTMF support to detect a caller's response using a Touch-Tone telephone. The voice-prompt menu design program is included with the software. It allows for complete design of the menu structure as opposed to the PhoneBlaster, where the menu structure is fixed. You need to record your own voice prompts using a microphone supplied with the product. Passwords can be used within the menu structure to limit access to particular documents. For example, end-user price lists can be generally available, while a password would be necessary to request OEM pricing.

Each line in a multiline system can be configured differently. For example, one line could be set up for tech support with associated documents, while another line is set up for customer service with pricing documents and testimonials.

RoboFax lets you track callers and document requests; this can be useful in determining what kinds of documents are requested most often. It can also assist in upgrade planning. Document files kept on a file server can be updated while the fax-on-demand server is running, but the documents are in a fax format so they must be converted before they are saved. The extra step is minor, but users that update files must be made aware of the requirement. RoboFax does no on-the-fly conversion of text files to fax files. For more automatic update procedures, check out Ibex's FactsLine product.

Callers use the typical fax-on-demand voice menu system to request a document. After placing the initial call, the caller hears a prompt indicating the kind of service being provided along with options that can be selected. Using the Touch-Tone telephone keys, a caller navigates through the menu system until he or she can select the desired documents. After the documents are selected, RoboFax will ask whether the fax should be sent immediately using the current telephone connection or as soon as possible after the caller hangs up. RoboFax can be set up to only send faxes to telephone numbers within specific area codes or with specific prefixes, or the call-back support can be completely disabled, forcing the caller to receive the fax using the same connection used to request it.

The FactsLine product line is rather extensive, and I will not cover it in detail. It is operationally similar to RoboFax, but the voice and fax boards can be separated. This architecture is more flexible and economical in larger installations, where incoming calls are always handled by voice boards and faxes are send by a bank of fax modems.

FactsLine includes a number of different products centered around the fax-on-demand module. FactsLine for Notes lets a Lotus Notes document database supply documents for faxing. A programming interface to FactsLine lets custom applications to be written. A custom application could allow a caller to request that the current status of the LAN be sent in a fax. The application would obtain the information about the LAN, print it to a fax printer driver, and direct the fax to the appropriate fax machine using the FactsLine server. Applications can also be written using Lotus Notes if the FactsLine for Notes product is used.

Some fax-on-demand products can be integrated with voice-mail systems, although most fax-on-demand systems are designed to be used with their own telephone lines. Larger companies can make it appear that the two are integrated by allowing the voice-mail system to forward a call to the fax-on-demand telephone lines, at which point the caller deals with the fax-on-demand system.

Fax-on-demand represents a popular way to access documents on a LAN. Unlike other remote LAN access methods, fax-on-demand can be used without a computer. In fact, if you use someone else's fax machine, all you need is a Touch-Tone telephone.

CHAPTER 7

WIRELESS CONNECTIONS

A wireless LAN connection is more than a dream. It is a reality in a number of different forms, from infrared systems to radio-based systems, including cellular telephone technology. Wireless technology lets you connect a computer to another computer without wires for at least part of the connection. For example, a standard modem can be attached to a cellular telephone to make a connection with a LAN. When you make a call, the connection is from the remote workstation, to the modem, and then to the cellular telephone; the wireless connection is between the cellular telephone and the telephone company's local cell, which contains a radio receiver and transmitter. The connection becomes wired at this point, and it goes through the local telephone company (possibly through a long distance network to the local telephone company), and then to the LAN modem that is attached to a workstation or communications server.

WIRELESS CONNECTIONS

There are three types of wireless technology appropriate for remote LAN access: cellular telephone, cellular digital packetized data (CDPD,) and wireless network interface cards (NIC).

Cellular telephone support uses the standard cellular telephone network used with voice cellular telephones. The cellular telephone and modem example just presented uses the modem with conventional modem-based applications. It is appropriate for any of the remote LAN access methods already presented in earlier chapters; the only difference is that the connection includes a wireless segment. A *cellular modem* includes both the modem and the cellular telephone in one handy package. They are often used with laptops, implemented as PCMCIA cards that plug into the laptop.

Cellular telephone–based systems have the advantage of being supported over a large area, essentially wherever cellular voice support is available (see Figure 7.1). They can be used for local calls or long distance calls. The disadvantage is the use of analog modems, which have a top speed of 28,800 baud with a V.34 modem. Cellular telephone connection quality is variable and often lower than a wired telephone connection, so maximum throughput is not always available. Newer digital voice cellular telephones provide better quality connections, but the modem connection is still analog. The digital cellular telephone converts the modem's analog signals to digital, then transmits the digital information to the cellular telephone company's nearest cell, where it is converted back to an analog signal. Actually, some telephone companies keep the digital information intact and pass it to the local telephone company in digital form, but it still gets converted to analog form when it reaches the modem at the other end of the connection.

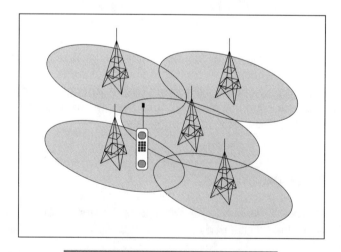

FIGURE 7.1 A CELLULAR TELEPHONE NETWORK.

CDPD uses the same kind of technology as the voice-based cellular telephones, except that the data from the remote workstation is not converted into analog form. The CDPD adapters are typically implemented as PCMCIA cards for laptops.

CDPD devices use their own cellular network, just like the voice-based system. Although a cellular telephone company can implement cells with both CDPD and voice support, they can also be implemented independently, possibly by different companies, because they use different radio frequencies.

CDPD support, at the workstation end, operates differently from a modem; software is specifically designed to work with current CDPD systems. The reason for this difference is the way CDPD systems operate. Voice-based systems require constant data transmission, but CDPD systems send and receive data in small blocks called *packets*. CDPD systems also handle reliable transmission from the mobile user to the cell. Data that is not received is retransmitted. The software that provides CDPD support is written for the CDPD hardware, not for a serial modem.

CDPD has found wide acceptance with remote mail support. Typically, a mail application resides on the remote workstation and uses the CDPD hardware to send and receive mail through a mail gateway (see Figure 7.2). The mail gateway is connected to a post office that the CDPD company maintains. Mail can be picked up using another CDPD-equipped laptop or from a workstation equipped with a modem. The modem is used to connect with another mail gateway for wired telephone connections.

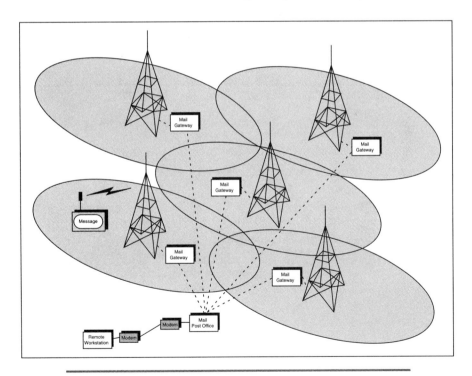

FIGURE 7.2 A CDPD NETWORK WITH MAIL GATEWAYS AND A POST OFFICE.

Voice-based cellular modems and CDPD setups are designed for medium to long distance wireless support; wireless NIC support is designed for very local connections, from ten to as much as a couple of thousand feet. The maximum distance is not far enough to travel across town, and it is often not even enough to travel across the street. The advantage over other wireless systems is speed: wireless NICs operate at speeds that are much faster than modems or CDPD systems. Wireless NIC speeds range from 100,000 bits per second to 2,500,000 bits per second (2.5 Mbps), which is many times faster than modem or CDPD connections, although it is slower than typical LAN NIC speeds such as Ethernet or Token Ring NICs, which run at 10 Mbps and 16 Mbps, respectively.

Wireless NIC support uses an architecture that is similar to cellular systems, as shown in Figure 7.3. The four main differences are speed of transmission, maximum transmission distance, data transfer protocol, and connection to a LAN. Cellular and CDPD data transmission speeds are low; distance is higher than a wireless NIC; they all use their own transmission protocols; and they do not connect directly to your LAN. Wireless NICs have higher transmission speeds, operate at smaller distances, use a LAN protocol, and are connected directly to a LAN.

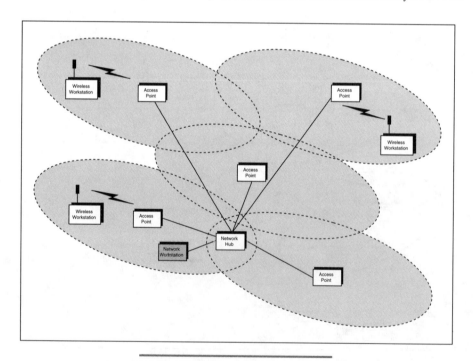

Figure 7.3 Wireless NIC architecture.

From a user's perspective, a wireless NIC operates the same way as one connected directly to a LAN. The user's workstation runs the same applications and accesses data directly from the LAN. A user logs in using the same procedure and network program on either a wired or wireless workstation.

This chapter concentrates on the wireless NIC products. Cellular and CDPD products involve a different class of problems. The methods presented in prior chapters can be used with these types of products; cellular telephones that are connected to a modem can be used with any method that requires a normal modem. The CDPD products normally integrate with a mail gateway, so Chapter 2 is the best place to look for more operational details.

Wireless NIC products can be divided into two categories: *infrared* (IR) and radio. IR wireless NICs use the same technology used by television remote control units. The main difference between the remote control and the IR NIC is that the NIC has both an IR transmitter and an IR receiver, while the remote control can only transmit. Transmission distances are typically limited to 25 feet, with transmission speeds being about 100 to 400 kbps. IR NICs consume very little power and can be very compact. IR radiation is harmless and can bounce off ceilings and walls, so a pair of NICs does not have to be within sight of each other to operate.

Radio-based NICs also do not have to be within sight of each other, since radio waves can pass through objects like walls and ceilings. Unfortunately, radio waves from radio-based NICs can be attenuated (weakened) or stopped by a variety of building materials, including concrete and most metals. Still, the coverage for a radio-based NIC is normally much greater than that for an IR-based NIC. A radio-based NIC has its best transmission distance out in the open (as in a field). Typically, such transmission distances are 1000 feet, but transmission distances in a typical office environment for the same hardware are about 250 feet.

Wireless NICs are not just for laptops. Wireless NIC products are useful alternatives to wired LANs for desktop machines under many circumstances. For example, do you need a temporary LAN connection for a new workstation before a network cable can be pulled to the workstation? Or is it impractical to run network cables? If you think the latter is unlikely, consider a rented office, where you do not want to have wires running all over the floor. Or consider a receptionist in the middle of an atrium in a historical building. There may be a telephone connection and power for a workstation, but you may not have planned for a network connection. A wireless NIC can handle these situations with ease and often at a much lower cost.

Of course, the typical reason for using wireless NICs is to support a mobile staff within the office. Hospitals are prime examples. Doctors and nurses travel all over the building, but they need access to patient information, usually kept in a database on the hospital's file server. Putting workstations at prime locations is one solution, but then a user must find an unused workstation to access the file server. A wireless system lets them carry a palmtop or laptop computer everywhere, providing instant access to the file server. Pen-based computers allow many tasks to be done in the same way as a hard copy environment. A doctor can write down a patient's status and have the information logged directly into the database.

Another environment where wireless NICs are ideal is in the home or small office. Home offices with networks or homes with a pair of computers (like a laptop and a desktop) are becoming more common, and wiring up your house with a network is not most people's idea of fun. I actually have part of my house wired, but I find wireless NICs to still be useful. There are no wires to pull, just another NIC to plug in. A small-office environment is also ideal for wireless NIC support because of the limited distance from one end of the office to the other. In fact, the entire network can be wireless. Unfortunately, larger office environments cannot be served in this fashion, and the lower transmission speed can also be a limiting factor. Luckily, there are alternatives offered by all wireless NIC vendors.

Most wireless NIC systems are built around devices called *access points* or *bridges*. An *access point* contains a wireless NIC and a wired NIC such as an Ethernet NIC. The access point is connected to a wired LAN and acts as a bridge between wireless workstations and the workstations and servers connected to a wired LAN, as shown in Figure 7.4. File servers can be located far away from the wireless workstations and the access point. The access point buffers the data going between the wireless workstations and the LAN, because the two normally operate at different speeds. A common configuration is a radio-based NIC with a 2 Mbps speed connected to a 10 Mbps Ethernet LAN. The *bridge* prevents the wired LAN from slowing down. Workstations connected directly to the LAN that access a file server directly connected to the LAN operate at the faster speed. A wireless workstation accessing a file server wired to the LAN sends data between the wireless workstation and the access point at the slower speed, and the access point then sends the data to the file server at the faster speed.

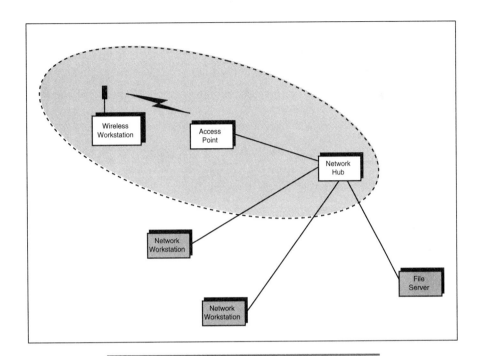

FIGURE 7.4 A WIRELESS NIC WITH A SINGLE ACCESS POINT.

Using multiple access points, as shown in Figure 7.5, is one way to support many wireless workstations. Placing all the access points onto the same LAN allows communication between wireless workstations that use different access points. It is even possible to have a wireless file server accessed from a wireless workstation with the wired LAN providing part of the connection. Multiple access points can provide coverage for an entire building or even a collection of buildings that also includes a wired LAN.

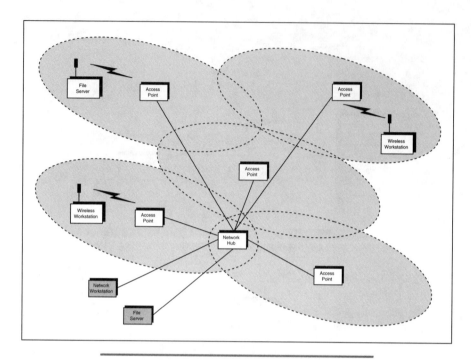

FIGURE 7.5 A WIRELESS NIC WITH SEVERAL ACCESS POINTS.

Almost all wireless NIC vendors provide access points that support *roaming*. *Roaming* with wireless NICs operates just like roaming in a cellular telephone network; a wireless NIC access point corresponds to a cell in the cellular network. A cell's reception and transmission area overlaps that of adjacent cells, so a person using a cellular telephone can always reach at least one cell. The same is true with wireless NICs and access points. The software in the NIC and the access points can allow the NIC to switch from one access point to another as the NIC, and the workstation or laptop to which it is attached, is moved, as shown in Figure 7.6. Good software makes the switch automatically and transparently, so a mobile user does not lose a network connection during the transition; poor software makes the switch but forces the mobile user to log onto the network again. Good software can also notify you, visually or audibly, when a connection is lost, and will automatically reconnect when you move back into an area where the connection can be restored.

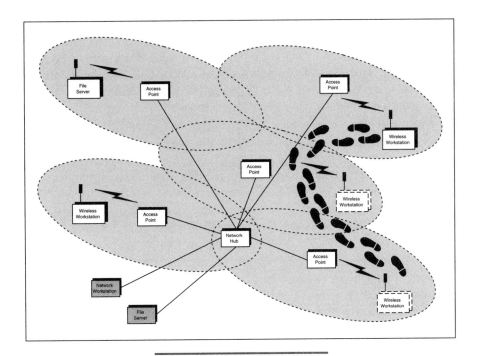

FIGURE 7.6 WIRELESS NIC ROAMING.

Access points are comparatively expensive and sometimes bulky devices. They typically cost two to four times what a wireless NIC alone costs. Hardware costs continue to drop, but at the time this book was written a wireless NIC would run you about $400, while an access point costs around $1200. A typical ISA Ethernet NIC costs less than $200, with inexpensive Ethernet NICs coming in under $60. Access point cost makes their placement critical, unless you can afford to install and maintain as many access points as are needed to easily cover a particular area. This is especially true for IR-based systems with a limited transmission distance. More IR access points are required to cover the same area compared to radio-based access points. Typically access points are placed in the middle of a work area or in key locations such as a conference room or auditorium.

Unlike some remote LAN connection methods, wireless NICs require network drivers that are compatible with the network operating system (NOS) used on the LAN. A network driver provides NOS support programs with access to the

NIC. Most wireless NICs come with the same type of drivers that come with wired NICs. The two most popular DOS drivers are Open Data Interface (ODI) and Network Driver Interface Specification (NDIS) drivers. ODI drivers are primarily used for Novell Networks. IPX drivers also provide access to Novell NetWare, but are superceded by ODI drivers. NDIS drivers can be used with almost any network operating system including Novell NetWare, although ODI drivers are preferable.

NICs used on a Novell Netware 3.x or 4.x file server need a server version of the ODI drivers; these are not always available and the DOS ODI driver is not inter-changeable with them. A wireless NIC that does not include a server ODI driver can still be used on a workstation and can provide access to a Novell file server though an access point. The same technique must be used for most other NOSes because the necessary drivers are rarely available. Placement of a wireless NIC in a file server is unusual, since the file server is rarely placed in a central location and users are better served by one or more centrally located access points instead.

Wireless NICs are not the remote LAN access solution for people who need medium to long distance connections, but wireless NICs are often the only alter-native for connections within the office and home environment. Although wireless NICs are more expensive and slower than their wired counterparts, they are often suitable for general use when you consider the ease of installation and the poten-tial mobility they provide.

A USER'S VIEW OF WIRELESS CONNECTIONS

For the time being we will assume that the wireless NIC has already been installed by the LAN manager. The procedure is actually no different from installing a NIC for a wired LAN like Ethernet, which users do all the time, but for this section we are concentrating on what a user sees when using a wireless NIC. For purposes of discussion we will refer to a workstation with a wireless NIC as a *mobile workstation*, even though it may be a desktop workstation that is never moved. A workstation with a NIC that connects to the LAN via cable will be called a *fixed workstation*.

The difference in what a user sees on a mobile workstation compared to a fixed workstation is almost nil. The status information displayed when the NIC device driver is loaded will be different because the NIC and driver are different, but that is about it; actually, there is another difference you don't see, related to the speed of the wireless NICs.

Because the wireless NICs transfer rate is slower than wired NICs, moving data between a mobile workstation and the LAN is slower than with a fixed workstation. The slower transfer rate makes file transfers slower, which will be noticeable when loading or saving documents. Database access programs that use data on the LAN will also run more slowly. Usually the difference in performance will be noticeable but not unbearable for files smaller than 1 MB. Larger files can extend the transfer time to impractical limits. This is especially true of today's programs, which themselves are larger than 1 MB and rely on additional modules, which also tend to be large. The trick to using the programs is to move large, often-used applications and support files from the network to the workstation to minimize the amount of LAN traffic generated. A desktop often has enough disk space to accommodate the application files, but laptop hard disks are often smaller, so the necessary files need to be selectively copied.

The wireless link is suitable for downloading the selected files, even if they amount to tens of megabytes since the transfer is only done once. Using batch files or a file-management program, you can start up the copy operation and let it run while you have a snack. An added benefit is faster application startup, since your local hard disk is faster than a LAN connection.

While slower access to LAN data will add a noticeable delay in the response time of your applications, the situation can get worse if you are a mobile user. Radio and IR signal strength diminish the farther you get from the transmitter. Wireless NIC throughput is not directly proportional to the distance between a transmitter and receiver, but they can change their throughput characteristics depending on the implementation. The worst case is all or nothing: either the NIC works at its specified speed or it does not work at all. Luckily most wireless NICs are more robust. As the distance between a transmitter and receiver increases and the quality of the signal at the receiver decreases, the wireless NIC reduces its speed. The reduction is normally done in fixed steps like 75%, 50%, and 25% of the maximum limit. The change in speed is automatic and transparent to the program, but not to you. Cutting throughput in half can significantly increase the response time delay, depending on how much of the response time is due to accessing LAN data.

Unfortunately, most software provided with a wireless NIC does not let you know when it changes its throughput or even when a connection is lost; often the only indication is slower response time or the NOS reporting a lost connection. Unfortunately, a user will often take a delayed response as a program or operating system failure and reboot the PC. Rebooting the PC can cause a loss of information or a corrupted database on the LAN.

There are ways to make using a wireless NIC easier, depending on your needs. For example, if your data files are small, then keeping them on the wireless workstation will be practical. The files can be copied from the network when needed and copied back to the network when you are done working with them. The advantage is fast and uninterrupted access to the data files while they are on the workstation. The disadvantage is the additional work required to copy the file to or from the network file server.

Copying data files is often impractical. The alternative is to keep a reliable connection with the network. For mobile users this means staying in a fixed location as much as possible, or else making sure that access points cover the area to be traversed, thereby minimizing the possibility of a degraded or broken connection.

The other alternative is to experiment. It is better to know where a problem might occur and what may happen. Often, a broken connection between a wireless workstation and the network will result in temporary inaccessibility; it can also result in the loss of data or, worse, the corruption of data on the network. The degree and possibility of problems vary greatly with the applications and data involved. For example, a word processor can often recover from the inability to save a file on the network and allow you to save the file on the wireless workstation. Unfortunately, many database applications will create a corrupted database if the connection breaks between the database application on the wireless workstation and the database file on the network file server. Some database applications are more robust.

Wireless NICs provide many advantages, such as mobility and elimination of wires. The tradeoff is speed and reliable connections. Being prepared for the disadvantages makes living with wireless support much easier.

A LAN Manager's View of Wireless Connections

Installing and managing a wireless LAN or adding wireless support to an existing LAN is not much different from adding additional workstations to a LAN. The NICs need to be installed and the support software must be set up on the wireless workstations. Access points must be installed and connected to the existing LAN. That's it.

Oh, if only using wireless networks were so easy! Actually, installing NICs and access points is just part of the job. The other parts come before and after the installation. Before installing a wireless LAN you will want to do some research into the advantages and limitations of the specific wireless NIC you will be installing. Transmission speed and distance will be readily available from product information, but these represent only the upper limit. Unlike wired LANs, wireless LANs usually operate under less than optimal conditions. Although optimal conditions are not necessary for maximum throughput, a wireless NIC's throughput will degrade when conditions become very poor. Transmission conditions are affected by a number of conditions, including distance, objects between the NIC and the access point, position of the antennas, and interference. A site survey program can help you figure out how all these variables will affect your wireless LAN.

Some vendors supply a site survey program with their products. You can also build your own without too much trouble, but more on this later. A *site survey program* runs on a mobile workstation, and it indicates the quality of the connection between the mobile workstation and the LAN. Unfortunately, the site survey program only tells you the quality of the connection for the workstation in a particular position; you need to move around and record the results to get an overall view of wireless LAN conditions. Doing a site survey for a small office with one or two access points should not take too long, maybe half an hour. Doing a site survey for a larger building will take longer. Figure 7.7 shows what a simple site survey result might look like.

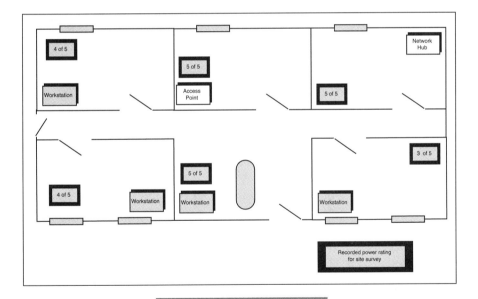

FIGURE 7.7 A SITE SURVEY EXAMPLE.

There are three problems with site survey results. First, you need to have the access points installed. Second, adding or moving an access point will change a site's wireless characteristics, although it should not affect locations that are *far* from the access point. "Far" indicates another access point is between the "far" location and the access point that is moved. For example, your workstation is near access point A. Access point A is between your workstation and Access point B . Your workstation is far from access point B and would be unaffected if access point B is moved. Finally, the site survey is specific to the time you make it. Usually the results and the operation of the wireless LAN will remain the same as long as the access points are not moved, but many other things can change the results. For example, adding a new wall or partition between an access point and a wireless workstation, or the addition of a device that adds interference, such as a cordless telephone, can change the results. Luckily most sites change little on a regular basis.

The site survey programs provided by wireless NIC vendors normally show signal strength and throughput, often as a percentage of the NIC's maximum throughput. Building your own site survey program is not too difficult. All you need is a way to copy data between the LAN and the mobile workstation, simultaneously indicating how the transfer is progressing. For a DOS-based workstation, I built a batch file that continuously copied a small file. The **Copy** command indicates when the operation is complete, so all I need to do is watch the rate at which the status indications are displayed to see when the transmission characteristics change. The following batch file was used for this test:

```
@ECHO OFF
:LOOP
ECHO Copying file
COPY F:\TEST.DAT NUL
GOTO LOOP
```

The network file server drive is **F:** and the **TEST.DAT** file can be any small file under a few thousand bytes. The **NUL** file is not actually a disk file. The **Copy** command copies the **TEST.DAT** file from the file server but does nothing with the data. It does copy the data using the network interface which is what we want. If the status is displayed too quickly, simply increase the size of the data file. This increases the transfer time and slows down the status display. The display looks something like this:

```
Copying file
1 File(s) copied
Copying file
1 File(s) copied
Copying file
1 File(s) copied
```

The batch file is not the greatest site survey tool but it is quite effective and it works. Positioning the access points and doing the site survey is just the start. You may have to reposition the access points or add access points after completing your initial site survey if the coverage provided by the site survey indicates potential problems.

Ok, you have the site survey done and the NICs installed, what next? You can let your users run, wild or you can educate them and help them understand the advantages and limitations of their new mobility. You may want to determine what applications and files will be placed on workstations, and what applications and files will be left on the file server and accessed from the mobile workstations. They must also be aware of the throughput limitations and distance limitations of the wireless network.

SHORTCUT

Providing a map of usable areas to users will help head off problems before they occur. No sense in getting a complaint that a wireless laptop does not work in the cafeteria when you never set up an access point to do so.

While working with users you will also want to find out what applications are in use and how they affect the LAN. You may already have this information available, but you should get it if you don't. Two aspects of LAN-application interaction need to be determined. The first is the amount of data transferred across the LAN by an application. Applications that transfer large amounts of data, either continuously or in bursts, need to be examined in the context of the wireless NIC's throughput capabilities. Users need to be made aware of any application which might cause unusual delays due to the amount of data and the NIC's maximum throughput. The second aspect is a bit more technical. Most applications deal with a file server an application server on a one-to-one basis, but some applications use a one-to-many, or *broadcast mode*, of operation.

Broadcast mode occurs when an application needs to communicate with many other workstations at one time. It does so by sending data in broadcast mode. All workstations receive broadcast messages but most typically ignore the messages. Only workstations that need the data will process it. The content of the message indicates which workstations need to process the message. The problem with broadcast messages on a wireless LAN is the amount of possibly unnecessary LAN traffic that is generated. Broadcast traffic that may cause a minimal load on a wired LAN may overwhelm a wireless LAN. For example, 10% broadcast traffic on a 10 Mbps Ethernet LAN uses 1 Mbps worth of bandwidth, but on a 1.5 Mbps wireless LAN it is over 60%. That does not leave much for non-broadcast traffic.

A further problem is that enough broadcast traffic to bring a wireless LAN to its knees can be generated by workstations on the *wired* portion of the LAN. Broadcast traffic is often generated by multiplayer network games or some network management tools. Preventing the use of these programs is one way to reduce or eliminate broadcast traffic. Another way is to split up the LAN into segments. Larger LANs are normally split into multiple segments for reasons of performance and reliability, because a file server will have one NIC for each segment. Broadcast traffic is often limited to or can be limited to the segment in which it is generated. Placing the wireless system on its own segment keeps broadcast traffic from other wired workstations from overwhelming the wireless portion of the LAN. Some NOSes let you logically partition a segment. The file server uses a single NIC to communicate with a single segment, but the workstations on the physical segment are assigned to a logical segment. Broadcast messages are sent to the logical segment, not the physical segment. For example, workstations A and B are on logical segment 1 and C and D are on segment 2. The file server sends a broadcast message to segment 1. Workstations A and B process the message while c and d ignore it.

I would like to digress for a moment. Most wireless NICs are installed on laptop or portable computers. Most NICs for this type of workstation are PCMCIA adapters. Unfortunately, the software drivers for DOS often use a large amount of low memory (low memory is the lowest 640 Kbytes). Low amounts of free low memory can cause problems with DOS and Windows applications. This might not be a problem if DOS and Windows combined did not make up the majority of operating systems found on wireless workstations, but they do. This particular problem is not specific to wireless NICs, but it is a problem that most LAN managers will run into when installing a wireless LAN.

Another issue with wireless NIC drivers is whether the NOS and the wireless NIC drivers gracefully handle a temporary break in the wireless connection, often encountered as a mobile user is working near the fringe of an area supported by an access point. Good drivers will let you know, either by a tone or a visual cue, when the wireless connection is degrading or lost. Better drivers will also automatically and transparently *restore the connection* when you move back into range. Poor drivers do neither and you may have to reboot the workstation to restore the connection, often losing any work in progress.

Finally, back to overall LAN management issues. Most access points come with or support remote management tools. These tools run on a workstation, wired or wireless, and let a LAN manager configure the access point or check its operation. SNMP support is often included, and it allows third-party products to manage the access point. SNMP support is useful if you use SNMP to manage other network devices.

Security is an item that is often implemented transparently to users. Network security handles a user's access to the network, but most wireless NICs will transmit unencrypted LAN information. In theory, it is possible to receive the information sent by a wireless NIC and examine it, although this can be difficult in practice, depending upon the wireless technology used. Some LANs require a more secure environment than this; if you need a higher level of security you can see if the wireless NIC will support automatic encryption or if the NOS supports encryption. Data sent from a mobile workstation to the LAN is first encrypted at the NIC using a key, so the data originally sent to the access point does not look anything like the data sent by the mobile workstation to the wireless NIC. Then the access point uses a matching key to decrypt the data and send it on its way. Network operating systems that use encryption do so at the device-driver level, and the data is passed across both the wireless and wired LAN in encrypted form. Encryption essentially prevents LAN eavesdropping.

As far as remote LAN access methods go, wireless NICs are the easiest to implement and the easiest to use. They do require user education, but this is also true for other remote LAN access methods.

WHAT ARE WIRELESS CONNECTIONS AND HOW DO THEY WORK?

There are two types of wireless LAN connection systems. One is based on infrared radiation (IR) and the other is based on radio. IR is the same technology used with most television remote control units. Although IR may sound threatening, it is harmless. It requires very little power to operate, making it an ideal candidate for laptop operation. Radio-based wireless NICs are implemented using one of two technologies: *fixed frequency* or *spread spectrum*. *Fixed frequency* uses one frequency at all times. *Spread spectrum* uses a number of different frequencies. The different frequencies are often a set of fixed frequencies, but the wireless NIC may utilize only some of these frequencies. The NIC may use one frequency at a time and rapidly switch between frequencies. Frequencies are chosen by a spread-spectrum NIC based on the quality of the connection for a particular frequency. Two different frequencies can have different performance characteristics, even though the NIC and the access point are in the same position. The difference is due to differences in attenuation. Spread spectrum tends to be more robust and less prone to eavesdropping.

Both IR and radio wireless NICs operate using the same general technique. The wireless NIC contains both a transmitter and receiver. These are used to communicate with another NIC within range or with an access point, which also contains a wireless NIC. The access point is a bridge between the wireless LAN and the wired LAN. The access point also has a NIC for the wired LAN. The access point passes data between the wireless LAN and the wired LAN. It buffers data going in either direction; it must do so because the two LANs operate at different speeds. Buffering at an access point allows wired LAN-based workstations or servers to send multiple data packets to the access point before the first has been completely sent to the wireless workstation as shown in Figure 7.8.

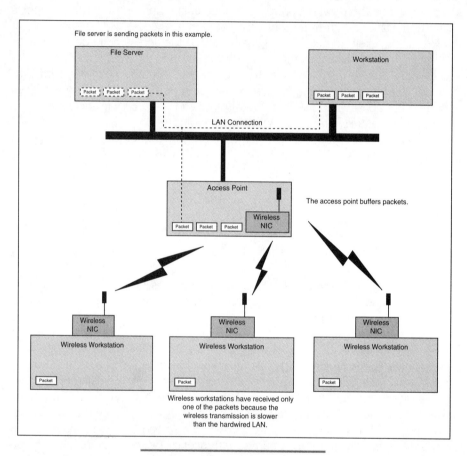

Figure 7.8 Access, point buffering.

IR transmitters and receivers are *optical* but IR is *invisible* to the naked eye. Ultraviolet and infared light are invisible but they are still light. If you look closely at an IR transmitter (no, it won't hurt you), you may be able to detect a visible flash but this is because the transmitter is also sending light in the visible spectrum as well. The optical aspect of an IR-based NIC explains its advantages and restrictions. An IR-based NIC will not work if you cover either the transmitter or receiver (yes, they are usually distinct although often adjacent). Most IR-based NICs work if the infrared radiation reflects off a wall or ceiling. To get an idea how this works, just consider a light bulb at the far end of the room. Even if you move out of the door into a darkened hallway, you will still see the light from the bulb, which may be reflected off many walls and even the floor and ceiling. IR reflects in the same ways, and the IR receiver works like your eye does, with visible light.

IR-based NICs will not transmit through walls, but you can bounce IR over partitions that are open at the top. Drop ceilings are fine for reflecting IR, but a recessed light, often found with drop ceilings, can trap IR as shown in Figure 7.9.

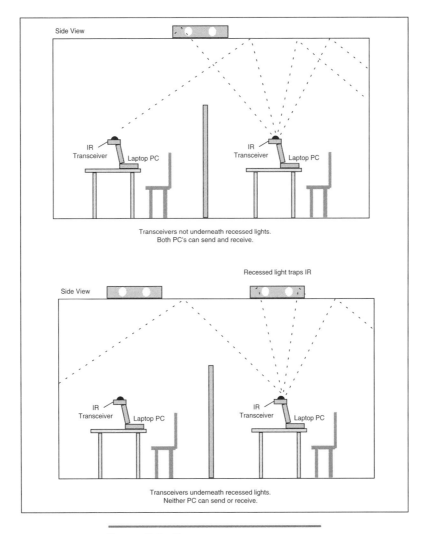

FIGURE 7.9 IR BOUNCE WITH DROP CEILINGS.

Radio-based NICs have a transmitter and receiver but both share a common antenna. The antenna often extends outward from the NIC, although some radio-based NICs incorporate the antenna into the body of the NIC, making it appear as if it has no antenna.

Radio transmission tends to be point-to-point, but radio waves can go through many materials with minimal attenuation. Drywall, wood and other building materials are almost invisible to radio waves, which makes radio-based NIC's a good choice for an office with lots of walls. Unfortunately, you also need to consider what else is in the wall. Metal can reflect or significantly attenuate radio waves. Metal beams and metal in concrete effective stop radio waves, at least those from the low-power transmitters found in wireless NICs. This is one reason why radio-based access points often work well within the same floor of a multi-floor office building but not between floors. The solution is to put access points on each floor.

WHY USE WIRELESS CONNECTIONS FOR REMOTE LAN ACCESS?

Wireless Connections have a number of advantages and disadvantages when used to remotely access a LAN. The following list summarizes these.

Advantages

Free connection time (does not require telephone)

Wireless operation

Reduced wiring costs

Transparent network access

Relatively high transfer rate compared to other remote access methods

Disadvantages

Limited distance

Relatively low transfer rate compared to wired LANs

Access point costs

Access points required to cover large areas

Limited number of users per access point

On the plus side, wireless connections normally have no connection time. Other remote LAN access methods utilize a telephone connection, which is usually charged on a monthly rate or by the minute. The amount is based on the distance of the connection. Wireless connections do not use the telephone company and typically have no operating cost associated with them. Like a wired LAN workstation user, a mobile workstation user will connect to the LAN arbitrarily and stay connected without concern as to cost.

Wireless operation is the main reason to choose a wireless LAN. Mobile users can access the LAN whether they are in their offices or down the hall in the conference room.

Wireless LANs reduce wiring costs, at least for the wireless workstations. Additional wiring may be necessary when adding access points, but often existing LAN wiring can be used for access points. The cost savings can often offset the cost of the wireless NIC.

Mobile users have the same form of network access as users of wired LAN workstations. LAN access is transparent to the fact that a wireless connection is used. Well, not fully transparent; it *is* possible to break a wireless LAN connection by moving the wireless workstation, which is not possible with a wired workstation.

Wireless NICs have a relatively high transfer rate compared to other remote LAN access methods. A typical wireless NIC throughput is 1 Mbps. The typical modem-based remote LAN access method using a V.34 modem runs at 28,800 baud, or almost 40 times slower.

On the minus side, wireless NICs have a limited operating distance, on the order of 500 feet. Other wireless technologies like CDPD operate at cellular telephone distances, but the throughput is significantly lower than wireless NIC throughput. CDPD-type wireless approaches are also more comparable to modem-based remote access systems.

Wireless NICs also have a slower throughput compared to wired LAN NICs. Typical wireless NICs operate at 1 Mbps, whereas Ethernet and Token Ring, the two most popular wired LAN technologies, run at 10 Mbps and 16 Mbps respectively. Wireless NICs are increasing in speed but so is wired LAN technology. 100 Mbps Ethernet is just one technology that is currently available.

The cost of access points can be an issue with wireless LANs. Many wired LANs employ hubs, which are conceptually the same thing as an access point. In theory, the cost of a wireless LAN access point can be offset against the cost of a wired hub. Unfortunately, the cost difference is often large. At this time an access point costs about $1500 while a basic 8-port Ethernet hub is one tenth of that.

Access point costs can actually be greater if the area to be covered is large. The area to be covered will be based on the needs of the mobile user population.

A user may make use of a number of access points on a regular basis. Some access points may be used only occasionally. Unfortunately, access points need to be in place even if they are not always in use.

Some access point products support a limited number of users; the number varies significantly, depending upon the product and the technology employed. The maximum number of users is usually greater than ten, but the impact of the limit will be based on the placement of your mobile user population. Some products allow multiple access points to be placed in the same spot but utilize difference transmission frequencies. This is the same as putting two FM radio stations in the same area with different transmitting frequencies; there is no conflict but you can listen to only one at a time.

Wireless LANs have relatively clear-cut advantages and disadvantages. Often the choice of using a wireless LAN is moot. Either wireless technology is feasible, technically or economically, or it isn't. Then the main choice is which product to use.

CONSIDERATIONS ON USING WIRELESS CONNECTIONS

There are a number of basic considerations which need to be examined before a wireless connections should be implemented. These considerations can help determine if wireless connections are suitable, practical and desirable. The following is a list of considerations we will examine in more detail.

Considerations

- ✧ Access to LAN users (full)
- ✧ Access to LAN services (full)
- ✧ Ease of use by remote users (good)
- ✧ Network operating system (important)
- ✧ Network protocol (accessible)
- ✧ Telephone time (none)
- ✧ Performance (very good)
- ✧ Scalability (good)
- ✧ Hardware requirements (medium to high)
- ✧ Client licensing (none)
- ✧ Cost (high)

✧ General maintenance (minimal)

✧ Security (good)

✧ Auditing (good)

✧ Automation (excellent)

Wireless NICs provide a mobile workstation *full access to the* LAN and its users as long as the workstation is within range of an access point that is attached to a LAN. Fully wireless LANs are possible, but most installations are a combination of wireless and wired workstations. A mobile workstation has the same LAN access as a wired workstation which includes all LAN services and LAN users.

Ease of use for mobile users is excellent, although the placement of access points limits the mobile user's location. The mobile LAN user can use the same applications and data files as users who are using workstations connected directly to the LAN. The difference in speed between the wireless and wired NICs can affect how a mobile user will want to operate his or her applications, as mentioned in earlier sections in this chapter.

The choice of the network operating system or the wireless NIC is important because the NIC must have a device driver that will work with the NOS used on the LAN and on the workstation. If the NIC does not have a device driver that is compatible with the NOS then the workstation will not be able to utilize the LAN. Novell Netware, IBM LAN Server and Microsoft Windows NT Server are NOSes typically supported by wireless NIC vendors. DOS and Windows are workstation operating systems also supported.

The network protocol is also an issue related to device drivers and access points. A wireless NIC provides the mobile workstation with access to the network protocol used by the LAN, but a device driver is specific to a particular protocol. As long as the proper device driver is available, the mobile workstation will work with a particular LAN.

Telephone charges encountered with other remote LAN access methods are not encountered with wireless NICs.

Wireless NIC performance is very good compared to other remote LAN access methods that utilize the telephone. Wireless NICs do operate at a speed slower than wired LANs, which can impact on what applications can be used on a mobile workstation. Applications that place a heavy load on the LAN may work well on a workstation with a wired NIC but not on a mobile workstation.

Wireless LANs scale well. An access point can handle dozens of mobile workstations, and more workstations can be supported with additional access points. Placing a large number of workstations in a confined area typically warrants a wired LAN, so the number of mobile workstations within the area covered by an access point is often comparatively small and well within the capabilities of an access point. Additional access points can also be used to cover more area and hence more workstations.

Hardware requirements are relatively high in cost. A wireless NIC is required on each workstation and one or more access points are needed to connect the mobile workstations to a wired LAN. A completely wireless LAN is possible as long as all mobile workstations are within an area about half the size of the area covered by an access point. The covered area is half the size of the access point coverage because each wireless NIC must be in range of all others within a completely wireless LAN. Workstation hardware requirements are no different from those of a workstation connected to a wired LAN. The main workstation requirement is the proper adapter and device driver.

Each wireless NIC comes with its own set of device drivers so there is no additional licensing costs; this effectively makes the client licensing cost zero. There may be a cost associated with the driver but it is hidden in the cost of the NIC, which is a required component.

Overall, the cost of a wireless LAN is higher than a wired LAN. Wireless NICs cost two to three more than their wired counterparts and access points cost more than a wired hub. Most wireless access points support remote network management, so an access point is comparable to a hub with remote network management support. Even so, an access point usually costs twice that of a hub with remote network management support.

General maintenance of a wireless LAN is minimal. Access points rarely need to be reset, and remote management tools can usually handle any changes or acquire any statistics needed by a LAN manager. Access points and wireless NICs require no adjustments. The principal problem a wireless LAN will encounter is rearrangement of access points or office walls; moving the office furniture usually makes no difference to the wireless LAN.

LAN security is good. It is based on the NOS. Eavesdropping on a wireless LAN connection is possible, although often difficult, and it depends on office security since an eavesdropping device must be within range of a wireless NIC or access point. IR-based NIC operation is restricted to a single room because walls, and ceilings block the signal. Radio-based NICs transmit through walls making them potentially less secure. For environments that must be more secure you can check out products that include encryption. Encryption encodes data before it is sent and decodes it at the other end. A key or set of keys is used with the encoding and decoding process. Encryption can be done through the NOS or the wireless software. Some, but not all NOSes and some, but not all, wireless NICs support encryption.

Auditing mobile workstation operation and usage can be done using standard network-based auditing tools. Access-point usage can be monitored using remote network management tools.

Automation support is excellent with a wireless LAN, since the mobile workstation has the same capability as a workstation wired to the LAN. Applications can be written in almost any programming language, including the macro languages found in many applications. The main limiting factor is the speed of the wireless LAN connection. A wireless system will work well as long as it can transfer the amount of data needed by the application in a reasonable amount of time.

WIRELESS CONNECTIONS: SOME EXAMPLES

Wireless connections support comes in a variety of implementations. Products from some vendors can be mixed, but they are typically the same products with different labels. There is no standard for either IR or radio-based NICs, so be prepared to purchase products from a single vendor. For example, CruiseLAN adapters will not work with NetWare access points.

We will take a look at three different products in this section. The first is an IR-based system from Photonics. It is a low-power device which is ideal for laptops. The throughput is low, with a top end around 450 Kbps. It is also limited in distance, with about a 25-foot range (which can be extended with additional access points).

The second product is from Zenith Data Systems (ZDS). It is a radio-based product called CruiseLAN. CruiseLAN is compatible with Proxim's RangeLAN2. It operates at 1.6 Mbps and comes in both PCMCIA and ISA adapter versions. Access points can extend the operating range of a mobile user.

Xircom's Netwave (not to be confused with Novell Netware) is another radio-based product that only comes in a PCMCIA version. In fact, the access point uses the same PCMCIA card used for a laptop. There is not currently a Netwave ISA NIC for a desktop workstation, but you can buy PCMCIA support for desktop workstations that a Netware PCMCIA card can be plugged into.

Of all the technologies presented in this book, the wireless technology has the greatest technological growth potential. Faster speeds, greater distances and lower costs can be expected, so check out any cost claims in this book against the prices in current catalogs and price lists, and compare performance characteristics against the latest product *spec sheets* and product reviews. You may be in for a pleasant surprise.

Photonics Collaborative

Photonics Collaborative San Jose, CA is an IR-based wireless LAN. It operates at up to 450 kbps with an NDIS device driver. Its range, 25 feet, tends to be the main limiting factor. An access point can easily cover a small office area or conference room, but a large open office area will require a number of access points for full coverage.

The Collaborative transceiver (transmitter/receiver, see Figure 7.10) is connected by a cable to the NIC. The cable allows the transceiver to be placed where it can operate properly. For example, in an office area with shoulder-high partitions, the transceiver can be placed near or on top of a partition. The transceiver can also be clipped to the top of a laptop workstation's screen. The transceiver version is available with a PCMCIA NIC and an ISA NIC suitable for use with most IBM PC-compatible workstations. A Macintosh product is available but it is not compatible with the Collaborative; the Mac version works with other Macs only. Photonics also sells an integrated PCMCIA/transceiver (Figure 7.11) product with a slightly more limited range (20 feet.)

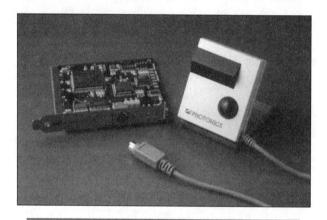

FIGURE 7.10 THE ISA PHOTONICS ADAPTER TRANSCEIVER.

FIGURE 7.11A+B THE PCMCIA PHOTONICS ADAPTER AND TRANSCEIVER.

The Collaborative Access Point (Figure 7.12) is a small IBM-compatible PC that operates without a keyboard or monitor, both of which can be added to observe and control the access point software. The Access Point is implemented with an ISA Collaborative NIC and an Ethernet NIC. The Access Point software is available as a separate product, so you can build your own access point. Often an unused PC can be brought back into service as an access point, thereby reducing the cost of implementing a wireless LAN. Roaming is supported, but a site survey tool is not included with the product.

FIGURE 7.12 THE COLLABORATIVE ACCESS POINT.

The Collaborative transceiver does not have to be in the direct line of sight of another transceiver; in fact, it works best with reflected IR light. High ceilings should be avoided, along with large or numerous windows. Windows do not reflect IR so the transceiver's signal literally goes out the window. A transceiver should not be placed directly beneath a recessed lighting fixture either. It can be placed to one side because the ceiling will reflect the IR light.

The Collaborative is not the fastest wireless remote LAN access system, nor is it significantly less expensive than the radio-based wireless solutions at this time. Its limited range can be a problem in large offices. It has the potential for being very inexpensive and the cost of electronic devices is continually dropping. IR is also more secure if the office environment is secure. Even windows are of little concern because of the limited range. Photonic's Collaborative product line does provide a reliable and robust remote LAN access method.

Zenith Data Systems CruiseLAN

Zenith Data Systems' (ZDS of Buffalo Grove, IL) CruiseLAN is a spread-spectrum radio-based wireless LAN that utilizes the 2.4 to 2.48Ghz frequencies. CruiseLAN is compatible with Proxim's RangeLAN2 and you can mix products from both companies in the same wireless LAN. Both use *frequency hopping* for a more robust system, and choose the best frequencies by monitoring the transmission quality while sending data. CruiseLAN has a maximum throughput of 1.6 Mbps but it will transmit at a slower speed if conditions warrant. Throughput speed switching is totally transparent. Unfortunately, there is no feedback when this occurs, so the increased response time delay due to a switch may not be apparent to the user. CruiseLAN transceivers run at 100mW, which is relatively low power for a radio transmitter, but the low power makes them suitable for use on battery-operated laptops.

CruiseLAN has a rated range of 1,000 feet at full speed with no obstructions. That is great if you are in the middle of a football field, but CruiseLAN's range in the typical office environment is still a respectable 100 to 300 feet. The wide variance is due to the variability of office environments. The more open the office area, the larger the operating range. A site survey is the only sure way of determining CruiseLAN's operating area.

CruiseLAN NICs come in two versions: ISA and PCMCIA. The ISA version (Figure 7.13) uses the same antenna as the CruiseLAN access point. The ISA adapter can be used in a workstation or a Novell Netware 3.x or 4.x file server. The main problem with using a server-based ISA card is that most file servers are not located in a central location with respect to mobile users. The file server is often off in a corner, away from most users. Even so, the ISA adapter is less costly than the access point and it may prove useful in a file server as an adjunct to access points.

The PCMCIA adapter version of CruiseLAN consists of two parts as shown in Figure 7.13. The PCMCIA card contains the basic hardware interface, which is connected to the transceiver and antenna combination by a cable. Putting the transceiver outside the PCMCIA card allows a more powerful transmitter to be included, along with a long antenna, which improves transmission and reception. Unfortunately the cable can get caught and tangled. The cable and transceiver can be removed without removing the PCMCIA card, but the wireless LAN is inaccessible without the transceiver attached. The PCMCIA adapter has the same range and capabilities as the ISA adapter. Status indicators on the transceiver let you know when it is transmitting or receiving. The PCMCIA adapter supports power management, which lets your laptop power down a PCMCIA device when it is not in use to reduce its power consumption.

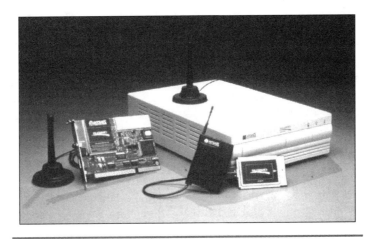

FIGURE 7.13 CRUISELAN NICS (ISA AND PCMCIA) AND ACCESS POINT.

The CruiseLAN access point is a large flat box (Figure 7.13.) It contains built-in Ethernet and CruiseLAN adapters with connections for both. You can change the access point's ID using switches (each access point must have a unique ID) and you can check its operation using SNMP. Installation is quick and simple. You change the ID (if necessary), plug in the antenna (which is the same one as in the ISA adapter), plug in the Ethernet connection, plug in the power cord, and the access point is operational. It can be mounted on the wall. A single access point will handle 25 to 50 wireless workstations depending upon wireless network traffic.

The ISA and PCMCIA adapters, at $595 and $695, are a bit more expensive than Ethernet adapters, but the prices are not extremely high. While Ethernet prices have leveled out at around $100, you can expect the wireless NIC prices to drop. The CruiseLAN access point is also pricey at $1895 (SRP) and its price will probably drop more slowly because only a portion is associated with the wireless NIC.

CruiseLAN comes with a good site survey tool that shows overall throughput statistics as well as the quality of the frequencies available for use. It is interesting to watch the frequency quality indicators as the test workstation is moved.

CruiseLAN supports roaming and *automatic reconnect* with some networks. *Automatic reconnect* occurs when a mobile user moves out of range of all access points and then moves back into range, often when an error is signaled, indicating the loss of the network connection. Without automatic reconnect support, you would have to move back into range and the reboot your workstation to make a new connection.

Xircom Netwave

Xircom's (Calabasas, CA) Netwave Credit Card Adapter comes only in a PCMCIA card with an integrated antenna (Figure 7.14). The antenna is a small stub that extends past the end of the PCMCIA card. It also contains a pair of status LEDs that blink when the transmitter and receiver are in use. The antenna is not removable, so you must remove the card if you want to close the PCMCIA slot cover found on most laptops. The integrated antenna and transceiver (contained in the PCMCIA card) make the Netwave NIC very easy to install and remove, but there is a tradeoff: the Netwave operates at a slower speed than the CruiseLAN NIC. The Netwave throughput is 1 Mbps and the average range is only 150 feet. The open-air range specification is 1,000 feet. Netwave uses half the power (50 milliwatts) of CruiseLAN, which accounts for most of the difference in performance. Netwave uses the same frequency bands (2.4-2.48Ghz) and spread-spectrum operating mode as CruiseLAN, but the two are not compatible. The PCMCIA adapter does not currently support power management.

Figure 7.14 Xircom NetWare Credit Card Adapter.

The Netwave access point is very small (see Figure 7.15), about the size of a 4mm hand-held camcorder. It is the same Netwave PCMCIA adapter used with a laptop and the access point easily mounts on the wall. There is nothing special about the PCMCIA adapter. I swapped the access point and laptop adapters and the LAN still ran fine. The access point will handle a maximum of 85 mobile users, but 10 or 25 is more typical. The Netwave access point supports roaming but it does not come with a site survey tool.

FIGURE 7.15 NETWARE ACCESS POINT.

The Netwave PCMCIA adapter currently has a list price of $599. Although the access point is small, it is pricey too at $1,499. The throughput of 1 Mbps is ten times slower than Ethernet, but as with most wireless systems, you learn to live with the speed limitation.

Like laptops compared to desktop workstations, wireless versus wired NICs will always be a tradeoff between flexibility, speed, power (or range), and cost. Laptops are almost to the point where they rival desktop workstations, but at a significantly higher cost. Even then, the laptop is often deficient in a number of areas compared to the desktop workstation. The same is true for wireless NICs. Their price will go down and their speed can be increased, but wired NICs are improving as well. 10 Mbps wireless NICs will be available but so will 100 Mbps—and higher—wired NICs. Applications will be written to take advantage of the higher speeds, which will leave wireless LANs in the same position they are in now, incapable of properly running some applications. The trick is to make the wireless LAN work with the applications you need.

SPECIALIZED TOOLS

Remote LAN access methods typically utilize modems for remote connections. ISDN connections and wireless NICs can also be used, but there are other kinds of specialized hardware and software that can enhance remote LAN access. The three kinds of products we will be looking at include whiteboard software, remote power control and voice/data modems.

SPECIALIZED TOOLS

Whiteboard software is a specialized remote control program used for group conferencing. Like a remote control program, whiteboard software lets two or more users see the same screen on their own workstations. The difference between a whiteboard program and a remote control program is what is being displayed and what kind of annotation, if any, can be made. The shared display in a whiteboard program is a blank area where annotations, including text and graphics, can be added by any whiteboard user. On the other hand, a remote control program shows an application. Annotations can be added to a document that the application displays if the application allows such annotations. For example, a word processor would allow the text of a document to be edited or added, but other programs may not. Even programs like word processors will not allow you to arbitrarily mark up documents, which is one of the main features of a whiteboard program. For example, most word processors will not let you draw a circle around text to highlight a change.

Remote power control hardware essentially lets you control the power switch for a workstation and its peripherals without being there. Remote power control hardware can save electricity by being used to turn on computer hardware only when it is needed. It is also valuable in resetting workstations and peripherals. Often power cycling—powering down and powering up a device—is the only way to properly restart the device. This is one way to force a device to restart regardless of the state that it is in when it is powered down. For example, a workstation may be running a program that crashes and locks up the workstation. There are two alternatives to restarting the workstation. The first is to physically press the reset button, if the workstation has one. The second is to run through a power cycle. Remote power control hardware lets you do the latter.

Voice/data modems are a special kind of modem. A basic data modem is used to send digital information over a telephone line. The current high-speed data modem standard is V.34. Fax modems are used to send or receive faxes to and from a fax machine or another fax modem. Data modems and fax modems are often combined. Both types of modems use a voice line but they do not let you use the same line to transmit voice. *Voice/data* modems let you use the same line for voice and data. This type of modem allows you to use a single telephone line with a remote control program or a whiteboard program.

Another trend in the hardware arena is the combo communication adapters. These adapters start with a data/fax modem and combine these features with voice and possibly multimedia support. They can turn a basic PC into an intelligent voice-mail system that also supports fax and data transmissions. The adapters are typically bundled with software that takes advantage of the hardware combination. The adapters are well-suited for single-user workstations or as a LAN gateway when the workstation with the adapter is placed on a LAN.

There are other pieces of useful hardware that we will not be taking a look at. For example, fax/data modem/voice switches (Figure 8.1) are inexpensive ways for different devices to share a single telephone line. The switch is a small box with multiple telephone jacks. The telephone line is connected to one jack and a fax machine, data modem and a telephone or telephone answering machine are connected to other jacks. The switch lets you place a call from any device and the first one used to make a call normally locks out other devices from making a call. Incoming calls are answered by the switch, which listens for a signal to determine what kind of call is being made. A fax machine has a distinct tone which causes the switch to select the device connected to the fax jack. Some switches have a prerecorded voice prompt and can detect tones from a Touch-Tone telephone. A tone from a particular key on the Touch-Tone telephone selects a particular jack, so you can actually have different kinds of devices attached to a single telephone line.

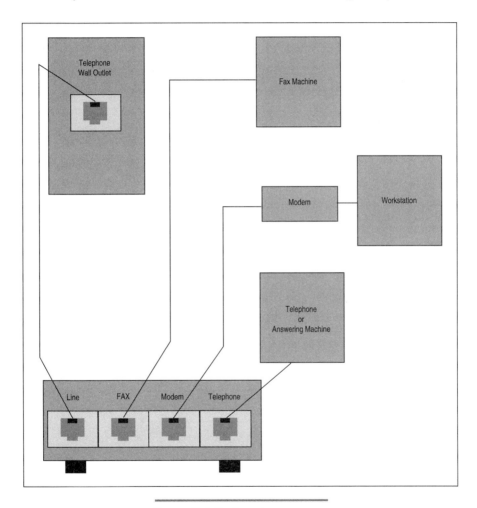

FIGURE 8.1 FAX/DATA/VOICE SWITCH.

Unlike the prior chapters, each section in this chapter is dedicated to a different product category, and examples of the products in these categories are included in the corresponding section instead of being collected together at the end of the chapter. The sections cover the following categories:

✧ Whiteboard software

✧ Remote power control

✧ Voice/data modems

✧ Specialized communications adapters

The hardware and software described in this chapter are not required for any of the remote LAN access methods described in previous chapters, but they can make the use of these access methods easier for the remote user or the LAN manager.

WHITEBOARD SOFTWARE

Whiteboard software is designed to provide graphical, screen-oriented, teleconferencing support on two or more workstations connected by a LAN or telephone connections. A common screen is displayed on all workstations involved in a conference, and each user can view and add annotations which can be seen by all conference attendees. Figure 8.2 shows a whiteboard conference using modems and a standard telephone line. This type of connection will work even if neither user is attached to a LAN. The telephone connection can also be used to transfer files and exchange messages.

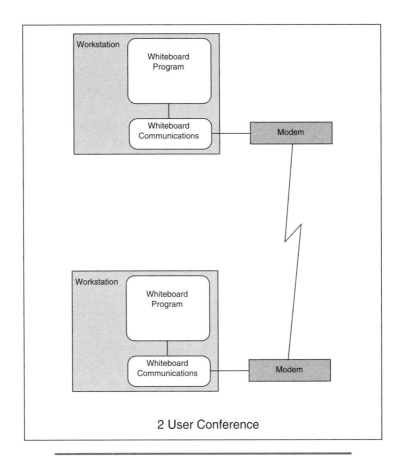

FIGURE 8.2 WHITEBOARD CONFERENCE OVER A TELEPHONE LINE.

Figure 8.3 shows a LAN-only configuration. Multiple users can participate in a single conference with a LAN connection. A user with a remote workstation, as described in Chapter 3, can also participate in a conference, as shown in Figure 8.4, providing an alternative to the dedicated whiteboard telephone connection as shown in Figure 8.2. Local LAN connections are fast compared to telephone connections, including both the remote workstation connection and the dedicated connection shown in Figure 8.2. The only difference in operation of the whiteboard software between a pair of attendees and multiple attendees is the number of people that can add annotations to the whiteboard. Some whiteboard products assign specific colors to pointers that users can manipulate on the whiteboard.

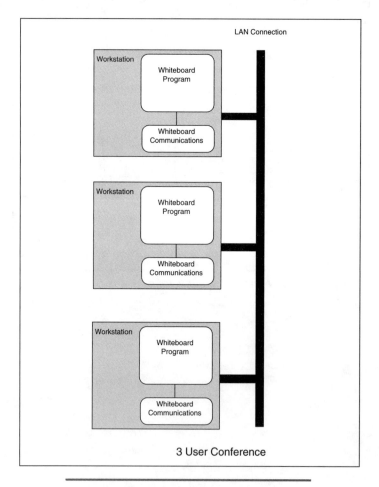

FIGURE 8.3 WHITEBOARD CONFERENCE OVER A **LAN**.

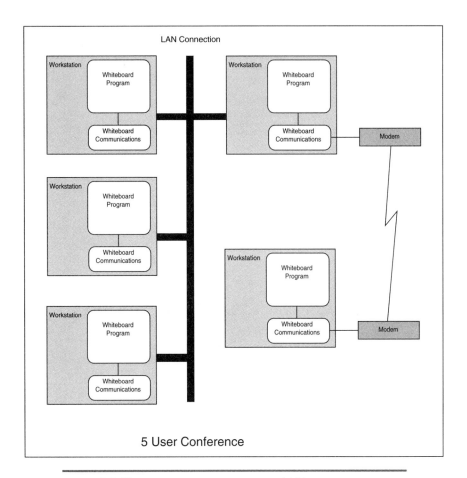

FIGURE 8.4 WHITEBOARD CONFERENCE OVER A LAN AND TELEPHONE LINE.

Figure 8.5 shows how specialized modems and additional hardware can augment a whiteboard program. Adding voice over the same telephone line is the first step. The third section of this chapter covers modems that provide this feature. Often a single telephone is all that is available at a location where one conference attendant is located. Without the voice/data connection there are two alternatives. One is to communicate using annotations or a chat mode built into many whiteboard products; the other is to use a second telephone line between the two locations and dedicate the second line for voice, often using a speakerphone. Audio adapters with speakers and microphones are often used at both ends with the voice data being transferred across the telephone line in digital form.

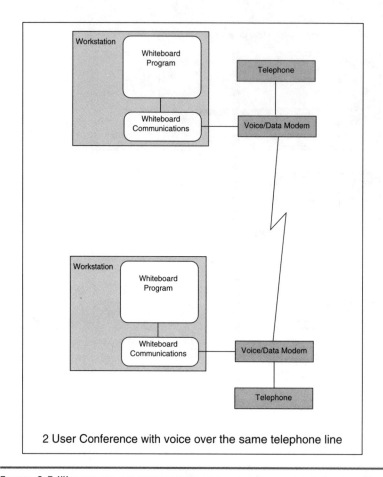

FIGURE 8.5 WHITEBOARD CONFERENCE WITH VOICE AND DATA OVER TELEPHONE LINE.

Adding video to the conference using the same connection is possible, but there are often limitations or additional requirements. A digital video camera is the minimal requirement, including its supporting adapter. A standard telephone connection does not have the bandwidth for full-screen, full-motion video support even when data compression techniques are used. If a standard telephone line is used there are two alternatives: to display video information in a small window, or to update the video window slowly. Displaying someone's picture in a smaller area reduces the amount of information sent. Often the hardware can display the same picture in a larger area, but additional detail is not gained through enlargement. A standard television refresh rate is 60 times (or frames) per second. A television set actually uses an interlaced technique which alternately updates half the screen at 60 half-frames per second, thus reducing bandwidth requirements, so 30 digital frames per second is the standard baseline for gauging digital video displays. Reducing the number of frames per second causes the movements to be jerky, or the display may appear to flicker, but you will still be able to see the other conference attendees as the conference proceeds. Of course, a faster connection, as found on a LAN or with an ISDN telephone line, means more information can be sent, thereby allowing the frame rate and the video window resolution to be increased.

Although whiteboard programs are conceptually simple and very similar, there are many ways to implement their various common features. The central feature is the whiteboard itself. The whiteboard is typically a window, which includes a toolbar where tools can be selected, as shown in Figure 8.6. A text tool lets you indicate where text is to be placed using a mouse, and then you type the text using the keyboard. The text placed on the whiteboard is displayed on every attendee's whiteboard. Drawing tools let you add lines, arrows and figures like boxes and circles. These can be used to highlight text or to draw pictures. Markers are drawing tools that use a transparent color, so you can still see things you draw over. Other tools let you capture the contents of the screen while using other applications, so you could grab a portion of a spreadsheet and place it on the whiteboard. More sophisticated whiteboard programs use embedded object technology such as Microsoft's OLE (Object Linking and Embedding) to actually include the item instead of just a picture of the item.

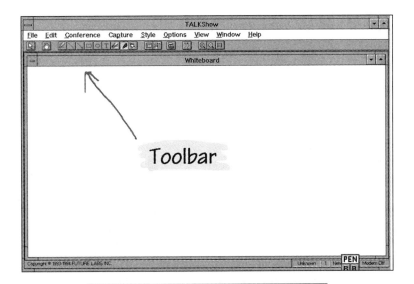

FIGURE 8.6 A WHITEBOARD SCREEN WITH TOOLBAR.

Some whiteboard products provide slideshow-style support using the whiteboard as the screen. The slides are prepared ahead of time and they can be displayed manually or automatically. The slides can usually be annotated when they are on the whiteboard, and a recording feature is often provided so that annotations can be easily saved. Intel's ProShare, a product we will look at in more detail later in this chapter, uses a different format for the whiteboard. ProShare uses a notebook paradigm. The notebook is common to all attendees, and you can view any page in the notebook independent of other attendees. This is handy if you want to prepare a page while someone else is working on another page.

The whiteboard area can be bitmap-oriented or object-oriented or a combination of the two. *Bitmap-oriented* whiteboard products are similar to paint programs; if you draw or paint over an area that had drawings or text on it, then the drawings or text will be lost; erasing an area is actually painting the area with the selected background color. *Object-oriented* whiteboard products are similar to CAD (computer-aided design) or technical drawing programs where each item is a figure, line or block of text. Figures are things like a box or a circle. You can move an item after is it's drawn and change its attributes. You can mark a region and move it in a bitmap-oriented product, but you cannot select an item as you can with an object-oriented product. To many users, the difference is not apparent until you need to make changes that are more easily accomplished using one type of product. For example, suppose you have some figures like a rectangle and a circle which obscure some text placed there previously. With an object-oriented product you can uncover the text by moving the figures; with a bitmap-oriented product you can never recover the obscured text.

Three other features found in whiteboard products include a chat mode, message facilities and file transfer. Chat mode is similar to the whiteboard in that every attendee gets to see the same thing. In this case it is a transcript of a typed conversation between attendees. Chat mode is often a feature found in remote control programs (Chapter 4) and bulletin board programs (Chapter 5.) The chat mode window, as shown in Figure 8.7, is divided into two areas. One area shows the transcript, and the other is an area where you can type a message that is to be added to the transcript. In a two-user environment the transcript is often just a copy of the other user's message area; in a multiple-user environment the transcript includes the name of the person who typed some text, followed by the text. The message area lets you compose the text before actually sending it. Once you type and send some text, it cannot be changed, whereas text on a whiteboard can be modified by any attendee. Chat mode can often be selective in a multiuser environment, so you can chat privately with another attendee. The transcript can sometimes be saved to a file, but often a whiteboard product will not be able to save the transcript, and it may not even keep it all, only the most recent text. Chat mode is typically text-only, and graphics or files cannot be embedded in the text.

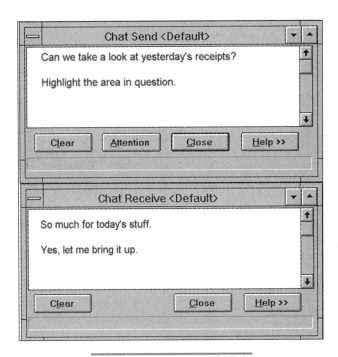

FIGURE 8.7 CHAT MODE EXAMPLE.

Messaging facilities may be combined with existing LAN mail systems or integrated with the whiteboard product. Messaging differs from chat mode in the way text is created and viewed. A message typically has subject and note areas with optional file attachments. It is prepared just like a mail message, but the recipients are conference attendees. Messages are handy when you want to keep a record of comments, as well as send files.

File-transfer support, as shown in Figure 8.8, allows a user to send one or more files to other attendees. Usually a whiteboard product will require a user to select the files to send, although it is possible to allow other attendees to see and select files on your workstation without your intervention. File transfers are often done in the background. You select the files to send and the person to send them to (in a multiuser conference) and the files and names are added to a transfer queue, often called an outbasket. The background transfer task removes entries from the queue and performs the copy. A matching inbasket can often be found at the receiving end, and the files are typically annotated with their original file name and the name of the sender. An alternative is for the whiteboard program to place all incoming files into a designated directory or to prompt the user when a file is received. Fancy file transfer systems let the receiver know the files and the size of the file to be received so they can cancel files that are too large or ones that are not needed. This feature is very useful in a multiuser conference environment, because the sender will often send files to everyone because it is easy to do.

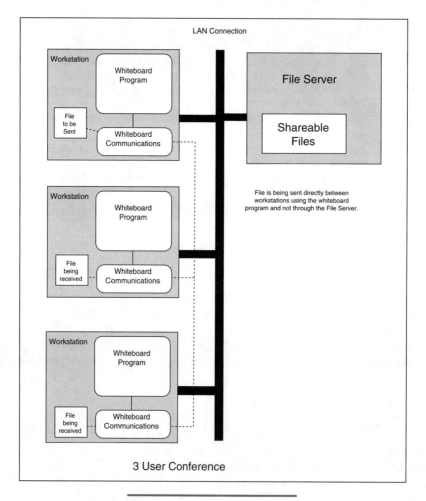

FIGURE 8.8 FILE TRANSFER EXAMPLE.

Most graphical interfaces use a pointing device, which is typically a mouse, but two other types of pointing devices are useful when using whiteboard software. These include light pens and pen-based tablets. Pen-based pointing devices are much better for use with whiteboard products because of the way in which most annotations are added. Drawing a straight line is much easier with pen than with a mouse. FTG Data Systems (Santana, CA) light pens can be attached using adapters or connections through the keyboard. Light pens work with most popular graphical user interface operating systems, such as OS/2 and Microsoft Windows. Many products, like FTG's, allow you to use both the pen and a mouse or trackball, so you can gain the best of both tools.

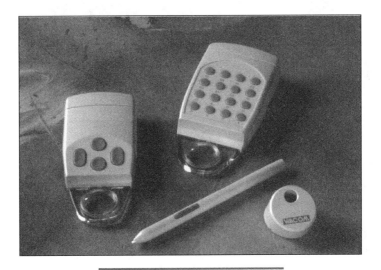

FIGURE 8.9 WACOM POINTING DEVICES.

Tablet-based pointers use a tablet with a sensing device and a special pen. The pen is sometimes connected to the tablet by a wire but most pen-based systems, like those from Wacom Technology (Vancouver, WA) use a wireless technology (see Figure 8.9 and Figure 8.10). The tablet is normally connected to a serial or parallel port on the workstation. Tablets are great if you want to trace an existing photo or drawing, and they are almost as easy to use for annotation as a light pen. Feedback is similar to a mouse, because you must look at the screen while moving the pen over the tablet, but it is a very natural movement. Drawing lines and circles for annotation is very easy with a pen and tablet compared to using a mouse. Like the light pens, many pen-based tablets let you use a mouse as well as the tablet. Some companies, such as Wacom Technology, also supply *pucks* as pointing devices. A *puck* looks, feels, and operates like a mouse, except that it must use the tablet as its work area. A tablet is typically the same size as a mouse pad and tablets are easier to move. Using a pen or puck with a tablet on your lap is practical, whereas a mouse and pad on your lap does not normally work well.

Figure 8.10 WACOM Pen and Tablet.

In the following pages, we take a look at three whiteboard products with different approaches to the whiteboard presentation. All three can be used with modem connections and LAN connections. Audio and video support is available, some-times through third parties. A number of other whiteboard products exist, and there are even whiteboard products that incorporate a real whiteboard; you use real markers but you have to erase the board when you are done—the computer will not do that for you.

The next three products presented include:

1. TALKShow from FutureLabs
2. Person-to-Person from IBM
3. ProShare from Intel

FutureLabs' TALKShow is the quintessential whiteboard program. It is centered around a whiteboard window with a menu and toolbar for calling up other options, including chat mode and file transfer. It supports multiple attendees.

IBM's Person-to-Person is a multiplatform whiteboard program built in a modular fashion. You can use Person-to-Person on Windows or OS/2. Person-to-Person has a module for each major feature, including making a connection, the whiteboard, chat mode, and file transfers.

Intel's ProShare was initially limited to a two-user conference, with future versions incorporating multiple-user support. ProShare's whiteboard paradigm is unique, replacing the single whiteboard with a multipage notebook. ProShare users can actually have two notebooks open at one time. One is a private notebook and the other is the shared notebook. You can copy items from the page of one notebook to another.

Whiteboard products provide an alternative to in-person conferences. They can reduce travel time and costs. They are unique as a remote LAN access because they require an active participant at both ends of the connection. Whiteboard software is groupware with immediate feedback. It can be used for brainstorming sessions, slide presentations, or marking up the latest document or spreadsheet. It can be a valuable tool between LAN and remote users or just across the LAN.

TALKShow from FutureLabs

TALKShow from FutureLabs (Los Altos, CA) is an excellent whiteboard product based on InVision from InVision Systems Corp. (Vienna, VA). They both are Windows-based products. The main window (Figure 8.11) is the whiteboard area, which is partially object-oriented. You can place some objects in the whiteboard area, such as items obtained from the Windows Clipboard, but the whiteboard is bitmap-oriented. Text can be overwritten by other figures drawn after the text. Likewise, text drawn over a figure obscures the portion of the figure that the text covers. Text and figures or objects can be removed globally using menu selections. This is handy for cleaning up the whiteboard. Objects can be items placed into the Clipboard, such as bitmaps, or you can use Microsoft OLE objects.

TALKShow supports synchronized and unsynchronized drawing; most whiteboard products just support synchronized drawing. *Synchronized drawing* causes any change made at any workstation that is part of a conference to update all other workstation whiteboards immediately. Staying in sync is nice, but often you want to make changes first and then present them to other attendees all at once. Sometimes you can use another application to create the drawing you want to present, and then copy it to the whiteboard. With TALKShow you can simply use the unsynchronized mode, and then select the manual synchronization button or menu option after your changes are complete. At that time the whiteboards on the other attendee's workstations are updated.

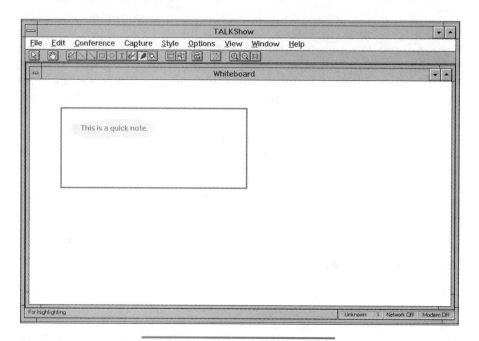

Figure 8.11 TALKShow main window.

Synchronized and unsynchronized updates are useful for on-the-fly creation and annotation, but TALKShow's slide show feature is more useful for prepared presentations. A slide show is a series of slides that are essentially the contents of a whiteboard, but the slide can be created when a conference is not in progress. During a slide show you can move backwards and forwards through the list of slides. Slides can also be annotated while they are in the whiteboard area, and the changes can be saved by the slide show creator.

You can save the contents of a TALKShow whiteboard in an archive file. Archive files are like slide shows, except that the archive is created by recording what is shown on the whiteboard. You can record a slide show using the archive, as shown in Figure 8.12, or you can record what occurs in the whiteboard when no slide show is in progress. The archive can be a sequence of incremental changes to the whiteboard, for example after you make some annotations, or it can be a record of each change made to the whiteboard, wherein you erase the whiteboard and start over. Unfortunately, you cannot convert slide show files to archive files or archive files to slide show files.

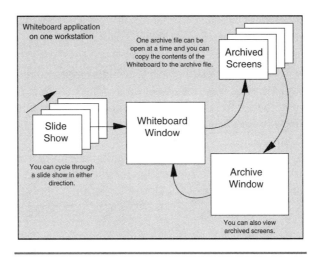

FIGURE 8.12 TALKSHOW SLIDE SHOW AND ARCHIVE FEATURES.

TALKShow handles different screen resolutions by allowing you to pan and zoom around the whiteboard. Often one attendee may be using a different screen resolution and zooming lets everyone see the same thing or a more detailed view of a section of the whiteboard. Panning lets you use more of the whiteboard without deleting what is currently drawn in another area.

One of TALKShow's strengths is its annotation tools (see Figure 8.13). While many whiteboard products let you draw text, lines, and possibly boxes, TALKShow can draw lines with arrows, solid and outline figures like rectangles, circles, and ellipses, and you can use paintbrushes and markers with different drawing sizes. TALKShow also supports the standard Copy and Paste operations, including the ability to copy the contents of another application's window.

TALKShow's chat mode is rather basic. It does use two panes but there is no way to save the transcript. The chat mode is designed for TALKShow's multiple-attendee support, so attendee names prefix each line of text. Files must be sent using the file transfer capability.

TALKShow's file transfer support (see Figure 8.14) is limited to a single file, and it must be sent in the foreground. In other words, you cannot use the whiteboard while the transfer is going on. JPEG compression is available, but it is a lossy compression algorithm suitable only for video or bitmap data. This is one area that is bound to improve with new versions of TALKShow..

FutureLabs has a great way of letting people use TALKShow. You can give a *guest* copy of TALKShow to anyone. The guest version is fully functional and there are no time limits for its use; the only limitation is that it can only be used with a licensed copy of TALKShow. FutureLabs has a rebate policy (which may still be in effect, so please check if you are going to use TALKShow), whereby you get a rebate for each user who buys a licensed copy of TALKShow to replace a guest copy that you gave out.

TALKShow works over a telephone line using a normal data modem. It can also use voice/data modems like those covered in a later section. A single line can be used to update the whiteboard as well as handle voice communication. Third-party products provide video support, although an ISDN line is more suitable for full-motion (30 frames per second) video. TALKShow also works on a LAN, where multiple users can attend a single conference. Multiple remote users can attend a conference based on a LAN if the remote users first call into the LAN as remote workstations. The LAN can be a clearing house for a remote-only conference if all the workstations involved in a conference are remote workstations.

Person-to-Person from IBM

IBM's Person-to-Person (P2P) whiteboard product runs under OS/2 and Windows. The OS/2 Warp Bonus Pack comes with a copy of P2P. Buy a pair of OS/2 Warp packages and you have a two-user P2P system for the price of an operating system, not to mention all the other goodies in the Bonus Pack. P2P is also available as a stand-alone product in single and multiple-license versions.

P2P consists of a number of integrated applets. They are typically found in the P2P folder under OS/2 and you can start any one individually or in concert. The applets include:

- ✧   Address Book
- ✧   Call Manager
- ✧   Chalkboard (aka whiteboard)
- ✧   Chat Mode
- ✧   File Transfer
- ✧   Clipboard utility
- ✧   Video and still Capture utility

The Address Book (Figure 8.15) contains entries for LAN and phone-based connections and is used by the Call Manager. The Call Manager (Figure 8.16) is used to make a new connection or wait for other attendees to join your conference. Once a conference is in progress the attendees can utilize the other applets. You can start the other applets before setting up a conference, but no one else will see what you doing until they join the conference. Applet support for other conference attendees can be controlled, so you can prevent users from sending files using the file transfer support or interrupting you with the chat mode.

FIGURE 8.15 P2P ADDRESS BOOK.

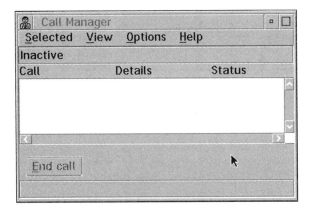

FIGURE 8.16 P2P CALL MANAGER.

P2P supports a diverse connection policy for conference attendees. The basic modem-to-modem connection using a telephone line is supported, as well as multiple users on a single LAN. P2P gets more interesting when you have a combination of the two techniques. Figure 8.17 shows how a LAN-based P2P workstation can host a connection to a remote P2P workstation. The entire group of P2P workstations is part of a single conference. P2P's ability to add and remove attendees as a conference progresses is not unique but it is very handy.

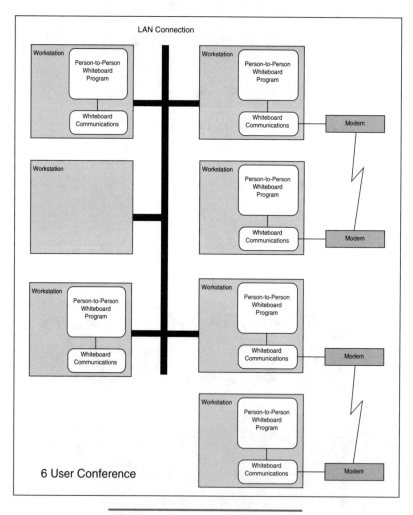

FIGURE 8.17 P2P CONNECTION EXAMPLE.

The main applet is the chalkboard which is P2P's name for the whiteboard window. There is no difference between the terms chalkboard and whiteboard. Figure 8.18 shows what a typical chalkboard looks like. P2P has an average collection of annotation tools on the chalkboard's toolbar. You can copy the contents of other application windows into the chalkboard or grab the contents of the entire screen.

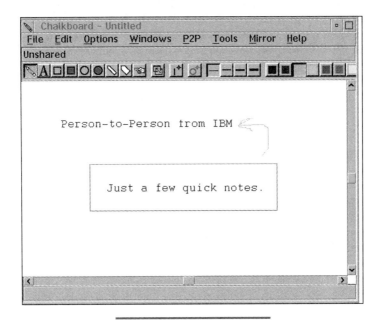

FIGURE 8.18 P2P CHALKBOARD.

The chalkboard is slightly different from other whiteboard applications. The P2P chalkboard is logically divided into two layers. The bottom layer contains text and graphics. The top layer contains annotations. You can erase either. P2P does not support objects yet. The P2P tools support various line styles and widths, but do not include the transparent markers found in other whiteboard products.

Unlike many other whiteboard applications, P2P lets you shut down and restart the P2P chalkboard during a conference. You might want to do so if you only need to use the other features, like the transfer or chat mode. You might restart the chalkboard after conversing with other attendees using the chat mode, make a few drawings and then shut it down again.

Figure 8.19 shows P2P Chat Mode. Like most multiuser conference products, P2P's chat mode transcript pane prefixes the lines with the name of the person who typed the line of text. P2P also lets you save the transcript to a file or copy it to the Clipboard, from where it can be put into another application. Chat mode can be used independent of the other applets once a conference connection is made.

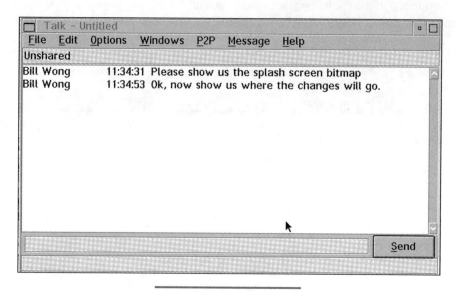

FIGURE 8.19 P2P CHAT MODE.

P2P's file transfer operates in the background. Figure 8.20 shows how you select files to be sent. The file names and the users to receive the files are placed into a queue, which is emptied as quickly as possible. Chalkboard and chat mode take priority, but any unused bandwidth can be used to transfer files. You can check the progress of the transfers and abort any transfers which have not completed. Incoming files are placed into a common directory, and you can specify the maximum amount of disk space to use, thereby preventing someone from sending a number of large files and filling up your hard disk. This is especially handy if you are using a laptop computer with a small hard disk.

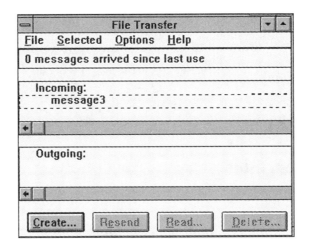

FIGURE 8.20 P2P FILE TRANSFER.

The Clipboard utility lets you share the chalkboard contents with other applications. You can automatically copy the contents to the Clipboard for a one-time transfer or set up a DDE connection for continuous updates. The Clipboard utility also lets you share a common Clipboard with all conference attendees. You would copy data to the Clipboard from an application you are running, and then other attendees can paste the data in this common Clipboard to their local applications. Delayed rendering is used, so Clipboard data is only sent if someone pastes the contents into their application.

P2P's video and still Capture utility works if you have a digital camera attached to a P2P workstation. The still capture mode is useful when you want to show a picture but do not need real-time update. Still mode uses less bandwidth and is practical across modem connections. P2P uses the same digital connection to send video data, so full-motion video can easily overwhelm a modem connection.

The main item missing from P2P is any form of slideshow support. The clipboard and chalkboard can be used to present a slide show but it is cumbersome.

You need to have the slide show available in another application, step to the next slide, copy the slide's contents to the Clipboard, switch to the chalkboard and paste it for all to see. Not a great idea, but it works. Keyboard macros can automate the process, but you need to set up the macros and the applications to make everything work.

P2P's ability to make diverse connections is probably its best feature. LAN and remote users can easily attend a conference.

ProShare from Intel

Intel's ProShare is available in a Personal Conference Edition, a Premier Edition and the Video System 2000. The first two support high-speed modems (V.32 and V.34) and ISDN links as well as LAN links; Video System 2000 requires ISDN or LAN links because it incorporates full-motion, real-time video. Video System 2000 includes a small camera that is normally placed atop the workstation's monitor, from where it can present a frontal portrait view of you. The Personal Edition is limited to a pair of users in a conference.

All three products are based around ProShare's whiteboard software, which uses a shared-notebook metaphor which I find more powerful than the more basic whiteboard metaphor. ProShare can actually open two notebooks (see Figure 8.21) at one time: one shared and one private. A notebook contains one or more pages which are essentially equivalent to a whiteboard in other whiteboard products. You can view one page of a notebook at a time, but each conference attendee can view any page in the shared notebook, regardless of which page is being viewed by other attendees. You can also copy items between notebook pages and between notebooks. You can copy items between notebooks using drag-and-drop techniques.

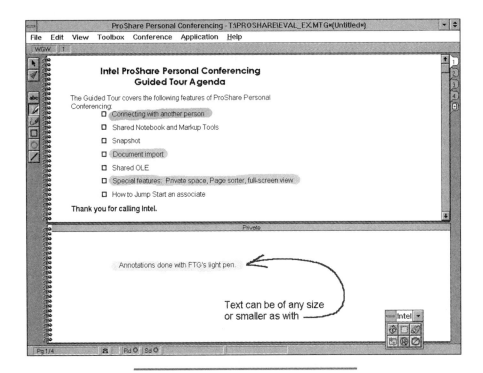

FIGURE 8.21 PROSHARE DUAL-NOTEBOOK VIEW.

Notebooks can be saved and created even if a conference is not in progress. A notebook is essentially a slide show that you can examine at your leisure. You can also synch up attendees so everyone looks at the same page at the same time. The really nice feature of ProShare is that all conference attendees wind up with a copy of the shared notebook.

ProShare is an object-oriented whiteboard product. Objects can be added from the Clipboard, or Microsoft OLE objects can be added as well. All annotation tools, such as the text and drawing tools, create new objects too. The drawing tools include pens and markers. Pens use opaque ink, while markers use transparent ink. Objects can be selected as a group and the group can be moved, copied or deleted. ProShare's drawing tools are fewer than other whiteboard products, but Intel did add straight lines to the Premier Edition.

ProShare does not have a chat mode but you can use a page in the notepad or part of the page currently being used. A second telephone line or a voice/data modem can let you use voice teleconferencing with ProShare.

ProShare does support file transfers. They can occur in the background, but the receiver must first acknowledge a transfer before it begins.

ProShare's guest licensing is not as generous as FutureLabs. ProShare's guest version can be given to anyone, but it times out 60 days after it is installed. You can reinstall the guest software again but this can get tedious. Intel is essentially trying to get you to buy a copy for each person using ProShare. Seems reasonable to me. The guest can only wait for a conference; a licensed version of ProShare can make a call or wait for a call. Calls can be placed using modems and a telephone line, an ISDN adapter and an ISDN telephone line, or a Novell Netware network connection.

ProShare's notebook metaphor and object-oriented whiteboard operation are definite advantages. Unfortunately, it is not as adept as other products when it comes to multiuser conferences and its lack of a chat mode can make a second telephone line a mandatory addition.

REMOTE POWER CONTROL

Remote power control is a way to save on electric bills and to remotely manage hardware, including workstations and peripherals. The primary purpose of remote power control is to provide a remote user with the ability to reset a device. This typically puts the device into a working state, even if it was not when it was turned off. The recommendation from the help desk to a user whose machine is locked up is typically: turn it off, count to ten, and turn it back on. With remote power control you can do this from across the room or across the country.

Remote power control comes in a number of forms to suit different needs. We will take a look at four different types of products, including:

- ✧ Remote Power On/Off from Server Technology
- ✧ Sentry from Server Technology
- ✧ InControl from Arvee Systems
- ✧ Smart UPS from APC

The Remote Power On/Off product from Server Technology is designed for use with a single device such as a workstation, router, or gateway that is attached to a modem. The typical configuration has power supplied to the device when an incoming call is detected, and power is turned off some time after the call is terminated.

Sentry is another product from Server Technology. It can control up to four devices, and multiple Sentry systems can be daisy-chained to control more devices. Although one of the devices can be configured to work in the same fashion as the Remote Power On/Off product, the primary purpose of the Sentry product is to control different devices. A LAN manager could call in and power cycle different workstations if they were known to be locked up.

InControl from Arvee Systems is similar to Sentry because it controls multiple devices. It differs from Sentry in two ways. The first is the power-handling capabilities and the second is the control mechanism. InControl is designed for high-power requirements and the control mechanism is through the parallel port of a PC, whereas the Sentry uses a serial port connected to a modem. InControl is more often found in LAN environments where file servers, routers, and remote control host workstations are located in a central area. A LAN manager can easily control all the devices from a central workstation, and a remote control program can be used with the central workstation to remotely control the power to the devices.

The Smart UPS from APC is a true UPS with added intelligence. It can be queried and controlled remotely from the LAN using SNMP. The UPS monitors incoming power and power used by the device. It can also turn off power, just like the Sentry and InControl products.

Each product has its own niche. Remote Power On/Off works well with single workstations and with workstations running remote control hosts. Sentry and InControl provide an economical and centrally managed method of controlling power to many devices. Finally, APC's SNMP support is ideal for large networks that need both the reliability provided by a UPS, as well as the remote management support provided by SNMP.

Remote power control is not just for controlling devices used for remote LAN access; it can also be used to control peripherals on a file server. For example, an external tape drive connected to a file server may only need to be turned on when a backup is about to occur. The LAN manager can use the remote power control system to turn on the tape drive before remotely configuring the tape backup process. The tape drive can be turned off when the backup is complete. It may even be possible to automate the entire process using batch files or other programming techniques.

Remote Power On/Off from Server Technology

Server Technology's Remote Power On/Off, shown in Figure 8.22, is a relatively simple device to use. It has a number of telephone jacks in the rear along with a set of switches for configuration. The front has a single button and two status LEDs. The button is a manual method of turning on the controlled device, and the status LEDs indicate when power is available to the Remote Power On/Off box and to the controlled device. The controlled device is plugged into an Intelligent Power Module (IPM). The IPM plugs into a wall outlet and provides a single controlled outlet. The controlled device plugs into the IPM. An IPM can handle up to 10 amps, which should be more than enough power for most workstations and peripherals. The IPM can be up to 1000 feet from the Remote Power On/Off box, although it is typically closed because the controlled device is normally attached to the modem which is also attached to the Remote Power On/Off box. Some laser printers may draw more power when first turned on, so check your peripheral's specifications before using a power control device.

FIGURE **8.22** REMOTE POWER ON/OFF (IPM IS IN THE CENTER).

The Remote Power On/Off box is connected to the IPM using a telephone cable. The modular connectors make setup easy, but you need to make sure you plug everything into the proper jack. The IPM does not send 110 volts through the cable, so you don't really need to worry too much about incorrect setup. The IPM will simply not turn on.

Figure 8.23 shows how the entire system gets wired. The workstation and modem are optional, but this is the typical configuration. The AUX port can be attached to another telephone device such as an answering machine or telephone. Using the AUX port is a bit odd. You need to call and hang up after the first ring and then call again immediately. The second call is routed to the AUX port instead of the main port where the modem is normally attached. The second call must be made within two minutes. Of course, you could change the connections and place the computer's modem on the AUX port instead. In this case, most calls wind up going to the telephone or answering machine, and the special sequence is required to get to the computer. This configuration is handy in a home where you have a single telephone line normally used for voice or a fax machine with the computer access as a secondary option.

The switches on the back control when the IPM turns on (after 1, 6, or 12 rings), how long it stays on after you hang up (15 sec., 2, 15, or 60 minutes), and whether power should remain on after a call. How you set up the Remote Power On/Off box depends upon what kind of software you are running on the workstation that is attached to the modem. The typical configuration is a workstation running a remote control host program. The Remote Power On/Off box is set up to turn on the IPM after the first ring, so the modem and computer power up almost immediately. There is a delay in answering the call, because the computer normally needs to run through its power-on and loading procedure. The call is typically answered by the modem after the fourth ring. Server Technology recommends that initial RAM checks be disabled if possible, to speed up the power-on and initial loading procedure.

The remote user can then utilize the workstation and hang up when done. The amount of time power should remain on again depends upon the type of software on the workstation. Remote routers are normally turned off almost immediately. Remote control hosts are typically left on so they can perform work while no connection exists, or to allow a user to call back in when a remote connection is accidentally broken. The power-down delay time is usually 15 or 60 minutes.

One trick I have used with the Remote Power On/Off box is the two call start-up. Often the software used to place a call to a device controlled by the Remote Power On/Off box has a limit on how long it takes to complete the initial connection. The time can be rather long if the power-on and loading procedure are long and if the call is placed through a PBX. In this case, I first place a call, either manually or using the software, to turn on the remote device. I then hang up, wait a minute and then call again. By this time the device has completed its power-on and loading procedure and is waiting for a call, so it picks up on the first ring.

Remote Power On/Off box is ideal for a single PC, even one used to provide remote LAN access. It is also suitable if you have multiple workstations providing remote LAN access, but you will need one Remote Power On/Off box per workstation.

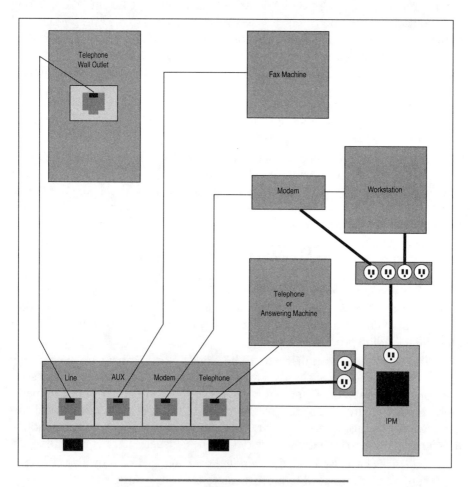

FIGURE 8.23 REMOTE POWER ON/OFF DIAGRAM.

Sentry from Server Technology

Server Technology's Sentry box, shown in Figure 8.24, looks a lot like the Remote Power On/Off box. It uses the same IPMs as the Remote Power On/Off box, but the Sentry box controls up to four IPMs. Multiple Sentry control boxes can be daisy-chained to control more IPMs. You can buy the control boxes and IPMs individually, so you only need to purchase what you will use. The maximum connection distance of 1000 feet from control box to IPM is more useful here than with the Remote Power On/Off box, because the controlled devices are often independent of the Sentry control box. The Sentry control box has four switches and four status LEDs to match the four IPMs that can be controlled. The buttons allow manual control of the devices.

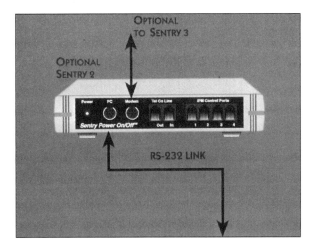

FIGURE 8.24 SENTRY.

Figure 8.25 shows a typical Sentry system layout. The Sentry box can be controlled through a workstation's serial port or from a modem. The modem can also be used in conjunction with the workstation and the Sentry, and one of the IPMs can be set up to operate like the Remote Power On/Off box.

Controlling the Sentry from the attached modem is similar to using a BBS. A microprocessor inside the Sentry provides a specialized BBS interface. A terminal-emulation program is used to call the Sentry's modem. When it answers the Sentry microprocessor sends a prompt to the terminal-emulation program asking for a password. After the proper password is given the microprocessor lets you send commands from the terminal emulation program to turn any IPM on or off. You can also reprogram the configuration of the Sentry box. The Sentry actually keeps track of two passwords. One lets you control the IPMs, while the other lets you also reprogram the Sentry. Only the latter lets you change the passwords. The same configuration procedure is used if you configure the Sentry from a workstation attached to the Sentry.

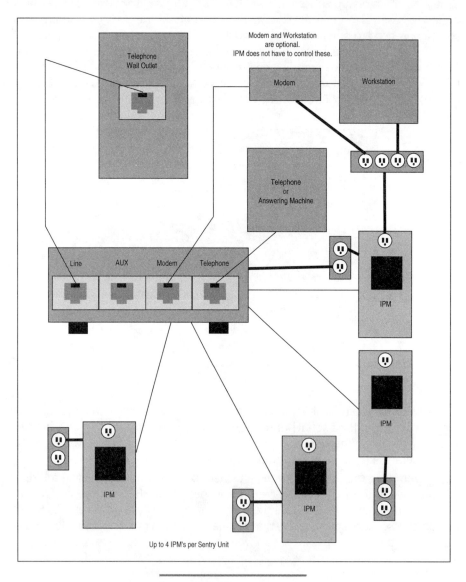

FIGURE 8.25 SENTRY DIAGRAM.

Sentry is an ideal system for controlling multiple devices remotely. All you need is a low-cost modem. It can be a low-speed modem if it is only used to configure the Sentry, because the user interface is character-mode only which works just fine with even a 2400-baud modem. Sentry can also be configured when there is no workstation attached to it. All configuration is done through the modem. In fact, there may not even be a workstation near the Sentry if the devices connected to the IPMs are not workstations.

InControl from Arvee Systems

InControl is designed for heavy-duty, LAN-based power control. The InControl box, shown in Figure 8.26, controls eight outlets. A single 20-amp fuse is shared by all outlets, but you don't have to fill up all the outlets to use InControl. If you have a device that requires 20 amps then you only use one outlet. InControl boxes can be daisy-chained to provide more outlets. Each outlet is individually controlled.

FIGURE 8.26 ARVEE INCONTROL.

Figure 8.27 shows a typical Arvee InControl configuration. The InControl box is connected to a workstation through the workstation's parallel printer port. The workstation must be near the InControl box, but it does not have to be immediately adjacent to it. The devices being controlled may be connected using extension cords, but I would not recommend running a lot of 100-foot extension cords to control devices that are far away.

Arvee has made the InControl box like a tank. There are no switches to manually control power to outlets and there are no status LEDs—just more things to go wrong, according to Arvee design engineers. Luckily, the control software is robust and easy to use. The supplied software can schedule when devices are to be turned on and off, and it is even possible to *down* a NetWare file server (shutting down a file server before turning off the power is the proper way of powering off a server).

InControl does require a workstation, but it is often the LAN manager's console. InControl can provide distant remote power control by running remote control host software on the workstation controlling the InControl box and running the remote control client software on a distant workstation.

InControl is expensive ($1,495) but its ruggedness and reliability can make it worth the money. The cost becomes comparatively less as you make use of more outlets.

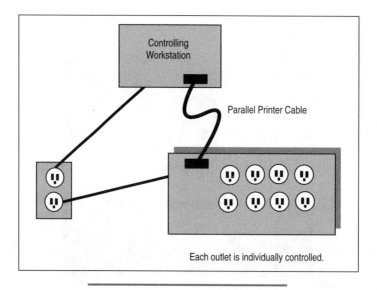

Figure 8.27 Arvee InControl diagram.

Smart UPS from APC

American Power Conversion (APC) makes a number of different UPS products. The Smart UPS systems include a *SmartSlot* that accommodates an SNMP module. The

SNMP module includes an Ethernet adapter. You plug the SNMP module into the SmartSlot and connect the module to the Ethernet, as shown in Figure 8.28. Turn on the UPS and you can now examine the UPS using an SNMP front-end application. An SNMP front-end application is typically a graphical program that can poll SNMP devices and display the gathered information. SNMP is typically used to watch for device failure or for potential network problems. For UPS devices the SNMP polling can check for power outages, power line fluctuations, and low battery charge. SNMP can also be used to control the Smart UPS. In particular it can simulate a power outage or even turn off the power to the devices plugged into the UPS. The UPSes have four or more outlets but they are not individually controlled.

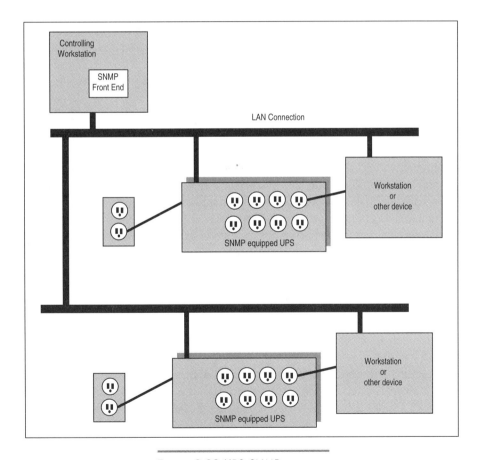

FIGURE 8.28 UPS SNMP DIAGRAM.

The Smart UPS with SNMP has the advantage of providing UPS support as well as remote power control and remote-power monitoring. It is ideal for medium-to-large LANs. Although you may not have a Smart UPS installed on all workstations, you may put one on each file server and each communications server or remote control host workstation.

SNMP front end programs include products like Hewlett Packard's OpenView and Novell Netware's Network Management System, which is now incorporated with Novell's ManageWise product. Front-end programs can be set up to track power outages, power usage, battery levels, and other aspects of a UPS in addition to any other SNMP device. SNMP devices can be anything attached to the network, including file servers, SCSI controllers on a file server, and workstations.

Remote power control systems can be combined with UPS support in a variety of ways. For example, a Sentry IPM could be plugged into a standard UPS, or a Smart UPS could provide power for an Arvee InControl box. No matter how you configure it, remote power control can be a valuable tool in providing remote LAN access.

Voice/Data Modems

Two remote LAN access methods can benefit from voice/data modems: remote control programs and whiteboard programs. Voice/data modems let you use a single telephone line for voice and data. They essentially let you talk while using a remote control program or a whiteboard program. The alternative is to use a second telephone line, which is not always feasible. For long-distance calls it is also not very economical.

Two basic technologies are employed for voice/data modems: simultaneous voice/data (SVD) and switched voice/data. The latter has been patented by Radish Communication Systems Inc. Radish has licensed the technology to a number of vendors. Figure 8.29 shows the difference between the two.

The Radish approach uses the telephone line for either voice or data, and it uses a handshake mechanism to switch between the two so the connection is not lost and you don't hear the data transmission. The two advantages are cost and full telephone-line voice quality. The cost is low because the modems only need to maintain a connection when not sending data; most modems can do this already, so it is just a matter of using the proper software. Voice quality is the same as the telephone-line quality because you use your normal telephone to talk and listen. The disadvantage to the Radish approach is that voice and data can share the line at the same time; for remote control and whiteboard applications this means the screen cannot be updated while you are talking. You can easily switch between modes but it must be done manually and intentionally.

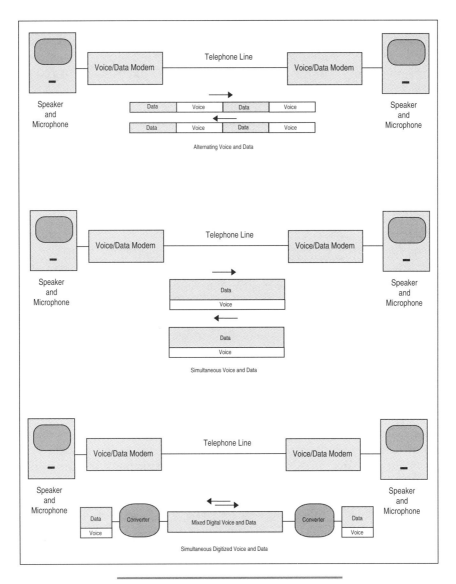

FIGURE 8.29 VOICE/DATA MODE TECHNOLOGIES.

SVD comes in a number of forms, but basically the voice and data information is sent across the telephone line at the same time. Some versions split the telephone line bandwidth into fixed partitions, with one for voice and another for data. Others dynamically change the partition based upon the amount of data being sent. Another way is to use digitized voice and send the digital data and digital voice using one communication link, and multiplexing and demultiplexing the two data streams in software. Digitized voice is digital data created by recording your via a microphone and sound board. Multiplexing is alternately sending data from the voice recording and from the application.

Multi-Tech's MultiModem PCS SVD is a high-performance, V.34, 28,800-baud, data/fax modem with SVD support. The alphabet soup stands for Personal Communication System (PCS) Simultaneous Voice Data (SVD). You connect the modem to a telephone line and you connect a telephone or speaker phone to the other telephone jack on the modem. The telephone or speaker phone can be used to talk and listen to the matching telephone at the other end of the connection. Oh yes, by the way, you need matching SVD modems at both ends if you are using the voice support. This is true for both SVD and Radish modems. Of course, the modems can be used with any other modem if voice support is not used.

The advantage of the SVD modems include the ability to send voice and data across the same telephone line at the same time. The disadvantage is a lower voice quality. In practice the difference in quality is acceptable.

The MultiModem comes bundled with a number of software applications that take advantage of the modem's features. The Windows-based MultiExpress FAX software and MultiExpress PCS (Personal Communication Software). bring the voice-mail capabilities of the hardware into play. The MultiModem cannot only provide SVD support, but also use voice digitization to play back messages stored on the Windows-based workstation's hard disk and to record incoming messages. FutureLabs TALKShow is also included and TALKShow makes use of the SVD support.

MultiTech includes some other nifty software, like its virtual modem driver for Microsoft Windows, which presents the modem as multiple modems attached to different COM ports. Each virtual modem is used for a specific purpose and with a specific application such as the fax support, TALKShow, or a terminal emulation. The virtual modem driver only lets one application use the modem at a time. It also detects the type of connection for incoming calls and routes it to the appropriate application.

SPECIALIZED COMMUNICATION ADAPTERS

Creative Labs (Milpitas, CA) PhoneBlaster represents one of many specialized communication adapters that incorporate a number of communications and multimedia features that can be beneficial to both individual workstations and those providing remote LAN access. The kinds of support provided by this class of adapters includes data modem support, fax modem support, DTMF recognition, and digitized voice recording and playback. These adapters often include multimedia support, including audio and CD-ROM drive support.

The PhoneBlaster (see Figure 8.30) includes all these features for the amazingly low price of $249 (probably less now), and this includes not only the adapter but some rather sophisticated software as well. The PhoneBlaster is a single ISA adapter that includes Creative Lab's SoundBlaster 16 plus an IDE CD-ROM adapter. The CD-ROM is not included but IDE CD-ROM drives are very inexpensive. On top of this the PhoneBlaster includes a 14,400-baud V.32 data/fax modem along with DTMF recognition, Caller ID support and digitized voice recording and playback. A microphone is included with the package. It is designed to work with the SoundBlaster 16 and, with the speakers you add, it combines to form a speaker phone system.

FIGURE 8.30 CREATIVE LABS PHONEBLASTER.

The bundled software takes advantage of all these features. The SoundBlaster 16 support includes drivers for environments like Microsoft Windows. Creative Labs' VoiceAssist and TextAssist also make use of the SoundBlaster 16 support. VoiceAssist is a voice-recognition program that runs under Microsoft Windows. It matches voice commands to program commands so you can speak to your computer and make it work for you. Unfortunately, voice recognition still needs a bit of work. Commands must be uttered as individual words, not as continuous sentences. Even so, it can be useful and entertaining. TextAssist works in the other direction. It will read text to you using a computer-generated voice. This actually works better than VoiceAssist.

The telephone features are used by Kalman's Ancilla program, which also runs under Microsoft Windows. Ancilla is a voice-mail system that includes fax support, an auto-dialer, and a terminal-emulation program. The voice-mail system uses a preconfigured prompting system. You can change the voice prompts (see Figure 8.31) and you can set up multiple voice-mail boxes, but you cannot change the general operation. It is rather simple in execution. An incoming call is answered. Ancilla first waits to hear if the call is from a fax machine. If so, it receives the fax and saves the fax file in the Inbox (see Figure 8.32) for later viewing. If not, the initial voice prompt is played. The caller can then select what to do, using a Touch-Tone phone. Ancilla uses the DTMF detection support to determine what key is pressed. As with most voice-mail systems, you hear additional recordings based on the keys you press. Eventually you can leave a message, in which case Ancilla records the message and saves the digitized version onto the hard disk. An entry is saved in the Inbox. You can also leave faxes with a voice message.

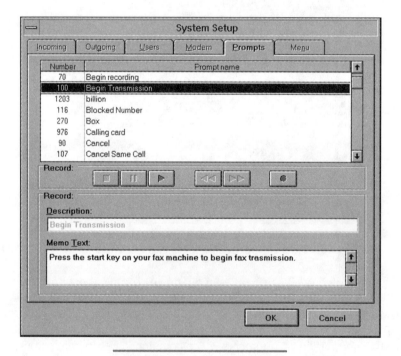

FIGURE 8.31 ANCILLA SETUP SCREEN.

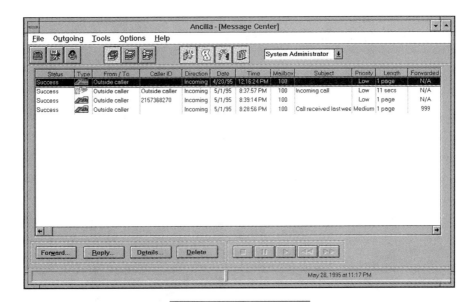

FIGURE 8.32 ANCILLA INBOX.

Ancilla also provides a limited fax-on-demand capability, as shown in Figure 8.33. Callers can select the document to send and have it sent using the same telephone connection. Ancilla works well if you have only a handful of documents that can be requested. If you have dozens of documents that must be available, then a dedicated fax-on-demand system is more appropriate. Ancilla can keep the faxes on a file server if the workstation is on the network. This lets any network user update the documents as necessary.

Just to make things interesting, the PhoneBlaster can utilize WAV and MIDI files as background music for the voice-mail system. It can even route audio from an audio CD-ROM if you have it in the CD-ROM drive.

Ancilla can also send faxes and voice messages. Incoming calls can also be screened using Caller ID if your telephone company supports it, and if you have the support enabled on the telephone line.

Creative Labs PhoneBlaster represents the low end of the multifunction communication products. It provides an ideal base for a small office LAN. If this is your work environment then keep an eye out for products like the PhoneBlaster, and third-party applications that are even more powerful than Ancilla. For environments with large LANs and heftier communication needs, look to the vendors of dedicated hardware and software products designed to handle multiple telephone lines and larger numbers of remote users.

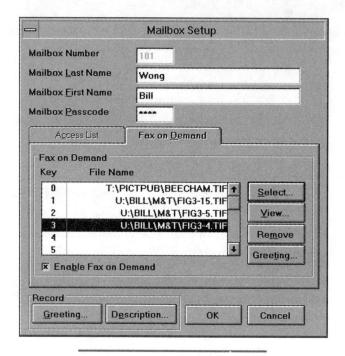

FIGURE 8.33 ANCILLA FAX-ON-DEMAND.

CHAPTER 9

THE INTERNET

The *Internet* is a public global-area network (GAN). It is currently the only one of its kind. The Internet is made up of many interconnected wide area networks (WANs) that are made up of many local area networks (LANs.) Some nodes in the Internet are actually single-user or multiuser systems, usually running UNIX, rather than LANs, but for our purposes we will consider them LANs.

THE INTERNET

The term *Internet* has several connotations associated with it. In reality, the Internet is a giant network that provides the same kind of transport mechanisms as a LAN. As such, many different services can be provided, but there are a number of services that have lately been associated with the Internet, including the World Wide Web (WWW, or simply the Web) and File Transfer Protocol (FTP) servers. Internet mail and related news groups are also very popular.

FTP actually came before the Web, but the Web is one of the hottest things around. FTP sites are similar to network disks on a LAN but data must be moved between FTP sites as files. Data within a file cannot be accessed directly. FTP site access used to be accomplished using command-line interfaces similar to UNIX and DOS, but today most FTP access is through GUI applications like the one shown in Figure 9.1. The initial connection is made using a name like **acme.com** or **whatsamatu.edu**. Once connected, a file management dialog box like the one in the figure is presented. Two panes are normally shown: one shows a local directory and the other shows a directory located at the FTP site. You can copy files in either direction and navigate through the directories, just as with a file management program using local disks and directories.

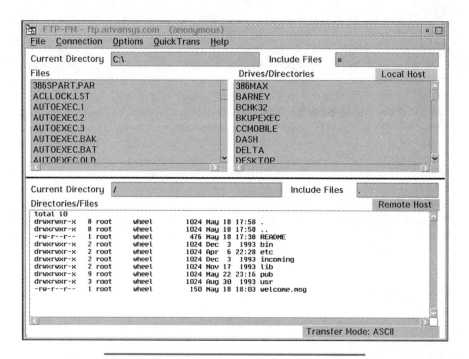

FIGURE 9.1 SAMPLE FTP GUI FRONT-END APPLICATION.

FTP support is one way to provide remote LAN access. A user needs a connection to the Internet and matching FTP software. The LAN needs to provide an FTP site and a connection to the Internet.

The Web is a very specialized, distributed, hypertext document store. The documents are written using the HyperText Markup Language (HTML). Web viewers programs allow users to locate HTML documents and display their contents, which can include text, graphics, audio, and video clips. Figure 9.2 shows a typical Web viewer displaying a page of text and graphics. Web documents are kept in FTP sites, and the hypertext links let you move from one document to another—even if the new document is located elsewhere on the Internet. To a user, the Web appears as one large collection of documents. Web documents are primarily for viewing, and you can often save the documents or portions of the documents on your workstation that is running the Web viewer. Some web documents can also present forms that can be filled out; the information is saved at a Web site, where it can be used for almost any purpose. For example, forms can be used for surveys or to request a fax document to be sent to a fax machine.

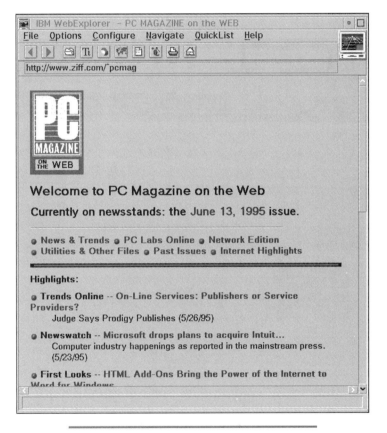

FIGURE 9.2 WORLD WIDE WEB VIEWER APPLICATION.

Internet mail operates like LAN mail. You create a message, add an address, and send it off. The Internet uses a store-and-forward system, so your mail message may stop at a number of locations before it arrives at its destination. You pick up your mail from a designated destination, which is effectively a post office. In fact, it is an FTP site, but for most users it is easier to call it a post office. Gateways that run on LANs and provide a link between the Internet post offices and mail post office products can be purchased. The gateways are usually bidirectional so mail can be sent from a LAN workstation, to a local post office through its gateway to the Internet to a person whose post office is accessible through the Internet (see Figure 9.3). Incoming mail goes in the reverse direction, with the mail gateway picking up mail for you from the Internet post office on a periodic basis.

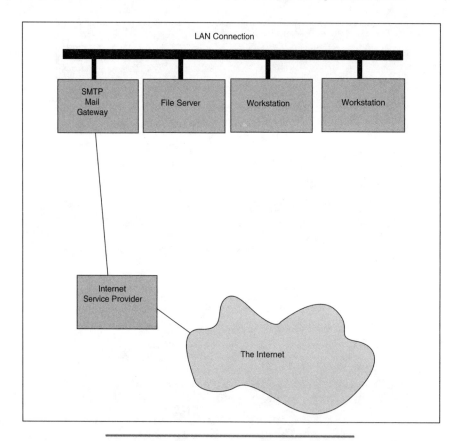

FIGURE 9.3 MAIL AND GATEWAYS TO INTERNET MAIL.

Internet *news groups* are a special form of Internet post office. A news group has a name like **alt.best.of.internet**. A news group is read using an Internet news reader application. Messages are added to a news section by sending mail to them. Anyone can read the messages in a news group. It is one way to stay up-to-date on different topics, although some news groups receive hundreds of messages daily.

The Internet can also be used for direct LAN connections. In this case, your workstation or local LAN can be connected to a remote LAN through the Internet. The underlaying TCP/IP support used in the Internet is used to accomplish this task. The local workstation or LAN and the remote LAN must also be using TCP/IP, although it is possible for TCP/IP to be used only at the gateway between the Internet and the LAN or local workstation. Some of the reasons for using the Internet rather than modems and telephones include the accessibility of the Internet, high-speed links, and a common access method to both the Internet and your remotely accessible LAN.

You can use the Internet to provide any or all of the services discussed here with the proper hardware, software, and service providers. Internet *service providers* let you get to the Internet. Although it is possible to have a direct connection to the Internet, these direct connections are normally limited to service providers, very large companies, large government organizations, and large educational institutions. Service providers sell access and services for the Internet. You would use a local service provider to access the Internet and to provide services such as an FTP or Web site. Although it might not be easy to find Internet service providers in your telephone yellow pages you can find some advertising in various computer and communication magazines.

The Internet is generally accessible, but it is not free, although some people would like it to be. You will pay fees to service providers to access the Internet and for other services the service provider may have, such as supporting a post office where your mail can be sent even when you are not connected to the Internet when the mail is received. The types of services and the pricing structure are often difficult to decipher but your service provider will usually be happy to explain the details.

There are books dedicated to connecting to the Internet, using Internet software and services, and doing all sorts of wonderful things with the Internet. This chapter is written only as an introduction to some of the things that can be done with the Internet with respect to remote LAN access.

Internet Basics

The basic network protocol used in the Internet is TCP/IP (Transmission Control Protocol/Internet Protocol). IP uses a 4-byte addressing scheme, which is usually written as 111.222.333.444, to uniquely identify each node in the Internet. TCP/IP can also be used in a LAN that is not connected with the Internet where each workstation has its own address. Two workstations on two different LANs can have the same IP address, but the LANs could never be connected together. Connecting a LAN to the Interent means that it is connected to the other LANs on the Internet. Therefore, a LAN's set of IP addresses must be unique when it connects to the Internet.

The standard IP addressing scheme allows for an extremely large number of addresses, but the number available for new users of the Internet is decreasing quickly. A number of proposed enhancements are being developed to create more addresses so more people can use the Internet. IP*ng* is one such proposal; it increases the addressing scheme to four 16-bit words instead of four 8-bit bytes. Although any change will probably not impact users directly in how their Internet and LAN applications work, LAN manager's will need to know about the difference and how it will impact their users. The issues involved are beyond the scope of this book, but LAN managers can find answers and information from their Internet access service providers and the Internet support application providers.

Most users never see the underlying IP addressing. Instead you will use names that are converted transparently to IP addresses by the software you use, just like the standard LAN software uses low-level NIC addresses. A typical user name looks like **user@foo.internet.org.** The portion to the right of the *at* (**@**) is the name of an organization and the portion to the left of it is a particular user. Multipart names are separated by periods. By convention, the last part of the organization name indicates the type of organization such as *edu* for educational institution, *gov* for government organization, or *com* for a company. User names are often single words that range from a person's surname to their full name. One special name, *anonymous*, is used when you want to use a public FTP site. FTP sites, and many other Internet services, can have restricted access; they require a name and password to access the service. *Anonymous* is used to distinguish between public and individual use.

Web and FTP sites have their own naming system that incoporates the organization names. The names look like UNIX file names:

```
http://foo.com/abc
ftp://foo.com/directory/news
```

The first name designates an HTML document used by the Web. The name is also called a Universal Resource Locator (URL), and the URL is used in an HTML document for hypertext links to other documents. The FTP name is a quick way to indicate to an FTP front-end application what FTP site to use and the directory path whose contents are to be displayed. Often the initial **http:** and **ftp:** are omitted because the application being used knows what prefixes are necessary.

Although HTML documents are text files, I am not going to cover the contents or makeup of HTML documents for two reasons. First, users never view the contents directly. Instead the contents are presented using Web viewer applications, which display the documents in a formatted fashion using scalable fonts and graphics, which may be included as part of the document. Second, people creating HTML documents typically use special editing applications that present the document in an application-specific fashion. An important thing to note is that a *document* is a simple file with links to other documents (see figure 9.4).

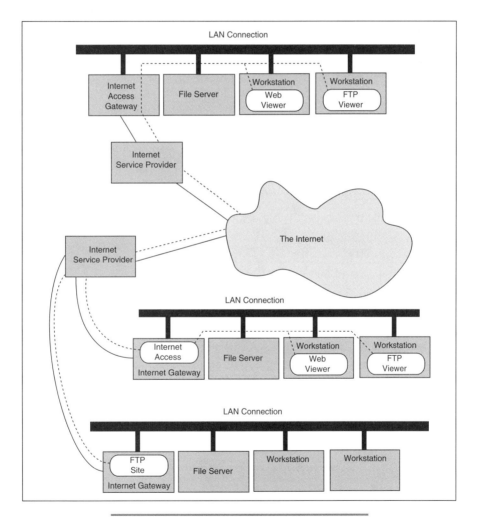

FIGURE 9.4 PROVIDING AND USING INTERNET SERVICES.

If finding information on the Internet is a chore you would rather not do, turning to a program is natural. Two popular Internet applications are *Gopher* and *Archie*. Actually, like other Internet applications, these are services; front-end applications provide access to them. Without going into too many details, these programs can be used to search the Internet for documents and files on specific topics. You can search specific sites and look for titles and text strings. Often, you can start a search that is actually performed after you disconnect from the Internet; you will get a mail message with the results of a search. The results of a search are usually the FTP site and file or Web URL names. These may be associated with a brief title of the item or a section of the text that contains the items that were used as the search pattern.

Types of Internet Connections

Connecting with the Internet from a workstation typically has little, if any, security issues associated with the connection. The Internet applications running on the workstation may require a user name and password to gain access to the Internet through your service provider. Connecting a LAN to the Internet is another matter. There are actually three ways to connect a LAN to the Internet (see Figure 9.4):

1. As an Internet site
2. As an access point to the Internet for users on the LAN
3. As part of the Internet

The three can be combined and a single connection used for all purposes, but this is best left to the product you choose to provide the connection. A fourth way to access the Internet is to use a mail gateway. From a LAN manager's viewpoint, the mail gateway is a special case of providing an Internet site, but to a user it will appear as another distinct access method.

An Internet site is one that provides services, such as an FTP site or a Web site. An Internet site is normally connected to the Internet at all times although it does not have to be. Of course, Internet users can only access an Internet site when it is connected to the Internet.

Individual workstations on a LAN can be connected to the Internet, just like a stand-alone workstation, but it is possible to use a single connection for one LAN. Although a single connection is used, LAN users can have individual accounts for mail on the Internet. A single connection can become overloaded if a number of users try to download too much information at the same time, but it is possible to upgrade to a higher-speed link. High-speed links cost more, but the cost may be worth it compared to using multiple telephone links that run at a slower speed. A single LAN connection is easier to support and manage.

Linking a LAN to the Internet lets Internet users access your LAN services directly. For example, a remote workstation could log in to your LAN's network operating system and access network disk files and printers. Providing direct access across the Internet should be done very carefully. It is possible to have secure connections, but it is just as easy to have an unsecure connection with potentially thousands of uninvited guests. TCP/IP is used as the main transport mechanism, so at least a portion of your LAN needs to be running TCP/IP and the remote workstation or LAN must also be running TCP/IP.

When investigating a LAN connection to the Internet you will hear the term *firewall*. A *firewall* may be software or a combination of hardware and software designed to limit the traffic between the Internet and your LAN (see Figure 9.5.) A firewall can limit access to LAN resources from the Internet and to the Internet from LAN workstations.

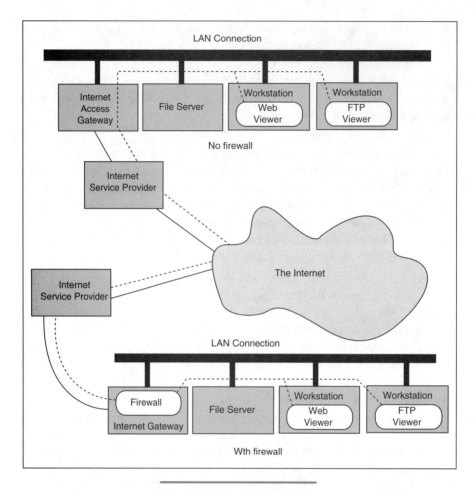

FIGURE 9.5 INTERNET FIREWALLS.

At a lower level, near TCP/IP land and the telephone, we have two popular protocols that are normally used between Internet service providers and workstations or LAN gateways. The first is called *Serial Link* IP (SLIP) and the other is called *Point-to-Point Protocol* (PPP). The actual protocol you need to use depends on the Internet software you run on the local workstation or LAN and the protocol required by your service provider. PPP is the newer and more flexible of the two protocols, although both operate over modems and telephone lines as well as ISDN and high-speed dedicated telephone lines.

Internet connections are becoming more common everyday. We will cover the many different ways to connect to the Internet in the following sections.

A USER'S VIEW OF INTERNET CONNECTIONS

A user can access Internet services, connect to a LAN through the Internet, and access services being provided to the Internet through the LAN as shown in Figure 9.6. A user accessing Internet services such as FTP sites, Web sites, and Internet mail and news groups uses front-end applications for either direct connections or LAN-to-Internet connections. For example, Figures 9.7 and 9.8 show what some front-end applications look like. There is no difference whether the connection is directly between the workstation and the Internet service provider or over a LAN through a shared Internet connection. The main difference between the two types of connections occurs when the user makes a logical connection to the Internet. With a direct workstation-to-Internet connection the logical and physical connections are the same. The typical modem connection is initiated using a connection application like the one shown in Figure 9.9. The required information includes the phone number of the Internet service provider, the user's Internet name, and a password. The LAN workstation-to-Internet connection uses a similar program, but the logical connection is through the LAN to the Internet gateway, which is normally already connected to the Internet service provider, or the connection can be made when a LAN user needs to access the Internet. In this case, the phone number of the service provider is maintained by the Internet gateway, which is configured by the LAN manager. The user needs to simply provide his or her Internet name and password.

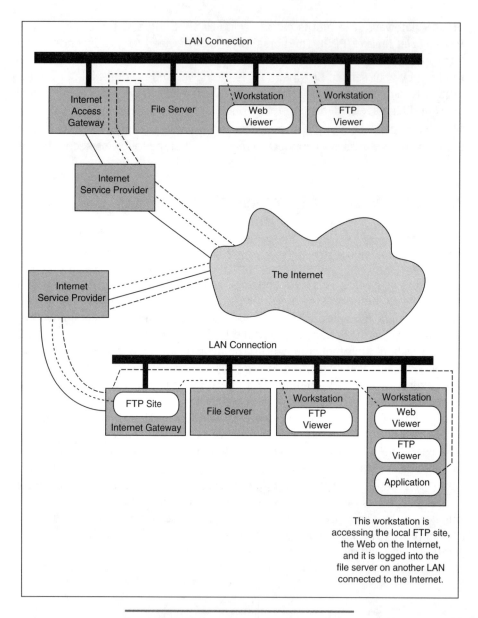

FIGURE 9.6 USER ACCESS TO INTERNET SERVICES.

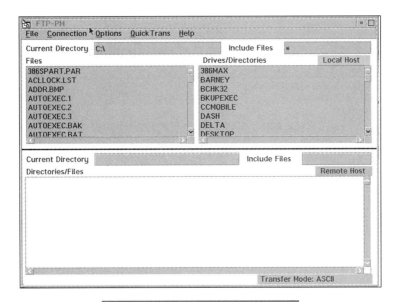

FIGURE 9.7 FTP FRONT-END APPLICATION.

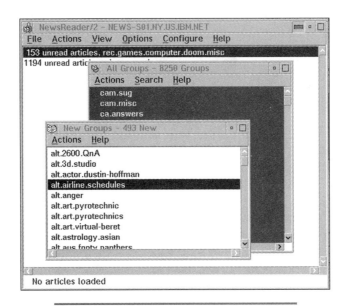

FIGURE 9.8 NEWS READER FRONT-END APPLICATION.

FIGURE 9.9 DIRECT INTERNET DIALER PROGRAM.

Sending and receiving mail across the Internet is possible using an Internet front-end mail application like the front-end applications already discussed. It is also possible to use a mail gateway to exchange mail. In this case, the LAN manager must set up the gateway prior to its use. The gateway simplifies a user's view of the mail system—and thus the LAN mail system and the use of Internet addresses. The advantage is the ability to send mail to LAN and Internet users simultaneously. From a user's point of view, there are no disadvantages.

Accessing a remote LAN as a remote workstation using the Internet uses a similar connection program. The main difference is the added information needed to connect to the remote LAN and what happens after the connection is made. The remote LAN's site name is needed so the LAN can be contacted when the remote workstation connects to the Internet. Once connected, the remote work-station acts just like a workstation on the LAN. The user must log into the remote LAN to gain access to the LAN's resources. The standard network operating system applications are used to access the resources. The main operating difference between a remote workstation connected through the Internet and a remote work-station calling directly into a LAN is the additional delay imposed on data going through the Internet. The delay may be minimal, but it can vary due to data traffic on the Internet. The delay is also based on how many hops the data must make between the remote workstation and the LAN. A *hop* is a connection between Internet routers. There are at least two hops involved in a LAN connection through the Internet. The first is between the remote workstation and the Internet and the second is from the Internet to the LAN. There is typically a third between the two routers on the Internet, as shown in Figure 9.10.

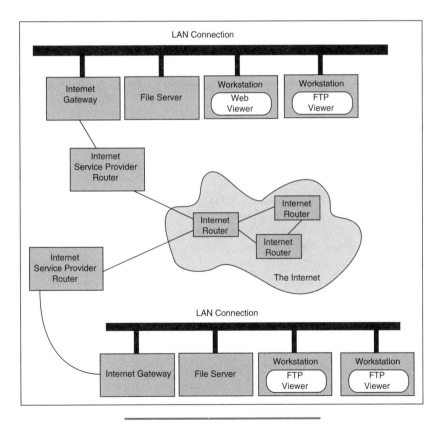

FIGURE 9.10 ROUTERS ON THE INTERNET.

The advantages of using the Internet are speed and the number of potential access points. The Internet uses very high-speed links between routers so it can handle quite a bit of traffic. Connections to service providers can also use high-speed links such as T3 and T1 lines. These connections are typically faster than what dial-up telephone lines can provide. A single connection from a LAN to the Internet can actually support multiple remote workstations connected to different access points on the Internet. In fact, access points are available worldwide. The main disadvantages of using the Internet are speed and security. The Internet is used heavily on a daily basis, so even its high-speed links can become heavily loaded with traffic from other sources. Security is an issue for both users and LAN managers; it takes a good deal of skill to tap into a LAN connection across the Internet. If you do not want other Internet users to see what you are sending, then encryption may be necessary. In this case, an additional password may be necessary for use with the encryption and decryption process.

A user on a LAN that provides Internet services such as an FTP or Web site may have access to the files and directories used by these services. The LAN manager may also have placed restrictions on these files and directories for security purposes. Users that have access can add files that Internet users can access and can copy files that Internet users have left, normally using an FTP front-end application. The directories used by the services will appear as normal network directories so conventional applications such as file managers can be used to access and update files.

Users with access to directories used by an FTP or Web site must be careful not to delete or update critical files such as the home page of a Web site. The *home page* is the HTML document that is presented to Internet users when they first access a Web site. Deleting this file means Internet users will not have access to the Web site because there is nothing to look at. Likewise, the HTML documents have links to other documents. Improperly constructed HTML documents can cause similar problems. Often the LAN manager will restrict access to critical files and directories to prevent such accidents.

Users have a fairly straightforward view of the Internet and Internet services provided from a LAN. Most of the difficult work is performed by the LAN manager in setting up the Internet support.

A LAN MANAGER'S VIEW OF INTERNET CONNECTIONS

While the user's view of the Internet and connections between their workstation and LAN are relatively simple, the LAN manager's view looks much more complicated. This is a slight exaggeration, and Internet access support is improving but

Internet access with a LAN is still a major job. It is also a critical job because Internet access opens up your LAN to the rather large Internet community as well as provides access to the Internet to LAN users. Security and Internet use are important factors, which the LAN manager must balance against flexibility and accessibility. The LAN manager wants to make access, both to and from the Internet, as easy as possible for valid users and as difficult as possible for invalid users. While many organizations provide unrestricted access to most of their services, most companies will do so only for a limited subset of services and resources. Firewalls play a critical part in maintaining limits.

As mentioned earlier, there are three kinds of Internet access that a LAN manager can install. The first is to make the LAN an Internet site that can provide services such as an FTP site, a Web site, or a post office for Internet mail. Internet mail uses the Simple Mail Transfer Protocol (SMTP), and many LAN mail programs provide an SMTP gateway to integrate Internet mail with LAN mail. The second type of Internet access allows LAN users to access Internet services. The third method is to allow a remote workstation or a remote LAN to become part of the local LAN. The mail gateway is viewed by a user as a fourth Internet access method.

We now take a more detailed look at the access methods and the LAN manager's involvement in installing and maintaining Internet support. This discussion is very general. The Internet and the products that support Internet access are advancing rapidly, especially in the areas of security and maintainability. Any kind of Internet access, with the exception of a single workstation accessing the Internet, involves a major commitment in time and money, which can vary depending on the level of involvement. Simply providing a low-volume FTP site will have a lower cost than a high-volume FTP site or a Web site. *Low volume* means that the number of Internet users accessing the site will be low and the amount of data transferred between the site and the Internet will also be low.

Providing an Internet site is a major commitment for a LAN manager, in terms of the initial setup. Many Internet service providers can configure and maintain various Internet services for you on their computers. In this case, you would be able to access and maintain information on this site through the Internet or you could send new information to the service provider who would install the information on its computers for availability to Internet users. The alternative is to use a computer on your LAN as an Internet site to provide the necessary services. A service provider will often be able to recommend software and hardware for this purpose. You will also need to negotiate price and support for the site. This includes the necessary Internet addresses to be used by your site. The minimum connection between your site and the service provider is a dial-up telephone line using a modem. The modem connection is suitable for low-volume applications, such as an FTP site to be used by a limited number of Internet users. Access will typically be restricted using passwords, and anonymous access will be limited or unavailable. Higher-volume applications or sites with multiple services will require higher-bandwidth connections starting with an ISDN line graduating to a dedicated T1 line. Initial startup costs, including telephone line hookups, run a couple hundred dollars for low-bandwidth solutions to thousands of dollars for high-bandwidth solutions. Monthly charges also need to be considered in the overall cost structure of the project but it is very difficult to give an estimate for these charges due to variability in costs based on service providers, telephone companies, and the estimated number of Internet users accessing the site.

Setting up an Internet site is getting easier. It used to require a computer running UNIX with a systems manager that understood UNIX, TCP/IP, and the Internet. Today you can buy a box that comes with software installed so that all you need to do is get the telephone lines installed, contract with a service provider, connect the box to the modem and the LAN, and run through a relatively painless installation procedure. Sun's Netra is one such product. Although a good understanding of the product and the Internet is needed, the background necessary to understand and maintain such a system is significantly less than that needed for a custom solution.

Security is a major consideration when adding an Internet site. Providing LAN-to-Internet access has its own security considerations, which we will discuss later, but providing an Internet site is riskier. There have been many published reports about Internet break-ins, worms, viruses, and other horrific security breaches. Many problems can be prevented, but the possibility of these problems occurring is often enough to scare away prospective site providers. A LAN manager needs to consider the risks, potential benefits, and the various configurations that are possible when adding an Internet site. Figure 9.11 shows possible configurations with different degrees of risk. The first shows a site that is not part of the local LAN. Compromising the Internet site does not compromise the LAN. The next alternative is to make a connection between the LAN and the Internet site using a connection that is not compatible with the Internet, such as a remote control program. The Internet site is on its own LAN, and a remote control host workstation is on the same LAN. This configuration allows a user on the local LAN to access the Internet site computer using the remote control host workstation. This configuration prevents an Internet user from accessing the local LAN through the Internet site. This remote access method is suitable for site maintenance but does not provide access to the Internet. The next alternative is to use a single LAN for both the site and local users but the LAN does not use TCP/IP. The Internet site computer will use TCP/IP over the connection to the Internet service provider. The

Internet site computer should also be different from the file server used by the LAN. Internet users will only be able to access information on the site computer and not the rest of the LAN. Finally, we have the firewall approach where the LAN also makes use of TCP/IP as a transport protocol. The firewall can be configured to limit traffic between the Internet and the LAN. While this configuration is the most flexible, it is also the most prone to abuse. Be careful when evaluating the firewall software and risks involved in making your site and LAN available to the Internet.

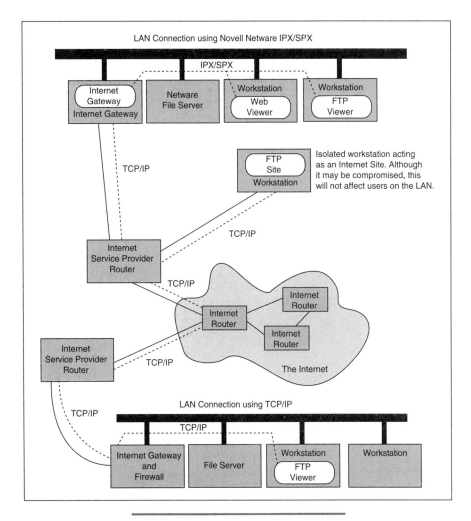

FIGURE 9.11 INTERNET SITE CONFIGURATIONS.

Implementing a mail gateway is often a viable alternative to a full Internet site. Internet mail can originate from anywhere on the Internet using almost any Internet-compatible mail program (see Figure 9.12). A LAN manager can connect a local LAN-based post office to the Internet using an SMTP gateway. Many mail vendors have their own SMTP gateway products, or you may be able to go through an intermediate post office such as Novell's MHS. In this case, the LAN post office needs a gateway to MHS and you will also need an MHS-to-SMTP gateway. The advantage of a mail gateway is security. The mail gateways are bidirectional, but only mail traffic is allowed. Direct access to the Internet or from the Internet to the LAN is not allowed.

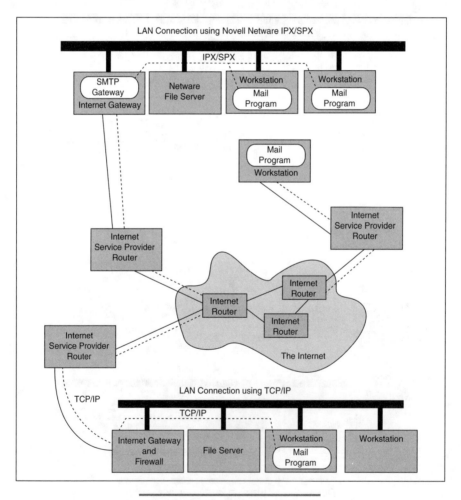

FIGURE 9.12 INTERNET MAIL GATEWAY.

Although a mail gateway is more secure than other Internet access methods you will still need to consider the ramifications of Internet access. The most common problem with a mail gateway is the accidental transmission of an important document or file to a user on the Internet. For example, most mail programs let you use aliases. An *alias* is a short name to be used in place of a users full mail address. For example **bill** may be used instead of **WilliamWong@company.com**. A LAN user may mistake the alias for someone on the LAN and accidentally send a message to the wrong person, or the alias may be included in a mailing list. In any case, users need to be made aware of what kinds of messages should be sent on the Internet and how to avoid accidentally sending a message to someone on the Internet. Luckily, it is usually impossible to accidentally send a message to everyone on the Internet or to someone whose Internet address is not part of the mail program's address book.

One way to help prevent accidental transmission to the Internet is to include a special character in the alias name of an Internet user. For example, ˜**bill** could be used instead of **bill** to indicate an Internet user. The same would be true for mail list names.

Setting up a mail gateway with a service provider is typically different than setting up an Internet site. Check with your service provider to see what kinds of services they can provide and what kind of requirements must be met by your software. Not all service providers and Internet packages work together.

Providing LAN users with Internet access is the next access method we will look at. In this case we want to let LAN users access the Internet using front-end applications such as FTP and Web viewers. These programs run on the user's LAN workstation and communicate with the Internet through the LAN's Internet access point, which is connected to your Internet service provider. There are really two ways of providing this service, as shown in Figure 9.13. The first is to use TCP/IP on the LAN and to provide a TCP/IP connection to the Internet service provider. The second is to use a LAN protocol such as Novell's IPX and to install an access point on the LAN that connects to the Internet service provider using TCP/IP. The difference between the two approaches is in how the front-end applications work with the access point. In the first case, the access point simply passes data through to the Internet. The front-end applications work with the Internet services using TCP/IP. In the second case, the access point is a more complicated piece of software. The front-end applications work with the access point, which then generates TCP/IP messages that are sent to the Internet services. Incoming information is received by the access point and sent over the LAN to the front-end applications. The second case essentially has a built-in firewall because Internet traffic on the LAN only occurs between the access point and the front-end applications. The rest of the LAN is isolated from the Internet and its users. It is possible to include a firewall in the first case, and most products do so.

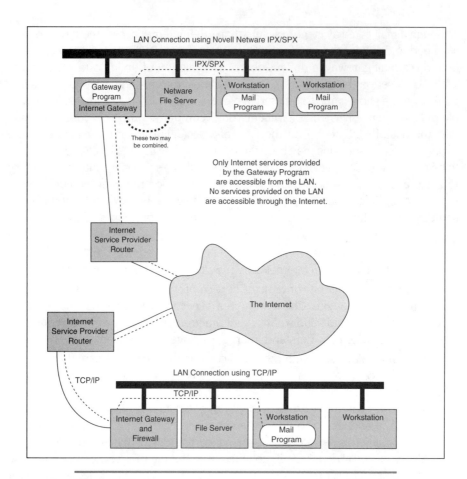

FIGURE 9.13 TWO WAYS TO PROVIDE LAN ACCESS TO THE INTERNET.

The most ambitious connection to the Internet provides remote workstation connections to the LAN and can even allow another LAN to be connected with yours over the Internet. The remote workstation or LAN and the local LAN must both be running TCP/IP. It is possible to use a technique called tunneling instead. *Tunneling* embeds one protocol in data using another protocol. For example, the local and remote LANs could use Novell NetWare's IPX. The routers connected to the Internet use TCP/IP and send IPX data in TCP/IP packets. The IPX data is restored at the other end. Although tunneling adds some overhead it can be more secure because TCP/IP traffic does not move on the LAN.

Firewalls and encryption can be used with LAN-Internet connections. These tools are actually more critical with this type of connection because it is more prone to infiltration by Internet users. TCP/IP traffic on the Internet can come from and go to any point on the Internet. Although you can control what occurs at the access points, you cannot determine where information is coming from and going to. It is possible for a sophisticated Internet user to *spoof* the Internet access point by appearing to be a valid user. While the techniques used to spoof and to prevent spoofing are beyond the scope of this book, you can find out more about security problems and prevention from other Internet books and from your product and service provider.

Internet connection methods can be provided individually or in concert with each other. The advantage of the latter is the ability to use a single connection to the service provider. The disadvantage is more complex security issues. It is possible to use multiple methods with their own Internet connections, as shown in Figure 9.14. The advantages of splitting up the connections are the added bandwidth with multiple connections and the ability to control security based on the type of connection.

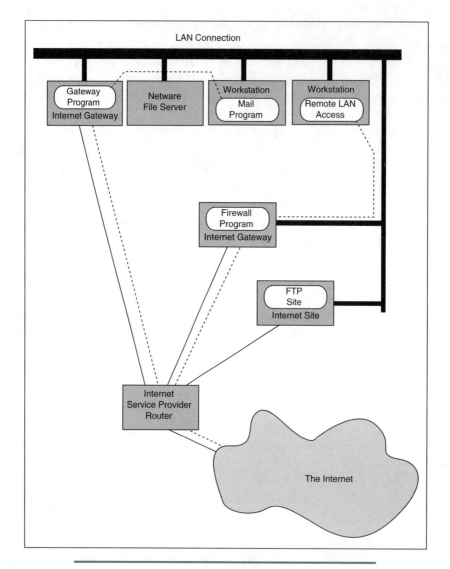

FIGURE 9.14 MULTIPLE SERVICES USING DIFFERENT CONNECTIONS.

Providing connections to the Internet is not something to do in a haphazard manner. Most other remote LAN access methods have significantly lower security risks simply because the number of users that can find the access point is lower. With a telephone-based remote LAN access method, such as the remote control remote

LAN access method, a remote user needs to know the telephone number and have the appropriate software, user name, and password to even attempt to access the LAN. With an Internet connection, however, an Internet user can more easily find an Internet site's address, equivalent to the telephone number, and they already have the applications that work with the Internet. All that is required is a valid user name and password, possibly obtained by nefarious means or a method whereby security can be breached without these. The public nature of the Internet is therefore both an advantage and a disadvantage. It provides many people access to Internet sites; whether it is an advantage or a disadvantage depends on which users gain access to which sites.

Your job as a LAN manager and Internet access provider is to provide the appropriate Internet access methods within the range of risks your company is willing to live with and within the capabilities of the products you can use to implement the connections.

HOW DO INTERNET CONNECTIONS WORK?

The Internet is neither magic nor extremely complex from a technical standpoint. There are many technical details involved with any kind of Internet connection, but not really any more than those encountered on a LAN or a WAN. Starting at the lowest level we have the TCP/IP transport protocol used on the Internet. This is the same protocol that can be used on a LAN and it is one reason that you can use the Internet to connect to a LAN as a remote workstation. The details of TCP/IP are about as important to most users and LAN managers as the details of any other protocol such as Novell NetWare's IPX, so we will leave these details to the designers, programmers, and sophisticated technical people that debug low-level LAN problems. For our purposes, we can view the Internet as a collection of LANs and routers, as shown in Figure 9.15. In fact, this view is relatively accurate, and it is the same configuration for a larger LAN that contains routers. The idea of a router is to move traffic from one area to another as needed instead of having one large LAN. Dividing the network into segments keeps local traffic moving quickly and lets long-distance traffic move through routers until it reaches its destination. The main difference between the Internet and a smaller LAN with a few routers is the distance between routers and the speed at which the throughput of the connections occurs. The Internet has a wide variety of routers and connection types. Very high-speed links connect larger routers together, which in turn exchange data with smaller routers that typically use slower connections. Eventually the connections from the access providers to your workstation or LAN come into play; often the slowest connections are found. Even these tend to be high-speed modem connections.

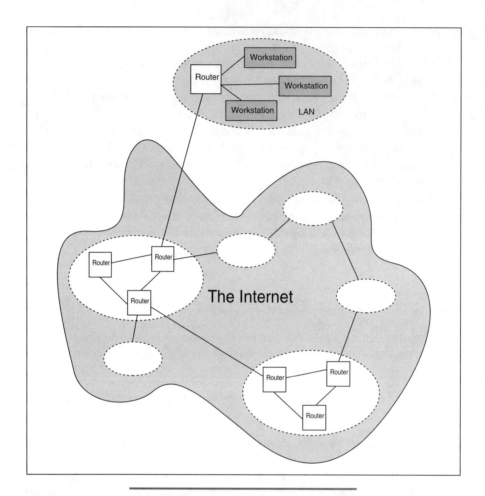

FIGURE 9.15 INTERNET AS LANS AND ROUTERS.

Other Internet services and remote LAN connections are built on top of this TCP/IP-router transport system. Although the transport system is really the Internet, the term I*nternet* normally incorporates the transport system, and the popular services now provided by the Internet include FTP and Web sites. The Internet is not really limited to these services, and new services are slowly emerging. Audio and video are becoming more common on the Internet, but like the World Wide Web, the services are a novelty at first; they may turn into a commonly used feature of the Internet later, however.

Since we started with the underlying TCP/IP transport system, we might as well look at how the transport system can be used to connect a remote workstation to a

LAN. Figure 9.16 shows how the Internet can be used to connect a remote workstation to some LANs connected to the Internet. The LAN and the workstation still use a higher-level protocol based on the network operating system but this uses TCP/IP as the transport system for moving data between the workstation and a file server. While most LANs are not connected to the Internet, LANs that are are potentially vulnerable to access by Internet users who should not be on your LAN. Firewalls and encryption of data sent across the Internet are two ways to prevent unwanted visitors from accessing LAN resources and viewing data sent across the Internet.

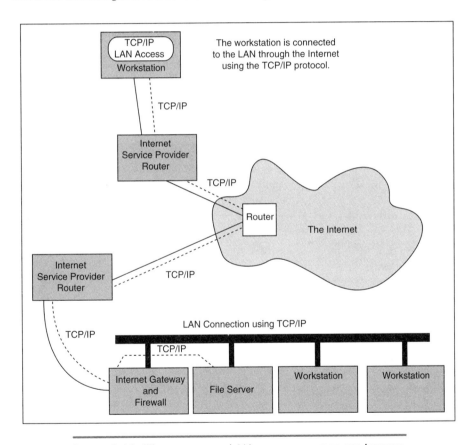

FIGURE 9.16 WORKSTATION-TO-LAN CONNECTION OVER THE INTERNET.

The two other Internet access methods provide opposite support. One, providing an Internet site, provides Internet users with access to your LAN, possibly indirectly. The other provides LAN users with access to the Internet. The latter is functionally identical to connecting a user's workstation directly to the Internet from a user's viewpoint.

Providing an Internet site involves connecting a computer to the Internet, usually through a service provider. The computer can be a stand-alone device, or it can be attached to a local LAN. From an Internet user's viewpoint, the computer is attached only to the Internet. There are a number of details involved in the support and connection process, which we shall ignore so we can concentrate on how the site provides its services to Internet users.

The three type of site services that are typically provided are FTP support, Web support, and mail support. Actually all three are fundamentally the same, as we shall see. There are many other types of services that can be provided using the Internet but we will not be looking at any of these. An FTP site provides a hierarchical file storage system similar to a network's shared disk. The main difference between the two is that an FTP site deals in complete files. You can get a list of files and directories from an FTP site, you can get a file from an FTP site, and you can send a file to an FTP site. User names and passwords can be used for security with the **anonymous** name and no password being the standard free access user identification. Like a network operating system's security system, an FTP site can restrict access to certain directories based on the user.

A Web site works the same way as an FTP site except that the files are HTML documents. In fact, Web and FTP sites differ only in the type of front-end application used to access the directories and files. A site that provides both services may even share directories and files. An FTP front end occasionally provides a text viewer for documents, but you normally transfer files using an FTP front end. A Web viewer presents HTML files in their intended graphical form, which may include different fonts, graphics, and even audio and video clips. More advanced Web viewers and HTML files support file transfers, forms, and other interesting features but the basic viewing of Web documents is the same.

Internet mail is based on standard message files; it uses directories to store incoming and outgoing messages. Incoming messages are normally stored in a directory that can be examined by the owner and no one else. Internet users can send files to the directory. In this sense, a post office is a computer that provides directories for each user. A program on the post office computer handles the movement of mail messages among users on the Internet. A message may pass through a number of post office computers until it reaches its destination. News groups are similar user directories, but they are accessible by the Internet community in general. The post office program typically cleans out messages in the news group after a predefined period of time.

Although all three services have different viewer architectures and the software on the site computer differs, the three are similar because they all use the TCP/IP transport system and they all use a hierarchical storage system.

WHY USE INTERNET CONNECTIONS FOR REMOTE LAN ACCESS?

Internet connections have a number of advantages and disadvantages when used to remotely access a LAN. The following summarizes these.

Advantages

Access to Internet services by LAN users
Access to LAN resources by Internet users
Variety of services can be provided to the Internet
Access available world wide
Access software general available
Good management tools

Disadvantages

Internet access provider needed
Telephone time not minimized
Manual connect/disconnect
Compatibility with front-end applications
Possible security problems

This section covers a mix of Internet connection methods such as providing an Internet site, connecting LAN users to the Internet, and using the Internet to connect a workstation or LAN to another LAN. Each of the advantages and disadvantages will be covered with respect to these methods.

Connecting LAN users or the LAN to the Internet provides users access to Internet services. While it is easy to let a workstation access the Internet directly, using a single LAN link to the Internet for many users can be more efficient and economical. Most Internet users access the Internet on a regular basis but do not transfer data continuously while connected. They may pick up mail or view a Web document but while they are reading the mail in the in box or viewing a page in a Web document the connection is not in use. Sharing the connection allows many users to access the connection and share the cost. This makes it more economical to provide a higher-speed link to the Internet.

Providing Internet users with access to LAN resources is another advantage to connecting a LAN to the Internet. In this case, the Internet's TCP/IP transport system is used to connect the LAN with a remote user's workstation or LAN. The Internet connection can be less expensive than a direct telephone connection, but this must be compared to sending LAN traffic on the Internet.

Providing Internet users with access to your LAN through Internet services such as an FTP or Web site or an Internet mail post office does not provide the same level of access as including your LAN as part of the Internet, but these methods do provide access to services in a more controlled and protected fashion. In fact, to Internet users, an FTP or Web site on a LAN will look the same as a stand-alone site attached to the Internet. LAN users can access the services to provide information to Internet users, and mail gateways allow LAN users to exchange information with Internet users easily.

Internet access is worldwide. Any Internet user can access any portion of the Internet—regardless of the location. Of course, there may be some delay because data may need to move through a number of routers if the two points are far apart with respect to the Internet's internal topology.

Providing Internet users with services such as an FTP or Web site does not mean that you will have to give them special software. Although most front-end programs cost money, they are available from a variety of sources. Your Web home page, an HTML document, can be viewed using any Web viewer program by anyone on the Internet. Freeware and shareware viewers are also available for the cost-conscious user, although using an Internet access provider incurs an additional charge.

The management tools for most products that provide Internet access to LAN users and Internet services are very good. Most are implemented on a GUI operating environment like Mosaic, Windows NT, or OS/2.

The positive aspects of using the Internet must be balanced with the negative. Internet access typically requires an access provider. This is akin to using a telephone company to access a long-distance carrier. While it is possible to connect directly to the Internet, the cost is normally prohibitive to all but very large companies or organizations. Luckily, most areas have more than one access provider, so you can shop around for the best price and features.

Telephone time is not minimized like other remote LAN access methods. In fact, many Internet connections are maintained year-round. This is especially true when providing services to the Internet. LAN users accessing the Internet can often initiate a connection only when they need to. Even transient connections are not always continuously used. The connection is used when transferring mail or a Web document, but while you are reading, the mail the connection is idle. A single LAN connection can be shared by multiple users, but idle time may still be a concern since more connection time costs more money.

While some Internet access products provide automatic disconnection when a connection is idle, most products do not. Manual disconnection means you cannot start a large file transfer using an FTP front-end program and let it disconnect when the transfer is done. You need to wait until it completes and then manually break the connection.

Compatibility with Internet front-end applications is not usually a problem, but as standards evolve older applications may not be able to access or present information developed with newer products; the Web's HTML documents are one example of this problem (HTML version 2 is the latest version of the document standard). Some—but not all—Web viewers can display the newer documents. Updates often provide support for the new formats, but determining what your Internet users can access is not always easy.

Probably the most serious potential problem with Internet access is security.

Considerations on Using Internet Connections

There are several basic considerations that need to be examined before Internet connections should be implemented. These considerations can help determine whether Internet connections are suitable, practical and desirable. The following is a list of considerations we will examine in more detail:

- ✧ Access to LAN users (variable)
- ✧ Access to LAN services (variable)
- ✧ Providing Internet services (good)
- ✧ Providing Internet access to LAN users (good)
- ✧ Ease of use by remote users (good)
- ✧ Network operating system (sometimes important)
- ✧ Network protocol (variable)
- ✧ Telephone time (variable)
- ✧ Performance (variable)
- ✧ Scalability (good)
- ✧ Hardware requirements (variable)
- ✧ Client licensing (variable)
- ✧ Cost (variable)

- ✧ General maintenance (minimal)
- ✧ Security (variable)
- ✧ Auditing (variable)
- ✧ Automation (variable)

Many of these considerations are annotated with the word *variable* because of the variability of connection methods and products. For example, access to LAN users by Internet users depends on the kind of connection provided. Internet mail exchange is one way to allow Internet and LAN users to interact. A mail gateway on the LAN can provide a good connection between Internet and LAN users. An FTP site on the LAN also provides a connection between Internet and LAN users, but it is more limited since users can only copy files to the FTP site. It is adequate for exchanging information but not as timely. At the other extreme is a direct logical connection between the remote Internet user's workstation and the local LAN. The Internet's transport system can provide a link between the remote workstation so that it is actually attached to the local LAN. The remote user then has the same access to LAN users and services as local LAN users. Access to LAN services is similar to access to LAN users. It all depends on how well-connected the LAN is with the Internet and how well the Internet user is connected to the LAN through the Internet.

Providing Internet services is one of the primary reasons for linking your LAN with the Internet. Although making sales over the Internet is just starting, supporting users and generating sales over the Internet is becoming more popular. Information can be provided using a Web site, and files can be made available to users using an FTP site. Providing Internet services is not easy or inexpensive compared to providing Internet access to LAN users, but Internet services can be a cost-effective way of providing customers and potential customers with information about your company and its products. A BBS and a tech support telephone line used to be the way to provide access to your company, but now commercial services like CompuServe and the Internet are important alternatives.

One advantage of providing services over the Internet is the ease with which remote users can access your Internet services. Gaining access to the Internet is relatively easy and cost-effective for most users. Once on the Internet, a user can access your services regardless of where they are located. Direct telephone access to your company by a remote user may incur a long-distance charge, but Internet access does not, unless it is a long-distance call to the Internet service provider for the remote user. Internet support makes good sense if your clientele is global.

The network operating system is important if you are going to provide Internet services or to connect your LAN to the Internet. While network operating systems that use TCP/IP as a transport system on the LAN will integrate easily with the Internet, other LANs using transport systems like Novell NetWare's IPX can still be integrated with the Internet using the (right Internet support software).

The network protocol on the LAN can be of importance if you are connecting a LAN to the Internet or providing Internet services. Using TCP/IP on the LAN can help make the connection of the LAN to the Internet, but the network protocol makes little difference when trying to connect LAN users to the Internet. In fact, many products work with a variety of network operating systems and protocols.

Most connections to the Internet are made using dial-up telephone lines. Dedicated telephone lines are used on higher-bandwidth connections so that connection time is of no concern here. Use of transient connections are more important when it comes to telephone time. Products that provide automatic disconnect when a line is idle or unused can minimize telephone time and charges.

Performance is normally measured as how fast data is exchanged with the Internet. High-speed modems are considered low-speed connections to the Internet. ISDN, T3, and T1 lines offer higher throughput at higher costs.

A variety of connection speeds lets you scale Internet connections and increase the number of lines. This is true for both LAN user-to-Internet connections and connections to Internet services that you provide. Although single-processor single-computer sites are sufficient for most companies that provide Internet services, multiple-processor and multiple-server sites can provide numerous services to many Internet users. Of course, such systems require a higher degree of expertise to install and maintain, and they will use a larger number of higher-speed connections to the Internet.

Hardware requirements vary depending on the kind of service and connection provided. At the low end, we have software-only products like Firefox's Nov*IX for Internet. It is an NLM that runs on your existing Novell NetWare 3.x or 4.x file server. All you need to add is a modem to connect to your Internet service provider. At the other extreme is a system that requires T1 connections and dedicated Internet servers. Your configuration may be somewhere in between.

Client licensing concerns the software used by Internet users that will access Internet services provided by you or remote users who will connect to the LAN over the Internet. Internet access products are available from a variety of sources with varying prices. Sometimes Internet access software is bundled with other products such as the OS/2 Warp Bonus Pack. Freeware and shareware products are also available. For the most part, users are charged with obtaining and paying for Internet access software.

The cost of installing and maintaining Internet connections for both users and LANs varies quite a bit. It depends on connection time, speed, and related services. The costs incurred can relate to software, setup charges, and telephone and service provider connection charges. Monthly costs may be as low as $35 for a single user using a high-speed modem, but higher charges can easily be incurred for dedicated connections and higher-speed links.

General maintenance for both LAN-to-Internet and Internet-to-LAN connections is minimal. Most of the work is done during installation. General maintenance usually involves checking usage logs and resetting modems when a connection locks up.

Security concerns vary depending on the kind of connection. Providing LAN users with access to the Internet has the lowest security concerns because most software has a built-in firewall. Security becomes more of an issue when Internet services are provided from the LAN because Internet users have access to the services. Name and password pairs can restrict access to services but data is still transferred over the Internet so encryption must be used for secure transmissions. Security becomes more of a concern if you move into purchase transactions over the Internet. The discussion of these issues is beyond the scope of this book.

Auditing Internet service and use varies from product to product. Some products provide no tracking abilities while others are quite extensive. The degree of auditing needed varies from organization to organization, so check your products carefully.

Automating access to Internet services and providing Internet services vary significantly among products. At one end, you have products that require manual intervention for all operations. This is especially true for Internet user access software. Most products are designed for active intervention by users. As software for the Internet matures, more user customization and automation will appear. For example, it may be possible to automatically make a connection at a particular time and have the software use the connection to pick up and drop off mail, copy files to an FTP site, and pick up messages from some news groups.

SOME EXAMPLES OF INTERNET CONNECTIONS

Many different products are available for the Internet. Some provide access to the Internet for stand-alone workstations while others provide access for LAN users. In this section we will look at a variety of options available for the Internet. Unlike other chapters, these products represent a very minor cross section of available products. The Internet has generated many interesting and powerful products.

For stand-alone workstations and LAN users, OS/2 Warp provides Internet access for a very low cost. Like most Internet access packages, OS/2 comes with front-end applications for FTP and Web sites and for exchanging Internet mail.

For LAN connections we look at two alternatives. The first is a box that plugs into your LAN and a modem connected to your Internet access provider. Performance Technology's Instant Internet includes its own set of Internet front-end applications that run on LAN workstations, so all you need to do is get an Internet access provider. Firefox Communication provides the same kind of service but through your Novell NetWare file server. It runs as an NLM. Front-end applications are also included to access Internet FTP and Web sites and Internet mail and news groups over IPX connections, which are more popular in NetWare LANs.

Finally, we get to an example of an Internet service site provider. Netscape Communications is well known for its Internet access products, but it also sells products that let you provide services such as a Web site.

Looking at the Internet as a remote LAN access method involves a number of major considerations; it should not be taken lightly. Most other remote LAN access methods can be installed and removed in a matter of days but an Internet connection typically takes more time and involves more people. The benefits of using the Internet are significant; don't overlook it. Likewise, be careful when considering products and examining the risks involved.

OS/2 WARP Bonus Pack Internet Support

There are a number of different Internet front-end products for almost any platform. One of the more interesting ones is included in IBM's Bonus Pack for its OS/2 WARP operating system. The Internet support in the Bonus Pack is interesting from two standpoints. First, OS/2 WARP is a 32-bit multitasking operating system, the ideal platform for an Internet access point. Second, the price of OS/2 WARP, which includes the Bonus Pack, is often lower than a stand-alone Internet access product. You effectively get alot for free if you compare it to other products. Depending on how you look at it, you get a free operating system and the rest of the programs in the Bonus Pack for the price of the Internet software or, for the price of an operating system, you get the Bonus Pack free.

The Bonus Pack also includes a CompuServe front end, a copy of IBM's Person-to-Person whiteboard program, multimedia support, FaxWorks for OS/2, HyperAccess Lite for OS/2 (a terminal emulator), IBM Works, and Personal Information Manager. IBM Works includes a spreadsheet, word processor, database program, charting tools, report writer, calendar, and phone book. This is a well-rounded bunch of programs for a bonus.

IBM's Internet Connection for OS/2, the formal name for the Bonus Pack Internet support, includes the major Internet access programs including a dialer,

Web, FTP, and mail viewer. IBM's mail viewer is called *UltiMail Lite*; it supports the Multimedia Internet Mail Extensions (MIME) protocol, which allows you to send and view multimedia mail that includes audio and video clips. Most video adapters can display video clips; a sound board is needed to play back audio clips. A microphone and sound board are needed to record audio clips and a video capture board and digital camera or VCR are needed to record video clips. Figure 9.17 shows how these programs can be running simultaneously under OS/2.

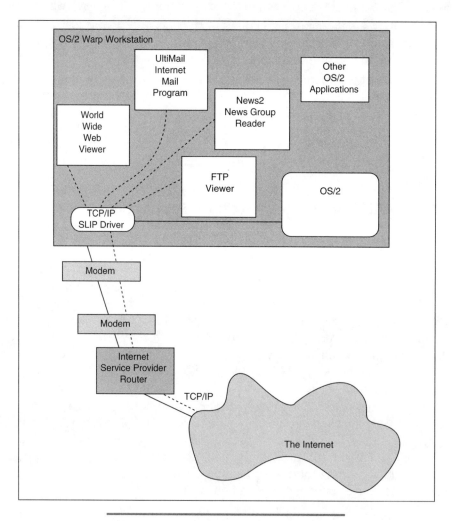

Figure 9.17 Warp Internet modem connection.

The Bonus Pack includes other Internet tools as well as the ones we will look at in this section. The tools not covered in more detail include Gopher, Telnet, Ping, and other tools that are used in special circumstances. *Gopher,* which lets you connect to sites on the Internet, can perform text searches for keywords so you don't have to browse FTP or Web sites one page at a time. *Telnet* is a terminal emulator that can be used to connect to multiuser systems on the Internet. You can run programs on the remote systems but normally you need a user ID on the remote system and a matching password. *Ping* is a simple program that lets you test a connection between your workstation and another system on the Internet. You need to know the TCP/IP address of the other system. Ping, like the other programs not discussed in detail, are used for debugging purposes. They are rarely used for daily access of the Internet.

The Internet applications can be started individually, but the first one that is started will start up the dialer program if you are using a SLIP connection through a modem. The dialer program (see Figure 9.18) makes a connection to your Internet service provider by dialing the modem and waiting for a connection. The same TCP/IP driver is used by all the Internet applications. The Internet applications can also be used with a network TCP/IP link to the Internet. In this case, a TCP/IP router on the LAN will be connected to the service provider, and each Internet application on the workstation will use the LAN TCP/IP support. The router connection must be made before the workstation's program tries to access the Internet. The Internet applications, except the dialer, operate in the same fashion regardless of the kind of TCP/IP support used to link the workstation to the Internet.

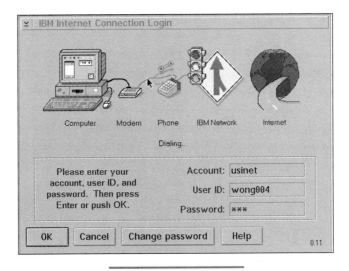

Figure 9.18 WARP dialer.

OS/2's Internet support makes good use of the program's *multitasking* (multiple programs) and *multithreaded* (programs that have multiple threads of execution) support. The World Wide Web viewer (Figure 9.19) is just one example of a multithreaded program. It is capable of downloading an HTML document while displaying it. Graphics and audio or video clips are downloaded asynchronously after the main document is sent. The multistep approach lets you see the text of a document before the glitter. Often you can determine what you need from the text alone and jump to another page using a hyperlink before the entire page is presented. The ability to view and use the document early is especially useful with modem connections, where the transfer rate is low (28,800 bps for a V.34 high-speed modem), and when documents contain large or multiple bitmaps that take a long time to transfer.

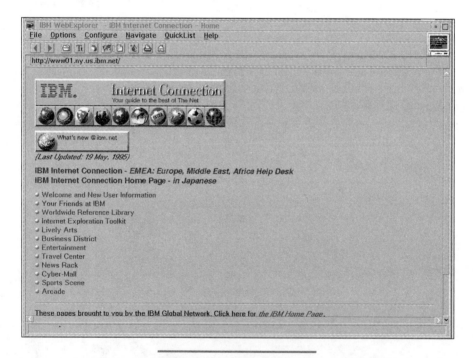

FIGURE 9.19 WARP WEB VIEWER.

The Web viewer keeps a copy of all the documents you have examined during a session so you can quickly see where you have been. Unfortunately, it does not automatically save the document for later examination, but you can manually save any page you view. These pages can be examined later, and you can use the hyperlinks in the pages that have been saved on a local disk if you are connected to the Internet. Like many newer Web viewers, IBM's can examine FTP sites and let you complete forms that are used by Internet sites to acquire data.

WARP's FTP viewer is a typical GUI FTP viewer. You can connect to one FTP site at a time. The bottom panel (see Figure 9.20) shows the directory of the remote FTP site while the upper panel is a directory that is accessible by your workstation. You can copy files between the two panels by selecting the names just as you would with a file browser application. Multiple files can be marked for transfer but the transfer occurs in the foreground with respect to the FTP program. This means the FTP program can be set up to transfer one or more files, but once you start the transfer, the program cannot be used for other duties such as selecting other files. The workstation is not dedicated, however, nor is the Internet connection; while an FTP transfer is occurring, you can switch to the Web viewer or another application on the workstation and use it. Of course, the FTP program is using some of the workstation's processing power, and the Internet connection is being used for a transfer operation. Two Internet programs that simultaneously use the Internet connection will have to share the bandwidth.

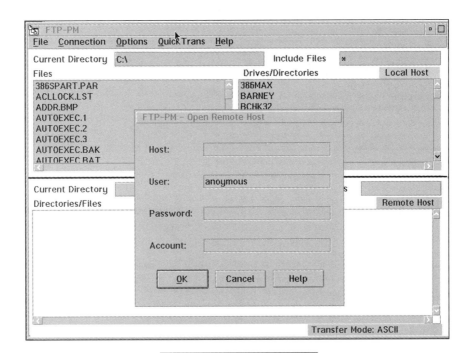

FIGURE 9.20 WARP FTP VIEWER.

UltiMail Lite, is WARP's Internet mail front end. The inbox and outbox are shown as OS/2 folders, but when you open a document you see windows like the one shown in the figure. Like most mail programs, UltiMail Lite provides an address book where you can keep Internet addresses of your favorite people.

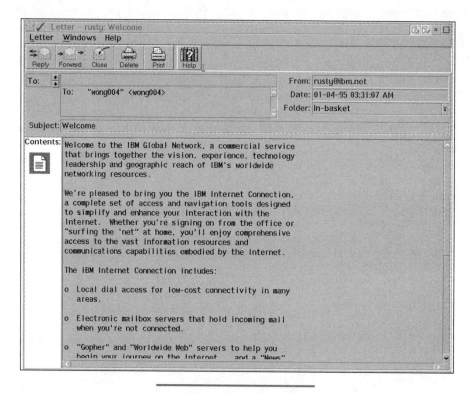

FIGURE 9.21 WARP MAIL VIEWER.

UltiMail supports MIME messages, so you can include multimedia information in your messages and view and listen to this type of information in messages sent to you. An audio board and speakers are required for audio support.

UltiMail Lite can also be used to send mail messages to news groups. You use the News Reader/2, included in the Bonus Pack, to read messages in a news group. The news reader downloads a list of all the news groups and updates it periodically when you connect to the Internet. You can scan the messages in a news group by title and view or save messages on the workstation.

UltiMail Lite picks up and delivers mail when you connect to the Internet. The process is automatic but you can view and create messages when you are not connected to the Internet. Overall, MultiMail Lite is a useful and easy-to-use mail program.

OS/2 WARP is a powerful operating system in its own right. The combination of OS/2 WARP and Internet support makes it an attractive package.

Performance Technology Instant Internet

Connecting to the Internet one workstation at a time can be quite tedious and expensive for companies. The solution is to make use of you LAN for part of the connection to the Internet. A single gateway between your LAN and the Internet can provide all the LAN users with access to the Internet. Performance Technology's (San Antonio, TX) Instant Internet is such a gateway.

Instant Internet is for use on LANs that use Novell NetWare or Performance Technology's own POWERLan. There are no special changes to be made on the file server or any of the workstations other than the installation of the Instant Internet software for workstation operation. The workstations must be running Microsoft Windows or Windows for Workgroups.

Instant Internet is a hardware and software combination. The hardware is a box that contains a standard PC-compatible workstation without a keyboard and monitor. It includes an Ethernet adapter and an internal V.34 modem from U.S. Robotics. You connect the Instant Internet box into an Ethernet LAN and plug the modem into a telephone outlet. The modem connection provides SLIP or PPP support. Plug in the power, turn on the box, and you are half ready to connect LAN users to the Internet. The other half is the workstation software installation.

The software comes on two diskettes and installs on a workstation running Microsoft Windows. It installs both the Instant Internet hardware management program and the workstation applications, including WinWeb, Eudora, and WinVN. WinWeb is a Web viewer that also provides FTP and Gopher support. Eudora is an Internet mail client, and WinVN is a news group viewer.

The software uses a Windows Socket (WinSock) transport system that runs on Microsoft Windows. The Internet workstation applications use the WinSock system to communicate with the Instant Internet box. WinSock is also used by some third-party Internet application vendors, which allows these applications to also use the Instant Internet access to the Internet.

The management program is set up immediately, and you can select connection scripts from an extensive list of providers. Custom scripts can be written, but Instant Internet is typically sold through VARs who will customize the unit before it reaches your LAN so that installation is quick and painless. All you need to add is the phone number of your Internet access provider, your account name, and your password. You get through the instant testing dialog box in an hour or less, which includes reading the short manual, plugging in the Instant Internet box, and installing the software.

Instant Internet has a main management screen that allows you to change the configuration of the Instant Internet box as well as add users and control security. Instant Internet provides an inherent firewall between the Internet and the LAN because the TCP/IP transport system used on the Internet is not used on the LAN when the internal modem is used. It is possible to use the Instant Internet box with a TCP/IP router that attaches to the LAN, but the NetWare or POWERLan network does not have to use TCP/IP, thereby isolating the LAN from the Internet even with TCP/IP traffic on the LAN's cable.

The Web viewer shows a typical page of an HTML document. Click on the hyperlinks and you move to another page, which may be obtained from a different location on the Internet. The Web viewer is customizable so you can choose the colors and fonts used on-screen.

The Web viewer program WinWeb also doubles as an FTP viewer. You can download files from an FTP site and save them on your workstation's or the LAN's hard disk. While the interface is different from a file management program, it is easy to use, and it gets the job done. Any kind of file can be downloaded from an FTP site, although large files (larger than 1 megabyte) can take a while using a modem connection, even the high-speed V.34 U.S. Robotics modem that comes bundled in the Instant Internet box.

The Eudora Internet mail program (shown in Figure 9.24) from Qualcomm Inc. lets you send and receive mail over the Internet. The mail program provides basic mail support.

The WinVN news group viewer lets you view messages in a news group and send Internet mail messages but not receive messages. You can send a message to anyone, not just to a news group; this is handy when you want to send a private response to a message you read in a news group message list. You can select which Internet site WinVN gets its news group information from. It takes longer to download news group information from busy Internet servers, so it can pay to chose a news group server that is not heavily used.

Instant Internet is an interesting solution to the LAN-to-Internet connection. As you may have noticed, I never mentioned what operating system runs on the Instant Internet box. It doesn't really matter because you never see it. The only interface is the Instant Internet management program, which is a very simple front end.

Instant Internet's simplicity should not detract from its power. It can be installed quickly, and it has a built-in firewall that allows LAN users to access the

Internet but prevents Internet users from accessing your LAN. Instant Internet can be set up to connect to the Internet automatically when a user needs a connection, and it can automatically terminate the connection after a predetermined idle time. The connection is restored when a user needs to access the Internet again.

While it is possible to use Instant Internet with an external Ethernet router, Instant Internet will most often be found using the built-in modem to support a small to medium-size LAN. The limited bandwidth of the 28,800-bps V.34 modem is adequate for a small workgroup as long as you do not have dozens of users simultaneously trying to access the Internet. The advantage of the Instant Internet solution when too many users need to access the Internet is that you just have to add an external router with a higher-speed connection. The Instant Internet box is capable of handling higher-speed connections like ISDN and T1 lines, although the level of sophistication of the LAN manager is higher.

For those needing quick access to the Internet or if you just want to let a few users try out the Internet, Instant Internet may be just what you need.

Firefox Communication Nov*IX for Internet

Nov*IX for Internet, from Firefox Communication (San Jose, CA,) provides LAN workstations with access to the Internet. Similar to Instant Internet, Nov*IX for Internet is designed to run on a Novell NetWare 3.x or 4.x server. It provides many of the same features and benefits as Instant Internet. LAN users can use the workstation applications to access the Internet through a NetWare file server. The workstations can do so without additional configuration changes because NetWare's native IPX transport system is used. Using the LAN's IPX transport system provides an implicit firewall between the LAN and the Internet.

Nov*IX for Internet's connection to the Internet can be a modem attached to the NetWare file server or an external TCP/IP router attached to the LAN. The modem connection is a good solution for small to medium-size LANs that require occasional Internet access.

Nov*IX for Internet is actually part of a larger product line from Firefox Communication. Nov*IX for NetWare provides the basic LAN-to-Internet support. Nov*IX for Client/Server is designed for custom client/server applications that may span the Internet. Firefox also has a SMTP gateway that supports POP3, the latest SMTP exchange protocol. The mail gateway lets you use Internet mail without the details associated with other Internet applications like Web viewers.

Nov*IX supports DOS and Mac clients as well as Microsoft Windows and Windows for Workgroups, which is necessary for running Nov*IX for Internet applications like the Web and FTP viewers.

Because Nov*IX for Internet is based on Nov*IX for NetWare, it provides a greater level of customization and control than Instant Internet. You can control the types of connections you can make between LAN workstations and the Internet, as well as where the connections can be made to.

Nov*IX for Internet uses a common front-end application. The toolbar buttons start the individual Internet applications like the Web viewer and Internet mail program. The status area displays connection information. The front end can be closed after you start running other Internet applications. Firefox Window's Internet applications use the same type of WinSock support as Instant Internet.

The Firefox uses the popular Mosaic Web viewer. Mosaic is available on a number of different platforms, including Microsoft Windows. Mosaic supports both a hot list and a history list. The history list is a list of HTML documents you have viewed during a particular session. The history list is automatically updated but it starts from scratch when you start running the program. You can jump to any document in the history list by viewing the list and selecting an entry. The hot list is like the history list, but entries must be added explicitly and it survives between sessions. You can also delete items from the hot list. The hot list is handy because you do not have to navigate through the Web each time to find documents that you have already found.

The Mosaic Web viewer can be used to view FTP sites. You can download files from an FTP site to your workstation, but the Firefox FTP viewer is actually a more powerful application for accessing FTP sites. The Firefox FTP viewer's file management windows looks almost identical to the Windows File Manager and operates in the same way. You can drag and drop files between windows to move or copy them, and you can run applications that have been copied to a local disk. The Firefox FTP program keeps track of hosts between sessions so you can quickly get to FTP sites that you access often. The Firefox Gopher program lets you scan the Internet for information.

The Firefox mail application includes a news reader application. The Nov*IX gateway on the file server can be set up to filter news groups so that users do not have unlimited access to the Internet. Together, these applications let you send and receive Internet mail messages and view news group messages. The mail program supports MAPI and MIME. MAPI is Microsoft's mail interface for applications; it can be used to send mail from a spreadsheet program and a mail program. MIME is a multimedia standard for Internet mail messages.

Nov*IX is an excellent solution for small LANs because a single file server can be used as an Internet gateway. Nov*IX uses existing IPX LAN support found on most NetWare workstations, and it isolates the LAN from the Internet. The ability to restrict LAN users to particular aspects or areas of the Internet makes

Nov*IX ideal for businesses that want to use the Internet but don't want users wasting time exploring it.

Internet Sites

Installing and supporting an Internet site is more complicated than connecting a workstation or LAN to the Internet. Conceptually connecting a server to the Internet is as simple as actually connecting a workstation to the Internet, but this simplicity is deceptive. Workstation and LAN connections can use dynamic IP addressing, while servers need to use fixed IP addressing. Dynamic IP addressing lets a service provider supply a workstation with an IP address when a modem connection is made between the workstation and the service provider. The workstation uses the IP address while connected, but it uses a different IP address the next time it connects to the Internet. This approach works because the workstation exchanges information between itself and Internet sites while it is connected to the Internet.

Internet sites need to have a fixed IP address so your workstation can connect to the same site each time it connects to the Internet. Internet sites keep a table of logical Internet names and fixed IP addresses, but these tables are relatively static; they are more like the yellow pages than a dynamically updated table.

In fact, a fixed IP address must be allocated for each Internet site. Internet access providers can often provide you with an IP address, but you should check with prospective access providers to see how IP addresses are obtained.

Internet sites can be based on stand-alone Windows workstations, but these low-end solutions are rare; workstations are often connected to the Internet using modems that do not have the horsepower to provide access to hundreds of users. For the higher-performance solutions, you need to look at servers based on high-performance 32-bit operating systems like Windows NT, OS/2, and UNIX.

UNIX is where it started, and most high-performance Internet sites run UNIX on symmetrical multiprocessing (SMP) systems. UNIX Internet software is available from a number of sources, and there also are public-domain products available. UNIX servers are used to provide all types of Internet services, from FTP and Web sites to Gopher and mail support. Most LANs that have UNIX servers and workstations use TCP/IP as the LAN's transport system so it is very easy to make a LAN part of the Internet.

Windows NT is becoming a popular platform for Internet sites for many of the reasons that made UNIX a popular platform. Windows NT has good TCP/IP support, excellent program development tools, and SMP support. While Windows

NT Internet site product offerings are not as numerous as UNIX solutions, the number of Windows NT products is growing faster.

OS/2 is a good Internet site platform, but the number of Internet support programs is more limited than UNIX and Windows NT. OS/2 also supports SMP, so it is possible to build rather sophisticated and powerful Internet sites on OS/2.

Is it possible to have an Internet site that is not at your site? Yes, many Internet service providers provide more than Internet access. Some providers maintain servers that provide multiple FTP and Web sites. You can deliver information to them by disk or over the Internet. The advantages are minimal maintenance on your part and usually a high-speed link between the Internet and the site. The service provider also provides the technical know how and support that you would need if you were to set up a local site.

Why would you want to have your own Internet site? Cost and control are two reasons, but speed of update and access are often just as important. Local sites can be accessed and updated more quickly than going over the Internet. The files or database on the Internet site computer often needs to be updated on a daily or hourly basis. The information on the Internet may also be heavily used by local LAN users, making a local site more practical.

Setting up an Internet site is a major undertaking. It should not be taken lightly, and security issues should be examined and addressed, especially if the site is part of your LAN. Firewalls can limit access to the Internet by LAN users and limit access from Internet users to your site and LAN.

Index